MILTON STUDIES

XV

MILTON STUDIES

XV   *Edited by*

James D. Simmonds

UNIVERSITY OF PITTSBURGH PRESS

MILTON STUDIES

is published annually by the University of Pittsburgh Press as a forum for Milton scholarship and criticism. Articles submitted for publication may be biographical; they may interpret some aspect of Milton's writings; or they may define literary, intellectual, or historical contexts — by studying the work of his contemporaries, the traditions which affected his thought and art, contemporary political and religious movements, his influence on other writers, or the history of critical response to his work.

Manuscripts should be upwards of 3,000 words in length and should conform to the *MLA Style Sheet*. Manuscripts and editorial correspondence should be addressed to James D. Simmonds, Department of English, University of Pittsburgh, Pittsburgh, Pa. 15260.

Milton Studies does not review books.

Within the United States, *Milton Studies* may be ordered from the University of Pittsburgh Press, Pittsburgh, Pa. 15260.

Overseas orders should be addressed to Feffer and Simons, Inc., 100 Park Avenue, New York, N.Y. 10017, U.S.A.

Library of Congress Catalog Card Number 69-12335

ISBN 0-8229-3174-5 (Volume I) (out of print)

ISBN 0-8229-3194-x (Volume II)

ISBN 0-8229-3218-0 (Volume III)

ISBN 0-8229-3244-x (Volume IV)

ISBN 0-8229-3272-5 (Volume V)

ISBN 0-8229-3288-1 (Volume VI)

ISBN 0-8229-3305-5 (Volume VII)

ISBN 0-8229-3310-1 (Volume VIII)

ISBN 0-8229-3329-2 (Volume IX)

ISBN 0-8229-3356-x (Volume X)

ISBN 0-8229-3373-X (Volume XI)

ISBN 0-8229-3376-4 (Volume XII)

ISBN 0-8229-3404-3 (Volume XIII)

ISBN 0-8229-3429-9 (Volume XIV)

ISBN 0-8229-3449-3 (Volume XV)

US ISSN 0076-8820

Published by the University of Pittsburgh Press, Pittsburgh, Pa. 15260

CONTENTS

MILTON STUDIES

XV

MILTON'S EPICS AND
THE SPANISH WAR:
TOWARD A POETICS OF EXPERIENCE

Robert Thomas Fallon

T HE BIOGRAPHICAL criticism of the nineteenth century has long
been laid to rest. The pedagogic practices that numbed the sensibilities of the youth of that age are no more, or so we fondly hope.
Jacques Barzun, in his incisive and engaging way, has described a professor steeped in that tradition, who after a lengthy discussion of the
poet's life and times finally came to the work itself, which he dismissed
with a shake of his sage head and a sigh of, "A gem, gentlemen, a gem,"
its beauties, it would appear, incommunicable to the uninitiated, to be
appreciated only by a select, learned brotherhood. Those who endured
his tutelage may recall him occasionally lingering over a work, but only
to dwell upon its veiled autobiographical allusions, the art thus serving
as a means to an end, a source for searching out the secrets of the artist's
life, filling in gaps left blank or inconclusive by an incomplete chronicle. His young scholars, as Barzun puts it, "were in no danger of becoming esthetes."[1]

The demise of this rambling pedagogue with his recital of the
loves, dates, and diet of the poet — "What porridge hath John Keats?" —
is mourned by few. The reaction to this tradition during the early decades of this century was swift, terrible, and apparently terminal. Its
passing, however, has left something of a hiatus in the spectrum of responses recommended to modern students of literature.[2] While most
scholars will accept the suggestion that a poet weaves into the pattern of
his art some threads from the experience of his days, there is still an understandable concern about how to discuss this influence without being
identified with that earlier tradition. So unfashionable are the methods
of biographical criticism today that no aspiring scholar would be so
foolish as to attach that label to his efforts; and if one does feel the com-
pulsion to interpret a work in its biographical or historical context, one
would be wise to keep such remarks brief, or better yet, relegate them to
the safe obscurity of a footnote.[3] This is not to say that such caution is

solely a matter of fashion, however, nor that it is entirely without substance; for many scholars have sincere apprehensions that in interpreting the art in terms of the artist's life one may diminish the aesthetic appreciation of the work, that in weighing down the lines of a poem with this burden of stolid fact, one may retard a critical imagination intent upon searching out its meanings and beauties.

Still, a knowledge of the life can be a key to a reading of the art; and in addressing a work of the scope and complexity of a *Paradise Lost*, for example, we need all the keys we can get. But how does one even approach the subject? We frown on the late, unlamented biographical critic's equation of a direct, one-for-one analogy between life and art; but since his fall from favor there has been no effort to replace that rather oversimplified formula with one more acceptable to modern critical theory. Having thrown the baby out with the bathwater in their enthusiasm for the New Criticism, twentieth-century scholars in general have simply chosen to ignore the subject.[4]

This study will propose a means of filling the gap left by the demise of the biographical critic without employing the more simplistic resolutions of his discredited method, in the hope that such an effort will encourage further analysis of the process whereby life is transfigured into art. A change of terminology will fool no one, of course, but I am proposing what may be called a "poetics of experience," that will help explain how, in the subtle chemistry of creation, some part of the poet's life emerges in the priceless amalgam of his art. Some works, of course, present little difficulty, as they are composed in a clearly identified historical or biographical context. Many of Milton's poems are unequivocally *about* an event, in the way that *Sonnet XVIII* records his reaction to the Piedmont Massacre; others make use of the occasion as a point of departure for creative expression, as he did the Christmas of 1629, the death of Edward King, and the confrontation at Turnham Green. Satire, to be at all effective, must depend on the reader's familiarity with the subject of the work; one needs some knowledge of just what the "New Forcers of Conscience" in the Westminster Assembly were forcing in order to appreciate Milton's distaste for that body.

Of greater significance than any specific event, however, are the more extended experiences of life, time spent in work, war, marriage, or aging—experiences which become part of the very fabric of the poet's being and which, having passed through the forge of his imagination, are transformed by some process into imagery that is often but a "shadowy type" of the original form. The influence of such experiences is of great importance, but it is not so clearly defined, nor is it so easily identified, since we have so little understanding of just what that process of transformation entails. An analogy with a more familiar literary influence may serve to clarify the distinction. Plato's presence is felt throughout *Paradise Lost;* it is not, however, as direct an influence as, let us say, that of Homer or of Genesis. The works of Plato may be said to "inform" the poem, but *Paradise Lost* is not *about* Plato in the same sense that it is about the epic tradition or man's first disobedience. Similarly, Milton's experience in the world may be said to "inform" *Paradise Lost,* but it is not a poem about the life of Milton in the same way that *Sonnet X* is about Lady Margaret Ley or *Lycidas* the drowning of Edward King. But to dismiss the influence of such experiences simply because it is more amorphous, more open to question, or more difficult to define is to deny ourselves an essential key to the appreciation of the poet's art.

This study, then, will begin with the premise that Milton's decade of service to the English government had a decided influence on his imagination; and it will proceed from there to consider, in a very tentative way, but one aspect of that service, in an effort to explore the process whereby his imagination reshaped the experience into matter for his art. The words "tentative" and "explore" are used advisedly, for a brief article can do no more than survey the ground for such a theoretical structure. Regrettably, limitations in space will not permit an analysis of what may prove to be the richest source of all in such an inquiry — the field of psychology.[5] These pages can only hope to open the door on the subject, persuading some perhaps that there are rich rewards in such an endeavor and that the risk of doing damage to the work or placing shackles on the critical imagination is worth taking, indeed may be no risk at all.

An analysis of the works of John Milton in terms of the experiences of his days does present some special problems, however. In the first place, we know so much less about him than we do of later poets, whose lives were more generously documented in correspondence and the works of contemporaries. Some of the essential facts of Milton's life are still open to question: How was he spending his time during those shadowy years, 1645–1649 and 1652–1658? And which wife was he referring to, anyway, in *Sonnet XXIII*? An even more formidable obstacle to this effort is Milton himself, for what we do know of his life and associations does not always paint the picture of an entirely agreeable figure. It may be unsettling, for example, to be reminded that he was a loyal and active servant of a government which can only be described as a military dictatorship, that he supported the wars of the Commonwealth of

England, to include the sack of Drogheda, and that he had great admiration for the soldiers of the New Model Army. If it is further suggested
that his works may be seen as reflecting some of these sentiments, one
can sympathize with those Miltonists who insist that biography is one
thing and art quite another. "Milton the man" has been much disparaged by T. S. Eliot, Robert Graves, F. R. Leavis, and many others, in
whose eyes he assumes the distasteful shape of the dour Victorian *pater
familias*.[6] They see him as a fundamentalist zealot, preaching the pun-
ishments of eternal damnation and the rigors of the strait and narrow,
an unyielding father, demanding husband, and unprincipled political
polemicist — in brief a figure from a stiff and colorless age who could
not be expected to elicit much sympathy from a forward-thinking
twentieth-century poet, critic, or student.[7]

In an effort to make the poet more acceptable to our age and to
correct some of these critical excesses, sympathetic scholars have tried
to soften this austere image, an effort which culminated in William
Riley Parker's brilliant biography, where he dwells at length on Milton's
humor, his humanity, and his wide circle of friends and admirers. The
poet emerges from those pages as a fond family man, a delightful host
and companion, and a wise counselor somewhat disappointed that his
advice is not more frequently sought. Parker attempts to dissociate Milton from the distasteful Puritan government which he served as secretary for foreign languages by diminishing him to a minor political figure who, untouched by the tainted ebb and flow of dictatorial power,
performed his slight function on the periphery of events.[8] Austin Wool-
rych goes further, suggesting that Milton chose to be remote from
events, particularly during the Protectorate, because he strongly disapproved of the policies of his government.[9]

The effort to restore Milton to his former stature has been resourceful and wide-ranging. James Holly Hanford drew attention to the pervasive literary and philosophical influence of Christian Humanism in
Milton's works, an influence which, Hanford argued, overshadows that
of the Puritan sensibility.[10] When the New Criticism appeared, it was
by nature ready-made for the cause: disregard the man and focus on his
words. But the dicta of Eliot and Leavis continued to rankle and in response scholars shaped a "new" Milton, one derived largely from the
evidence of his works. Out of the ashes of the disagreeable Puritan there
arose Milton the Whig,[11] Milton the Liberal, and finally Milton the
Pacifist.[12] Evidence for these more satisfactory alternatives was found
either in his works or in the books from which he drew his inspiration,
and persuasive indeed was the argument mounted on the basis of his

wide reading and remarkable mind. So a very different Milton emerged, one whom Eliot would find more likable and with whom the modern academician and his students could be more comfortable. As Joseph H. Summers remarks, "It is a rare critic who can resist the tendency to reduce an admired figure to his own image,"[13] and this may well explain the "new" Milton, for he resembles no other figure so closely as that of a late twentieth-century, liberally oriented university professor, who, safely insulated from the dust and heat of the race, is free to pursue his studies, surrounded by his beloved books and admiring students — a very comfortable figure, indeed.

The emergence of this more attractive figure, however, has yet to excite any new interest in identifying the works with the life of the man who walked the streets of London in the mid-seventeenth century. Modern critical attention focuses almost exclusively on the books he read, or on other forms of art. Scholars today accept almost any suggestion for a source or analogue of a great work if it comes from literature, painting, music, theatre, sermon — anything that appears in print. At the moment there is a lively interest in iconography and it is not difficult to find interesting and persuasive collections of paintings and illustrated manuscripts that Milton may have had an opportunity to see, which therefore might possibly have inspired his work.[14] Studies abound which suggest sources in the Talmud, Cabalistic texts, little-known philosophers, obscure Eastern European epics, and archaic musical forms with which the poet was "probably" familiar, and each is heard with the sympathy and respect it deserves. Inspired by E. M. W. Tillyard's discussion of "unconscious meanings" and the appearance of Anne Davidson Ferry's seminal book,[15] modern scholars have become fascinated with the many voices which emerge from the text of *Paradise Lost*.[16] We may be entirely deaf to these several voices, but we accept the sincerity of colleagues who say they hear them and we will listen with sympathy while they tell us what they say. Structuralists find forms and shapes in the work which we may be blind to, yet we will sit patiently and strain to see.[17]

This study will ask only that the reader assume that same openness of mind when it is proposed that art does not always arise from art alone, that poets are something more than the sum of the books they have read, and that the artistic vision can be inspired as well by events that take place beyond the walls of their libraries.[18] In brief, it is requested that this method, which I have chosen to call experiential criticism, be permitted to take its place among the many critical approaches which provide keys to the understanding of art. In his vivid portraits of warfare Milton was surely indebted to Tacitus, Homer, the Bible, Robert Ward, and the iconographic traditions of the Renaissance. It should not be too difficult to accept the suggestion that his imagination was as deeply moved by Oliver Cromwell and the wars of his country. It is proposed, simply, that life and art are symbiotic spheres of experience which a powerful imagination can encompass in a single vision, and that the artist who records that vision in the pages of a book is not limited for inspiration to the pages of another book.

The reader who is uneasy with this proposal will be even further disquieted by the suggestion that the familiar "new" Milton is perhaps not an entirely accurate representation of the historical figure. This study deals specifically with Milton's years as secretary for foreign languages under the Protectorate and it is assumed in these pages that he was as alert to the activities of his government in the latter years of his decade of service as he had been before the onset of his blindness, when, in Don M. Wolfe's words, he was "a prompt, resourceful coworker in the immense variety of duties imposed upon the Council by the daily issues faced by the new republic."[19] He was surely less active in the late 1650s but, as I have proposed elsewhere, he was hardly the detached, unconcerned figure that Parker and others would have him.[20] One is most reluctant to disturb that very agreeable image of the sequestered scholar, safely insulated from the turmoil of his time, by intruding upon his quiet study with all of this distasteful talk of politics and warfare; and one would not think of doing so had not the unquestioned acceptance of that figure given rise to interpretations of his works which seem clearly inconsistent with the historical Milton. For example, commentary on the function of the military imagery in Milton's works — the figure of Satan, the War in Heaven, the warrior angels — has suffered by neglecting to take into consideration the role that the soldier played in his life.[21] Such neglect often produces a single-dimensional oversimplification of the poet's art and thought. Edward Wagenknecht, for example, in a recent book wherein he accepts the currently popular figure of Milton the Pacifist (*Paradise Regained* "is certainly one of the great pacifist books of all time") devotes three pages to *Of Education* without a single reference to the military nature of the academy.[22] It is almost as if Milton had never defined its purpose as that of preparing men to perform the offices of peace *and war*.

Such limited perspectives sometimes have ancient roots. Critics since the time of Dr. Johnson have expressed themselves dissatisfied with Milton's angels. The guardians of Eden, it is said, are put to an impossible task and when they fail are hauled back to Heaven and told not to worry because there wasn't anything they could have done about it anyway.[23] John Peter sees them as "a group of minstrels armed with toy spears."[24] Again, A. J. A. Waldock describes Raphael's account of his voyage to the gates of Hell during the days of Creation as an example of "sheer clumsiness on the part of the poet."[25] Such ceremonial trappings may, indeed, seem indecorous, but only if one views them in isolation. When considered in the total context of the war between Good and Evil, such small incidents find their place and take on meaning. These pages will propose that, during the years when Milton was a respected figure in the Cromwell government, England was involved in a war which in its broad design was quite similar to that which he describes in *Paradise Lost*, one which, moreover, contained incidents — the withdrawal of ambassadors and Blake's mission — which are suggestive of the actions of the angels. Further, a grasp of the shape of that historical war provides a rationale for the appearance of these small figures on Milton's canvas of cosmic conflict.

Further parallels between the historical events of Milton's time and the shape of that imagined conflict will be developed below. Once more, to trace these analogies is not to exclude other sources, parallels, and influences which emerged from his reading. Milton may well have found vivid models for his vision in Tasso's treatment of the Moslem-Christian struggle for the Holy Land or in Polybius' account of the wars between Rome and Carthage for the possession of Sicily.[26] He may have found in Procopius a graphic example of a "foothold" (discussed below) in the Greek Exarchate of Ravenna during the fifth and sixth centuries.[27] History, like art, has a way of repeating itself, so it should not be surprising that the European conflicts of the 1650s assumed those same ancient patterns. Our concern here is not with those classic accounts of old wars but with the impact of contemporary events on Milton's vision.

John Milton entered vigorously into the controversies that marked his era, and in his capacity as secretary for foreign languages in the English government sat close to the centers of power of his country, where he watched and served England's leaders as they shaped his world. Through his attendance at debates in the Council of State and through his contacts in the inner circles of that government, he maintained an intimate knowledge of the issues of his times and shared in the frustrations and triumphs of his fellow servants.[28]

When he came to the composition of his two epic poems this experience was a part of the fabric of his imagination and he drew on it, consciously or unconsciously, to shape his concept of the cosmic struggle between Good and Evil. In defining this struggle he makes extensive use of the language of diplomacy and the imagery of warfare, and one can find in the diplomatic and military history of his decade as a public servant events which correspond suggestively with this language and imagery.

It is not surprising that Milton so frequently uses the harsh colors of warfare to define this eternal struggle, for during the poet's mature years, that period when he was actively involved in the affairs of his country, England was seldom at peace. The decades from 1638 to 1658 record the two Bishop's Wars, the two civil wars, the Irish campaign, the Scottish campaign, the Anglo-Dutch War, and finally the Spanish War. This almost constant military activity etched itself in the imagination of the poet. If readers will consider the action of *Paradise Lost* visually, for example, they will discover the stage crowded with uniforms. Over 3,000 of the 5,429 lines in the first six books describe military ceremonies, conferences, confrontations, and battles. There is less in the final six books, surely, but Michael, as he talks with Adam in Books XI and XII, is under arms the entire time, and his revelations include graphic descriptions of warfare. Milton, though he declared himself "not sedulous by Nature to indite / Wars" (IX, 27–28), certainly did a great deal of it.

Indeed, a close look at Heaven and Hell in *Paradise Lost* will find them both described at one time or another as nations in arms. Prior to the war in Heaven, God summons his angels, who appear

> Under thir Hierarchs in orders bright;
> Ten thousand thousand Ensigns high advanc'd,
> . Standards and Gonfalons, twixt Van and Rear
> Stream in the Air.   (V, 587–90)

As night falls "the Angelic throng / Disperst in Bands and Files thir Camp extend" (V, 650–51) while Satan dislodges "with all his Legions" (V, 669) on a "flying march" (V, 688); and we may safely assume that his were not the only angels organized on that day as a military unit. Indeed, when Abdiel returns the following day, he finds "the Plain / Cover'd with thick embattl'd Squadrons bright" (VI, 15–16). Following his fall from Heaven, Satan arouses his fallen forces from off the "fiery Gulf" and sets about to organize what is essentially an armed camp. He directs his troops to reform into their units and march in review. He then delivers a stirring, militant speech which ends in his vow that "War then, War / Open or understood, must be resolv'd" (I, 661–62). In dramatic response his followers

> fierce with grasped Arms
> Clash'd on thir sounding shields the din of war,
> Hurling defiance toward the Vault of Heav'n.   (I, 667–69)

After the expulsion of the rebel angels, Heaven presents the picture of a secure and peaceful kingdom where the "Powers of Heav'n" resume their role as proper angels, equipped with harps and halos rather than swords and helmets. Hostilities do not cease, however, for though Heaven itself is safe from incursion, a new arena of battle develops beyond those "ever-during Gates." Chaos is a cosmic no-man's-land, where angels venture only in military formation, armed to the teeth.[29] At the Creation the Son does not appear in martial guise, of course; but there is, it seems, a need for escort. He leaves Heaven attended by "Chariots wing'd / From the Armory of God" (VII, 199–200) and Raphael is sent

> on a voyage uncouth and obscure,
> Far on excursion toward the Gates of Hell;
> Squar'd in full Legion (such command we had)
> To see that none thence issu'd forth a spy
> Or enemy, while God was in his work.   (VIII, 230–34)

Thus, Heaven and Hell seem locked in cosmic conflict, one which will persist until the end of time. Some of the imagery that Milton employs to define and enrich that struggle has suggestive parallels in one of the conflicts of his own age. The last of England's wars to take place during Milton's period of public service was that with Spain, which lasted from late 1655 until the Peace of the Pyranees in 1659. Cromwell involved England for a brief time in what was actually a century-long struggle between two great powers, France and Spain, for control of the hereditary Hapsburg possessions in the commercially rich provinces of Flanders known as the Spanish Netherlands, an area roughly included in the borders of modern Belgium. By the end of the Thirty Years' War in 1648, Spain had lost its position as the undisputed major power of Europe. She had been forced to recognize the independence of the United Netherlands but had been able to retain control of the Spanish Netherlands. France, growing in power even as Spain was declining, was reluctant to give up whatever claim she had to those provinces and so persisted during the 1650s in efforts to secure them. England entered the war after a long period of diplomatic maneuvering, during which both Cardinal Mazarin of France and Philip IV of Spain actively courted an English alliance. In the end Cromwell threw in his lot with the French. The terms of the alliance included a secret agreement that Charles II was to be denied his political haven in France and that certain towns on the coast of Flanders were to be given to England upon their capture from Spain. The English agreed in turn to deploy their fleet against Spain itself and to land an army in Flanders to assist the French. Cromwell's strategy in the war was to concentrate energies in the Netherlands while Admiral Blake skirted the Spanish coast, interrupting the flow of gold from the New World and preventing the intrusion of enemy forces by sea. The enterprise met with considerable success, for Blake kept the Spanish fleet from taking any part in the fighting in Flanders, Charles and his itinerant court were forced to seek refuge first in Germany and then in Spanish territory, and after the Battle of the Dunes Cromwell gained control of Dunkirk, thus reestablishing an English presence on the Continent for the first time since Mary Tudor had surrendered Calais a hundred years earlier.[30]

It is difficult to say how much Milton actually knew of the Spanish War. The blind poet was surely not as active in government as he had been earlier, but in his capacity as secretary for foreign languages he continued to be responsible for the preparation and translation of numerous letters and documents. He was a respected member of the Cromwell administration, his home in Petty France but a short walk from Whitehall; and during the years when the alliance was being debated and the war fought, it can surely be assumed that he was as interested as any public official in its outcome and would have kept abreast of events through his social and official contacts in government circles.[31] He was very decidedly involved in one of the climactic events of the war. In May–July 1658 he was called upon to prepare thirteen letters in a period of six weeks, including ten to France alone.[32] The numbers are somewhat deceptive, since the protocol of the time required that any letter to Louis XIV have a companion to Mazarin, but seven of these letters make mention of Dunkirk and the last four concern the surrender of that city and its immediate assignment to England.[33]

The balance of this study will propose certain parallels between the events of the Spanish War and the struggle between the forces of Good and Evil in Milton's epics. The real and the imagined conflicts have suggestive similarities, first, in their general outline; in each, two large powers are struggling for control over a smaller, disputed possession. Second, each includes images of a foothold, or bridgehead, in enemy territory. Third, in both event and imagery each incorporates elements of that theory of international dynamics to which modern historians have attached the label, "the balance of power."

A few remarks about method will be helpful before we proceed. The informed reader may be uncomfortable with the analogies proposed here in that they will seem to lack the complexity one is accustomed to find when examining an artist's use of sources. The effect is not without design. It seems more important at this stage of the inquiry to demonstrate that a relationship between images and events does indeed exist. Thus the analogies are presented without adornment, their lines in such sharp relief that, it is hoped, even the most critical eye can acknowledge them. Further, this study is more concerned with process than with meaning and so must forego for the moment the many delights of pursuing all the political, ontological, ideological, and philosophical implications of the correspondences. Such restraint is necessary if we are to avoid clouding our perception of what is going on in the creative process.

A brief consideration of a more familiar controversy will serve to illustrate. The figure of Satan has perplexed Miltonists since the days of Addison, and some more daring scholars have attempted to come to terms with him by suggesting that he is drawn from life.[34] There are, indeed, times in *Paradise Lost* when he does seem to resemble Cromwell:

> his face
> Deep scars of Thunder had intrencht, and care
> Sat on his faded cheek, but under Brows
> Of dauntless courage and considerate Pride.   (I, 600–03)[35]

The impatient pursuit of the political and ideological implications of this comparison has produced at least two very different schools of thought. If, as one group has argued, Satan is analogous to Cromwell, then it can be safely said that Milton disapproved of Cromwell, a view certainly sympathetic with that comfortable figure, Milton the Pacifist. On the other hand, it can be argued that since so much evidence seems to indicate that he admired Cromwell, we are free to conclude that he approved of Satan, a view which the Romantics found attractive. Our knowledge of Milton, of course, persuades us that both these conclusions are open to serious question. These contradictions are indeed frustrating; and in the face of them there is an understandable temptation simply to dismiss Cromwell as a source, with the result that we are denied what may be a valuable key to the complex figure of Satan.

Further confusion has arisen from the rather naive assumption that since Satan is the archetype of Evil and morally corrupt, he must therefore be a bad general, an inept leader, and an intellectual lightweight, deficient in all dimensions.[36] But life does not work that way, and neither should we expect it of art. For the present purpose it is sufficient to note that all successful leaders, however questionable or admirable their cause or moral persuasion, be they Ghengis Khan, Bonaparte, John Kennedy, Mao Tse-tung, or Martin Luther King, have certain qualities in common which equip them to sway large bodies of people and achieve a position of political prominence. Milton observed the leaders of his day at close range and noted some of those common qualities: a tendency toward extravagant gesture, a mastery of rhetoric, physical courage, and an unswerving dedication to their cause, among others. Not infrequently, he was able to observe, the burdens of office weighed so heavily that "care / Sat on" their faded cheeks. This experience helped him to define the figure of Satan, not as an incompetent bungler, but as an effective leader. After all, one must ask, is Satan an inept general? Surely not; he commands a third of the Heavenly Host and effectively revives a defeated and completely demoralized army in Hell. Is he an intellectual lightweight? Again, surely not; the only thing he doesn't understand is omnipotence; but then God alone knows what that means. He is pretty shrewd about all the rest and shows it as he manipulates his lieutenants, deceives Chaos, eludes the celestial guards, discovers Eve's weakness, and conquers the world. He is a competent leader in the same way that Cromwell was a competent leader, and this need not imply that Milton either admired Satan or disparaged Cromwell. It simply means that he was artist enough to create such a commanding figure from the materials of his experience; and in exploring that process little is to be gained by stretching the analogy out or reading into it the full burden of all that significance.

To return to the proposed parallels between the real and the imagined wars, the diplomatic and military activities of France and Spain in their struggle for control over the Spanish Netherlands are in some respects quite similar to those of Heaven and Hell as they contend for control over "this pendant world." In *Paradise Lost* the world, once created, takes on many of the characteristics of a frontier post or colony of Heaven, where Adam acts somewhat in the fashion of a governor-general. Satan sees him thus; God made Man, he says, and

> for him built
> Magnificent this World, and Earth his seat,
> Him Lord pronounc'd.   (IX, 152–54)

Raphael defines Adam's role for him in much the same terms. Man is to subdue the Earth and "throughout Dominion hold" (VII, 532) over all its creatures. God looks upon the world as "th' addition of his Empire" (VII, 555) with Adam as a trusted subordinate whom the Father has made "chief / Of all his works" (VII, 515–16).

Control of the world is to remain in dispute, however, for by divine ruling Satan is free to act outside the walls of Heaven. When he refers to the world, it is in terms of conquest. It is a place, he tells his followers in Hell, where

> may lie expos'd
> The utmost border of his Kingdom, left
> To their defense who hold it;   (II, 360–62)

and later, as he gazes on the pleasures of Eden, he speaks of "conquering this new World" (IV, 391). The two kingdoms meet at a hostile boundary and prelapsarian man is protected by armed sentries in this outpost of Heaven; Gabriel, "Chief of th' Angelic Guards," sits outside Eden with his troop of the "Youth of Heav'n" equipped with "Celestial Armory, Shields, Helms, and Spears" (IV, 549–53). Under their watchful vigilance there is easy access between Heaven and Earth. Uriel is unarmed and Raphael makes the trip without incident, passing by the sentinels' "glittering tents" on his way to Eden. Satan at this stage of the hostilities must come in disguise, a spy intruding on enemy land; and only when he is confronted by the sentries does he assume his accustomed warrior posture, springing up to threaten battle: "On his Crest / Sat horror Plum'd; not wanted in his grasp / What seem'd both Spear and Shield" (IV, 988–90).

There are occasions in the epics when both Satan and God engage in diplomatic maneuvering of the type that preceded the Spanish War. Prior to the Fall Satan has need of assistance on his cosmic voyage and in the process of enlisting aid runs the gamut of diplomatic posturing, from his effort to bully Sin and Death into opening the gates of Hell to his subservient fawning before Uriel, whom he praises with all of the flowery hyperbole of a seventeenth-century courtier. One of his most effective performances is in the court of Chaos where he finds that monarch unhappy about the recent incursions on his realm, territorial encroachments, he complains to Satan, that are

> Weak'ning the Sceptre of old Night: first Hell
> Your dungeon stretching far and wide beneath;
> Now lately Heaven and Earth, another World.   (II, 1002–04)

Satan, the skilled diplomat, asks assistance in finding that world. Disguising his full intent, he promises that if successful he will seek to return that usurped region to Chaos, who can then "once more / Erect the Standard there of ancient Night" (II, 985–86). All Satan wants really, he says, is revenge; he has no territorial ambitions.

Similarly, Raphael's role may be seen as that of an envoy from a great power. His diplomatic mission is to convince Adam of the benefits

of his continued allegiance to his God and to inform him of the dangers
inherent in defection of any kind. For a time, he tells Adam, the world
is to be like some territorial possession of Heaven which may eventually
achieve the status of statehood. Human beings will live on Earth

> till by degrees of merit rais'd
> They open to themselves at length the way
> Up hither, under long obedience tri'd,
> And Earth be chang'd to Heav'n, and Heav'n to Earth,
> One Kingdom, Joy and Union without end.   (VII, 157–61)

but only "if ye be found obedient" (V, 501). Should Adam choose to violate the terms of his allegiance, however, the consequences are clear.
Raphael's account of the defeat of Satan is a vivid enough lesson for any
statesman pondering alternative alliances.

In *Paradise Regained* the imagery of contending nations persists,
binding the two works with a pattern of events which identifies them as
parts of a single vision. As a consequence of the Fall, Satan and his de-
mons are in firm possession of the world and are comfortably enjoying
"this fair Empire won of Earth and Air" (I, 63). The grand councils are
no longer held in Pandemonium but "in mid air" (I, 39), and it is here
that Satan gathers his followers to discuss what appears to be a threat to
their control. His talk is all of conquest and dominion, of

> How many Ages, as the years of men,
> This Universe we have possest, and rul'd
> In manner at our will th' affairs of Earth.   (I, 48–50)

His position is comparable to that of a distraught Philip IV confronted
with the French threat to the hereditary Hapsburg possessions in the
Spanish Netherlands. Satan continues in this vein during the second
council held in "the middle Region of thick Air" (II, 117), where he reports that

> an Enemy
> Is ris'n to invade us, who no less
> Threat'ns than our expulsion down to Hell.   (II, 126–28)

Once more, we hear almost the same words from the mouth of
God, who boasts of his son as a man who will resist all of Satan's forces
and eventually

> drive him back to Hell,
> Winning by Conquest what the first man lost
> By fallacy surpris'd.   (I, 153–55)

But first Christ must be exercised in the wilderness, where he will

> lay down the rudiments
> Of his great warfare, ere I send him forth
> To conquer Sin and Death the two grand foes.   (I, 157–59)

Christ's exercise is an encounter with a Satan appearing in the guise of a skilled diplomat, one who offers aid, conceals designs, and misrepresents his position as he did with Chaos in *Paradise Lost*. He is feeling out a potential enemy, assessing strengths and probing for weaknesses, making threats and suggesting alliances. Satan is at his most devious when offering Christ a kingdom. There are only two worth having, Rome and Parthia, and Satan shows him the weaker first, the one destined to earlier extinction. With a show of grave concern, he counsels:

> one of these
> Thou must make sure thy own; the Parthian first
> By my advice.   (III, 362–64)

It is bad advice, of course, worthy of the Devil, and only after Christ refuses does Satan reveal the glories of Rome.

When Satan falls from the temple's pinnacle, the angelic hosts descend to succor Christ; and in this, their only visit to Earth in the poem, they carry out the imagery established in *Paradise Lost*. It is a military formation:

> straight a fiery Globe
> Of Angels on full sail of wing flew nigh,
> Who on their plumy Vans receiv'd him soft.   (IV, 581–83)[37]

And when the choirs raise their voices, it is to sing of victories, the first in Heaven and now this, in which Christ has "regain'd lost Paradise, / And frustrated the conquest fraudulent" (IV, 608–09). He is the "heir of both worlds, / Queller of Satan" (IV, 633–34).

Of particular interest is the appearance in the poems of the image of a foothold, or bridgehead. One of the fruits of the Spanish War was the English acquisition of Dunkirk. This "footing in the continent," as it was called, was to be a "sally-port by which his Highness may advantageously sally forth upon his enemies," a base of operations, in Thurloe's words, "which might be made use of to the overthrow of France."[38] The rebel angels in their deliberations in Hell speak of the world in just such terms. It is an outpost of Heaven which, once occupied, may even be used as a bridgehead for further operations to regain their "ancient seat." Beëlzebub tells them that from there

> with neighboring Arms
> And opportune excursion we may chance
> Re-enter Heav'n.   (II, 395–97)

The bridging of Chaos after the Fall is, of course, an imaginative visual realization of this language, establishing the world as a literal "bridgehead."

God and Satan, as we have seen, often use similar language to define their relationship with Man; and in depicting the war Milton frequently employs the same military image on both sides. The foothold is no exception. After the fall God instructs Michael to return to Earth, reoccupy Eden, and deny the forces of Evil and the progeny of Adam access to "all my Trees" (XI, 124). Milton enriches the biblical source by designating Michael as commander of a military unit and emphasizing the martial nature of the mission, thus heightening the impression that the angels are entering a hostile environment and adapting the incident to fit the larger image of cosmic conflict.[39] Michael comes with a "Cohort bright / Of watchful Cherubim" (XI, 127–28); he wears a "military Vest of purple" over his "lucid Arms" and at his side "as in a glistering Zodiac hung the Sword, / Satan's dire dread, and in his hand the Spear" (XI, 240–48). Their mission is to establish a "Cherubic watch, and of a Sword the flame / Wide waving, all approach far off to fright" (XI, 120–21). The archangel obeys, ordering "his Powers to seize / Possession of the Garden" (XI, 221–22), thus creating a Heavenly foothold in the Satan-infested World.

After the war in Heaven there are no more pitched battles in the cosmic conflict, but there are further victories and defeats. Milton continues to use the language of conquest, as we have seen, but in the absence of military confrontation he turns to the imagery of international diplomacy to define the changing fortunes of the two powers. The two pivotal events in the history of man, which alter both his role in the war and the relative strength of the antagonists, are his fall from grace in the Garden and his redemption through the ministry of Jesus Christ. In his epics, Milton describes these two turning points in the war in terms of the shifting balance of power among nations.

The middle of the seventeenth century presented a vivid model for such a shift. Until the Treaty of Westphalia in 1648, Spain had been considered the strongest power in Europe, but once its weaknesses were unmasked that nation entered a period of sharp decline during which the powers of Europe scrambled for pieces of its crumbling empire. The United Netherlands sat confidently behind its dikes and built a fleet which made it the strongest naval and commercial power in the Western world.[40] France began a policy of territorial expansion which was eventually to unite all Europe against it, and for a short time ambitious princes found that they could not ignore the rising star of Cromwell's England.

Shifts in the balance of power among nations are marked by many seemingly unrelated and inexplicable changes in official policy, whose significance skilled diplomats are quick to read. Old enemies are embraced and recent allies spurned, ambassadors are recalled and state visits cancelled, letters are exchanged, the wording of which is carefully analyzed, fleets are moved and tariffs raised — all outward manifestations, the "body language" of international affairs, reflecting changing alliances and shifts of power. When Catholic France signed a commercial treaty with militantly Protestant England in 1656, Cromwell dismissed the Spanish ambassador, Cárdenas, and warmly greeted Mazarin's envoy, Bordeaux. Earlier, Charles II had been denied his sanctuary in France, where he had been a welcome guest for a number of years. Any alert statesman would conclude that if Cromwell had the power to force Charles to quit Paris and seek haven in Cologne, he could do much more. When England gained possession of a few square miles of Flemish coast in 1658, this small victory had repercussions that went far beyond the actual value of the place. Cromwell was hailed as the arbiter of Europe with, in Thurloe's words, "the keys of the continent at his girdle,"[41] praise which is not as excessive as it first sounds, for such small conquests are often the prelude to larger events.[42]

When Milton describes the consequences of the Fall of Man, it is in terms of just such a shift in the balance of power. As a result of this small act of eating, it appears, to Satan at least, that God "hath giv'n up / Both his beloved Man and all his World" (X, 488–89). And so it would seem, for the act is followed by a series of events, each minor in itself, whose sum is the inescapable conclusion that Adam's world has passed under the hegemony of the forces of Evil. Sin mysteriously senses "new strength" as a result of the distant victory, and "Dominion giv'n me large / Beyond this Deep" (X, 243–45). The bridge over the turmoil of Chaos is symbolic of this authority, even as Cromwell's power reached across the stormy Channel after the occupation of Dunkirk. It creates, in Satan's words, "one Realm / Hell and this World, one Realm, one Continent" (X, 391–92), invalidating forever God's offer of "One Kingdom, Joy and Union without end." Satan is now powerful enough in his own right so that he has no further need of old allies. He passes over his bridge, paying no heed to Chaos, who is raging against broken promises:

> on either side
> Disparted Chaos over-built exclaim'd,
> And with rebounding surge the bars assail'd
> That scorn'd his indignation.   (X, 415–18)

In Pandemonium, Satan tells of his conquest and urges his followers to "possess, / As Lords, a spacious World" (X, 466–67), concluding with the triumphal words, "What remains, ye Gods / But up and enter now into full bliss" (X, 502–03).

The actions of Heaven reflect this same shift. God withdraws Gabriel and the angelic guards, an outward sign as tangible as the withdrawal of Charles II from France or Cárdenas from England that there has been a change in the subtle and hidden chemistry of the balance of power. Earth holds some dangers now, and it is the mighty Michael who returns to occupy Eden, not with Gabriel's beardless "youth of Heav'n" but with his

> choice of flaming Warriors, lest the Fiend
> Or in behalf of Man, or to invade
> Vacant possession some new trouble raise.   (XI, 101–03)

"In behalf of Man" is surely interesting. God lends emphasis to the fact that man is no longer under his dominion, and that it is Satan now who acts in the name of his new subject.[43] Adam is diminished. No longer lord of an outpost of Heaven, protected by celestial guards, he and Eve are banished into a world where Satan rules. Subduing the earth seems beyond him now. The ground is cursed and man will eat only in the sweat of his face. He will end his days as dust, reduced to the element he was destined to rule.

In *Paradise Regained* there is another subtle shift in the cosmic balance of power, defined chiefly in terms of man's new role in the war. Christ is a pattern for the triumph of man, and the political and military imagery is particularly effective here, as it places the inner struggle in the perspective of the world. Michael had told Adam that Christ, when he came, would arm man "With spiritual Armor, able to resist / Satan's assaults, and quench his fiery darts" (*PL*, XII, 491–92). Christ, as man, provides an example for the race, showing them that they need no longer be subject to the tyrant. The world is like a long oppressed nation that, newly armed with hope, can rise up and strike back at the occupying power; and Adam's progeny are now strong enough to reject the despotic commands of the usurper to "fall down / And worship me" (IV, 166–67), or "cast thyself down" (IV, 555). Thrice-armed by Christ's ministry, man can now enter the lists on his own behalf; and though

Satan is still powerful, his rule over the conquered territory need no longer go unchallenged. As God predicted even before the Fall,

> Upheld by me, yet once more he shall stand
> On even ground against his mortal foe,
> By me upheld. (*PL*, III, 178–80)

It is a role such as that which England anticipated the Flemish would assume, inspired by the presence and example of the English army in Dunkirk. Cromwell's ambassador to France, William Lockhart, for example, expressed the hope that "many of the people of Flanders and those parts kept under [by] Spanish severity might declare themselves Protestant, and several of the great towns be induced to throw [off] the Spanish yoke."[44]

The perceptive reader will be troubled by these analogies, for if one pursues the suggested parallels between the real and the imagined conflicts, some serious contradictions surface, of the type that obscures the Satan-Cromwell analogy, discussed earlier. If, for example, the war between Spain and France for control of the Spanish Netherlands is comparable to the struggle between the forces of Good and Evil for control of Adam's world, then Milton would seem to be equating Spain with Heaven and France with Hell. The same difficulty presents itself in the analogy with the balance of power, where God surrenders the world to Satan's forces after the Fall in the same manner that Spain surrendered portions of the Spanish Netherlands to France at the Peace of the Pyranees in 1659. Given Milton's attitude toward Catholic Spain, the bulwark of the anti-Christ, the author and fomenter of popish plots, and England's ancient enemy on the seas, is it possible that he could have considered Spain as analogous to Heaven? Again, victorious France seems comparable to victorious Hell, but Milton's England was allied with France in the war. Does this mean that Milton perceived the Protectorate government as an ally of the devil?

The two images of the foothold described are equally troublesome, for they would appear to contradict one another. In the first, Satan describes Adam's world as a bridgehead to be used for further incursions on Heaven. In the second, after the Fall, God reoccupies Eden, thus maintaining a foothold in Satan's world. The latter, postlapsarian image provides a much more satisfactory correspondence with the historical event, the return of the armies of Protestant England to reoccupy a part of its former territory in Catholic Flanders, for Cromwell here is more appropriately comparable to God, England to Heaven, Spain to Hell, and Flanders to the fallen world. The two are, however, the same image — a foothold. Can the reader reject the former and accept the latter analogy as valid, simply because one happens to conflict with our concept of Milton's values and allegiances and the other does not?

This is not to suggest, however, that it is fruitless to pose such questions, no matter how they may seem to leave us in "wand'ring mazes lost." The very contradictions help define what may be called an axiom of the poetics of experience: whatever the process whereby life is transfigured into art, it is not always by direct, one-for-one analogy. Milton himself said as much: "Who would claim that things which are analogous must correspond to each other in every respect?"[45] One should not demand of an historical analogy a degree of congruence that one would never require of any other source, be it literary, biblical, iconographic, or musical. Indeed, it was the insistence on this strict correspondence that cast the nineteenth-century biographical commentaries in such a bad light in the first place. If it could be shown that the analogy is apt in every way, the poet would be open to charges of slavish imitation, political propaganda, or at least a decline in creative energy.[46]

Somewhere in that maze of contradictions there surely lies a core of truth; but the pursuit of all the implications of the alternative correspondences, Cromwell-Satan or Cromwell-God, can only confuse the search for understanding of process. For the moment it is sufficient to observe that all political or military leaders, whatever their ideological orientation, when planning to expand their authority or secure their borders, will express themselves in terms of occupying bridgeheads, establishing footholds, or upsetting what we have come to call the balance of power. Milton, in his epic poems, was describing a war, an immense struggle raging in the cosmic vastness and in the heart of man, between the forces of Good and Evil; and he was seeking ways to depict man's role in that struggle so as to provide his reader with a vivid warning of its crucial consequences for the seed of Adam. To this end he defined the spiritual struggle in terms of armed conflict, as have many before and since; and he drew on all the biblical, literary, historical, and iconographical resources of his vast learning to make that warning a compelling one. He also enriched this image of warfare with the language of real life. He drew on his period of government service, when England was party to a war which in its broad outline was comparable to many others of which he had read, a war in which, moreover, there were events whose inclusion would add to the vitality of his imaginative account. In his use of this experience he does not necessarily reflect his attitude toward Spain, France, Cromwell, Philip IV, or his verdict on war itself. The astute reader will observe that Milton's moral judgments of the nations and figures in his epics are predicated on more substantial factors than their resemblance to the heroes or villains of his own day — factors such as their obedience or disobedience to the will of God or how faithfully they follow the light of right reason.

By this point in the argument scholarly readers may begin to feel slightly uneasy, sensing perhaps that they have been pretty well boxed in. If, on the one hand, they are asked to reject the simplistic and unimaginative one-for-one interpretations of the biographical critic and, on the other, to abstain for the moment from pursuing the more complex implications of the analogies, one of the true pleasures of the profession, they may well ask what there is left to consider. First, it is hoped, this analysis has been persuasive in demonstrating that the parallels are valid ones. The effort to isolate the analogies, however, has a more important function than simply identifying them. In exploring the influence of life on art it is necessary first to single out the essentials of that life and that art, so as to establish a foundation upon which to build a more elaborate analysis of the relationship between the two. One must first penetrate to the core of the artist's experience, to that point where the bright arc of inspiration bridges the gap between fact and fancy, before attempting to understand how he shapes and colors it into his art. That moment is brilliant and simple, like a pure beam of white light before it is refracted by the prism of the imagination into the multicolored spectrum of expression in word, oil, or sound. To see it then is to see it whole.

To isolate the relationship in this way makes it possible to examine it and to venture one or two proposals for the formulation of a poetics of experience. Basic to any understanding of the influence of life on art is the realization that the process is almost entirely dependent on the faculty of memory. Experiential and literary sources of poetry differ in that the latter are so often close at hand and hence remain unspoiled by the passage of time; one need only pull a book from the shelf or recall the words and a work, no matter how ancient, may be said to live and participate in the moment. Should Milton have wished to make use of the wrath of Achilles in his lines, Homer's hexameters were but an arm's reach away, to read or have read, if they were not already etched in his mind. But how could he consult the experience of a London of 1643, Essex's army in decay, Rupert's cavalry cutting ever closer to the city, the parliamentary forces everywhere in retreat? And what of 1660? If Milton wished to convey some of the true shape of his own experience of fear or despair, he had no sources upon which to call save the dying coal of his own days. No experience can be retrieved with the same precision as a literary source — the memory fades, the mind plays tricks, lingering over some favored detail, leaving another in shadows. The particulars grow dim and over the years one recalls not so much "what it was" that happened as one does, more generally, "how things were" at the time.

In a way, it is this quality of the memory that makes experience something of a touchstone for the artist, for that question is just the one we ask: "How were things?" or better, "How are things?" It is the generic perceptions of the creative mind that we most admire, for it is in them that the artist touches the truth of our nature. We expect the artist to see in the particular acts of human beings a pattern common to the race and to define it in art, stripped of parochial or transitory trappings, in such a way that we may recognize it as universally true. We expect the artist, in brief, to transcend the particular and show us the shape of things. Artists will, of course, define that vision in terms of particulars, and the aptness and decorum of detail are marks of artistic achievement. But it is that generic shape for which the reader searches; for while the particular may catch the attention and delight the eye, it is the vision that enlarges the spirit. Further, it is the vision that directs the choice of detail, either consciously or unconsciously, not the other way around. It is a commonplace that time glosses over the experience of the past. If it was a happy time, one forgets the sadness; if a period crowned with triumph, the doubts and uncertainties of the trial will fade with the years and the moment of victory remain bright in the mind. If called upon to give an account of an event long past, one will recall those particulars that convey the quality and tone of the time as one remembers it. The creative vision will pierce to the meaning of that event and the artist will select the detail that gives expression to that meaning.

This study suggests that something of this order was going on in the imagination of John Milton as he searched for ways to define his vision of the war between Good and Evil and to warn of its grim consequences. As his mind reached back, he recalled the shape of war: two great powers contending for control of a small corner of Europe, one a fading giant, the other a swelling youth, proud in its vigor and ambition. The choice for England was whether to support Spain and maintain for a time the delicate balance of power in Europe or to throw in her lot with the aspiring French in exchange for a foothold on the Continent.[47] The issues were debated for months, in both public forum and the inner councils of the Protectorate government. We do not know how the secretary for foreign languages stood on the issues, nor is it important that we do. What concerns us is that in later years Milton recalled, through the veil of memory, that spectacle of controversy and conflict and saw in it how "things are" with fragile man at such a time: Great powers clash. Some wax. Some wane. In the end, "what I will is Fate"; and so we take our solitary way, "hand in hand with wand'ring steps and slow."

La Salle College

NOTES

1. "Biography and Criticism — A Misalliance Disputed," *Critical Inquiry*, I (March 1975), 479–80.

2. In *Milton Studies*, VII, ed. Albert C. Labriola and Michael Lieb, (Pittsburgh, 1975), for example, the editors published ten essays, each illustrative of a critical approach currently employed in the study of Milton's works. Biographical criticism is not included in this very useful volume. An essay on psychobiography is about as close as they come.

3. The "MLA Newsletter" of November 1973 reports on the results of a survey of members in which only 236 of 42,383 (0.5 percent) responses indicated "biographical study" as an area of interest. "Literary criticism" and "literary history and criticism" combined polled 50 percent of the responses.

4. Christopher Hill's provocative *Milton and the English Revolution* (New York, 1978) represents the most recent effort to break the silence. Reception has been mixed, however, perhaps reflecting the current status of the method. Reviewers in general praise his history but dismiss his analysis of the poetry in the light of it. See Frank Kermode, "A Moderate New Notion," *The New York Times Book Review*, 5 March 1978, p. 10. Some view with alarm this apparent disinterment of the long discredited approach. In "Milton among the Radicals," *TLS*, 2 Dec. 1977, p. 1395, col. 1, Blair Worden warns that "Hill wants to redirect the course of Milton studies. If he succeeds, we shall know that literary criticism has lost its nerve." The works of Leon Edel and W. Jackson Bate are encouraging, as both include critical passages in their biographies. Bate, in *Samuel Johnson* (New York, 1977), p. xx, proposes that we "try to heal the split between 'biography' and 'criticism.'"

5. Psychology has been a matter of interest to Miltonists, of course, since E. M. W. Tillyard first wrote of the "unconscious meanings" in *Paradise Lost* and found Satan to be an "insubordinate creature of Milton's imagination," *Milton* (London, 1961), p. 289. The need is for a psychological study of the creative imagination that does not depend for its terminology upon the pathology of abnormal behavior.

6. The list is long. The sentiments seem to be summed up in Eliot's confession that he entertained "an antipathy toward Milton the man" in "Milton (1947)," *The Proceedings of the British Academy*, Vol. XXXIII, as published in *Milton Criticism*, ed. James Thorpe (New York, 1969), p. 312.

7. This view of life during the Interregnum has been corrected somewhat by Lady Antonia Fraser in her superb *Cromwell, The Lord Protector* (New York, 1974), pp. 455–83.

8. *Milton, A Biography* (Oxford, 1968), II, 95, 481, and passim.

9. *The Complete Prose Works of John Milton*, ed. Don M. Wolfe et al. (New Haven, 1963–), VII, 2–3, 47, and passim — hereafter cited as *YP*. See also his "Milton and

Cromwell: 'A Short But Scandalous Night of Interruption'?" *Achievements of the Left Hand: Essays on the Prose of John Milton*, ed. Michael Lieb and John T. Shawcross (Amherst, 1974), pp. 185–218.

10. *John Milton, Poet and Humanist: Essays by James Holly Hanford*, ed. John S. Diekhoff (Cleveland, 1966), passim.

11. George F. Sensabaugh, *That Grand Whig, Milton* (Stanford, 1952).

12. Too numerous to list. See, for example, B. A. Wright, *Milton's "Paradise Lost"* (New York, 1962), p. 129, where he describes Book VI as a satire "on war in general"; Edward Wagenknecht, *The Personality of Milton* (Norman, Okla., 1970); Stella P. Revard, "Milton's Critique of Heroic Warfare in *Paradise Lost* V and VI," *SEL*, VII (Winter, 1967), 119–139, in which the two books are described as a "full length critique of war, both earthly and heavenly" (p. 122).

13. "Milton and the Cult of Conformity," *Milton: Modern Judgments*, ed. Alan Rudrum (London, 1968), p. 30. E. M. W. Tillyard says of another group of scholars, "People are so fond of Shakespeare that they are desperately anxious to have him of their own way of thinking"; in *Shakespeare's History Plays* (New York, 1947), p. 204.

14. Roland M. Frye's *Milton's Imagery and the Visual Arts* (Princeton, 1978) is a brilliant and most fascinating study of the subject.

15. *Milton's Epic Voice: The Narrator in "Paradise Lost"* (Cambridge, 1963).

16. In the most recent major conference on Milton, held at the University of Wisconsin–Milwaukee in November 1974, there were three papers on the subject alone: John R. Mulder, "The Narrator in *Paradise Lost*"; Roger B. Rollin's discussion of Mulder's paper; and Roger H. Sundell, "The Prologues in *Paradise Lost*"; as well as frequent reference in other presentations. All were interesting and provocative.

17. Two recent studies are Donald F. Bouchard, *Milton: a Structural Reading* (Montreal, 1974), and Ralph Waterbury Condee, *Structure in Milton's Poetry* (University Park, Pa., 1974).

18. Jackson Campbell Boswell, *Milton's Library* (New York, 1975). The author lists 1,520 separate works, some multivolumed, which scholarship has either confirmed or suggested that Milton read.

19. *YP*, IV, 144.

20. In "Filling the Gaps: New Perspectives on Mr. Secretary Milton," *Milton Studies*, XII, ed. James D. Simmonds (Pittsburgh, 1979), pp. 180–90.

21. Robert Thomas Fallon, "Milton's Military Imagery: Its Growth and Function in his Art," Diss. Columbia 1964, in particular pp. 65 and 103–08. See, more recently, Jackie DiSalvo, "'The Lord's Battells': *Samson Agonistes* and the Puritan Revolution," *Milton Studies*, IV, ed. James D. Simmonds (Pittsburgh, 1973), pp. 39–62, in which Ms. DiSalvo discusses the play in the same context.

22. *The Personality of Milton*, pp. 41–43.

23. Robert H. West discusses the subject helpfully in *Milton and the Angels* (Athens, Ga., 1955), pp. 106 ff.

24. *A Critique of "Paradise Lost"* (New York, 1960), p. 24.

25. *"Paradise Lost" and its Critics* (Cambridge, Eng., 1951), p. 106.

26. Milton quotes Polybius in *Of Reformation*, *YP*, I, 599, and *A Defense of the People of England*, *YP*, IV, 439.

27. There are two references to Procopius in the Commonplace Book, *YP*, I, 416, 488, and others elsewhere.

28. J. Milton French, *The Life Records of John Milton* (New Brunswick, N.J., 1956), III, 75–205. The Mylius papers record eleven separate occasions in 1651–1652 when

Milton attended meetings of the Council of State: Oct. 16, 20, 25; Dec. 31; Jan. 2, 6, 8, 19; Feb. 4, 9, 22.

29. With the exception of Raphael, "the sociable Spirit," and "th'Arch-Angel Uriel." All quotations of the poetry are from *John Milton: Complete Poems and Major Prose*, ed. Merritt Y. Hughes (New York, 1957).

30. Charles H. Firth, *The Last Years of the Protectorate, 1656–1658* (New York, 1964), II, 182. Blake's mission was in some ways similar to Raphael's during the days of Creation when he was sent to preclude any "eruption bold" which might have interrupted the divine work. Indeed, at one critical point in the campaign the presence of the English fleet prevented the dispatch of Spanish reinforcements from the port of San Sebastián to the Netherlands.

31. See Fallon, "Filling the Gaps," p. 190 and n. 91.

32. State Letters 146–51 and 154–57 in *YP*, V, 823–46.

33. Some scholars have suggested that Cromwell's Spanish Declaration of 26 October 1655, in which he announced his opposition to Spain, may also be Miltonic. John T. Shawcross, in "A Survey of Milton's Prose Works," *Achievements of the Left Hand*, finds the ascription to Milton "noteworthy" (p. 363). *YP*, V, 711–12, rejects the document.

34. One of the most rewarding of recent efforts to identify Satan with a historical figure is Joan S. Bennett's "God, Satan, and King Charles: Milton's Royal Portraits," *PMLA*, XCII (May 1977), 441–57. Prof. Bennett, however, does not propose that Satan is modeled on Charles himself. The figure is rather drawn from Milton's fiction of the king in *Eikonoklastes*, which is in turn a reply to Gauden's fiction in *Eikon Basilike*, thus thrice removed from the historical monarch.

35. In *John Milton: "Paradise Lost," Books I–II*, ed. John Broadbent (Cambridge, Eng., 1972), Prof. Broadbent notes that "Milton admired leadership, like Satan's, in Cromwell" (p. 39). William Empson, in *Milton's God* (London, 1961), p. 74, is uncertain whether Satan is a satire on Charles II or on Cromwell. See also James Holly Hanford, *A Milton Handbook* (New York, 1954), pp. 191 and 238.

36. See, for example, C. S. Lewis's judgment that Satan represents the "co-existence of a subtle and incessant intellectual activity with an incapacity to understand anything," *A Preface to "Paradise Lost"* (London, 1960), p. 99.

37. See Hughes, p. 528 n., where he identifies "Globe" as a "circular phalanx of troops," and p. 244 n., where he refers to *OED* (8).

38. Firth, II, 218.

39. Genesis iii, 24.

40. Charles Woolsey Cole, *Colbert and a Century of French Mercantilism* (New York, 1932), p. 343. Colbert estimated that by 1665 Dutch vessels were carrying three-fourths of the trade of Europe.

41. Firth, II, 218.

42. A year earlier, Cromwell had been negotiating with the King of Sweden for control of yet another foothold on the Continent, the Duchy of Bremen. Firth, II, 27 n., 226.

43. See "behalf" in *OED* I.2.a.

44. Firth, II, 219.

45. *YP*, VI, 547.

46. Two recent books, widely different in orientation, address the question of the artist's use of his sources. Arnold Stein, in *The Art of Presence* (Berkeley, 1978) proposes two Miltons, the person and the poet, and concerns himself only with the latter. The poet, as a "presence" in the lines, is the pure, disembodied artist who accepts the challenge of composing a long, narrative poem about the myth of the Garden and delights himself and

his reader with his ingenuity in overcoming the difficulties presented by the materials: "the man, Milton, approved the judicious reticence of the poet, letting his character speak freely and well" (p. 143). One of Prof. Stein's unique contributions is to find Milton very much at ease with his artistic self, unlike more psychologically oriented studies which propose that the poetry is a product of a subconscious clash between the two. The figure is far removed from the Milton proposed in these pages, of course, but the book is a gracefully written and valuable study of the process. On a different level, though more to the point, John Irving, in *The World According to Garp* (New York, 1979), illustrates the writer's effort to create art from the materials of his life. The accounts, though admittedly antic, provide valuable insights and deserve attention. See particularly pp. 263–274, which make a shambles of the biographical critic's close analogies.

47. Fraser, *Cromwell*, p. 552. Ludlow's criticism, quoted here, is perceptive. The French alliance, he wrote, was ill-conceived, for "by it the balance of the two crowns of Spain and France was destroyed, and a foundation laid for the future greatness of the French, to the unspeakable prejudice of all Europe in general, and of this nation in particular."

"THY HUMILIATION SHALL EXALT":
THE CHRISTOLOGY OF *PARADISE LOST*

Albert C. Labriola

I N *PARADISE LOST* Satan's relationship with the fallen angels is described in various ways. Fraudulently he professes to be their judge, savior, and creator, the same roles undertaken by the Son and prefigured by certain Old Testament prophets and patriarchs, most notably Moses. Confronting the fallen angels still "covering the Flood" (I, 312), Satan seeks to raise them from oblivion.[1] In the posture of an *orant*, he judges the angels who will not be raised as "for ever fall'n" (I, 330). The others, who rally to his voice and presence — "thir liveliest pledge" and "surest signal" (I, 274, 278) — will constitute the "remnant" populating the hellish domain he intends to create. In great detail Satan's raising of the fallen angels (Book I) and the formation of their society (Book II) closely parallel the description of Moses' leading the Israelites through the Red Sea and toward Canaan (Book XII). These resemblances acquire greater meaning when related to the prophecy of the Son's temporal ministry — namely, his intervention for the "multitude of [his] redeem'd" (III, 260).

Because of Satan's "cunning resemblance" to Moses and the Son, scholars have commented on Milton's technique of characterizing the archfiend. They view him as a demonic parody of Moses and the Son. If the Son is the *imago*, then Satan is the *eidolon*.[2] Still to be explained is Milton's use of the interrelation of Moses, the Son, and Satan to elaborate a fundamental concept of his epic, its Christology. That is my topic.

As his followers perceive him in Book I, Satan is paradoxically described: "Dark'n'd so, yet shone / Above them all" (599–600). While Satan appears dimmed, like the sun partially concealed by mists, clouds, or an eclipse (I, 594–97), he still shines forth. Elsewhere in the epic there are similar accounts of Satan's appearance. When he returns to hell in Book X, Satan mounts his throne:

> Down a while
> He sat, and round about him saw unseen:

29

> At last as from a Cloud his fulgent head
> And shape Star-bright appear'd, or brighter.   (447–50)

Describing Satan's presence and self-disclosure to the fallen angels, these images are adapted from the Old Testament — for example, the cloud and column of fire marking the guiding angel at the Exodus or indicating the presence of the deity when he communicates with Moses. Among other passages, Exodus xxiv, 15–18 and Deuteronomy v, 22 describe God's presence at the mountaintop as a "cloude" and "fire."[3] Similarly, *Paradise Lost* uses images of cloudlike concealment and sunlike illumination to describe God's manifestation of himself, and at times the images paradoxically converge. The epic narrator explains that

> when [the Father] shad'st
> The full blaze of [his] beams, and through a cloud
> Drawn round about [him] like a radiant Shrine,
> Dark with excessive bright [his] skirts appear,
> Yet dazzle Heav'n.   (III, 377–81)

Images of darkness and light also characterize Moses' appearance to the Chosen People. Exodus xxiv, 18 recounts how "Moses entred into the middes of the cloude, & went up to the mountaine" to hear the Lord. Descending from Sinai after having received the Commandments (Exodus xxxiv, 29), Moses appears radiant. In this passage the word "KRN" from the Hebrew Bible has been translated to mean "shone" or "horned," indicating that Moses' countenance and head sent forth sunlike rays or horns of light. The Latin Vulgate translates the Hebrew as *cornuta*, so that artists, including Michelangelo, have depicted Moses with horns coming from his forehead. After his meetings with the Lord, including those in the tent, Moses became so radiant that he wore a veil when speaking with the people. But he too, like the Father in *Paradise Lost*, remains noticeably brilliant even while somewhat concealed. Because of Moses' ascents to the mountaintop, proximity to the Lord, and radiance, he undergoes virtual divinization. Certain passages in Scripture (Exodus iv, 16; vii, 1) indicate that in his meetings with the pharaoh Moses was to present himself "as God."

These and other passages in Scripture use images of descent and ascent, darkness and light, concealment and disclosure to describe Moses. If such imagery calls attention to similarities between Moses and the God of the Old Testament, it also highlights his relationship with the deity of the New Testament — in particular, with the Son who undergoes the cycle of humiliation and exaltation. Their relationship is nowhere more graphically illustrated than at the Transfiguration, an episode recounted in the Synoptic Gospels (Matthew xvii, 1–8, Mark ix, 1–7, Luke ix, 28–36). Depicting the Son's transition between states of humiliation and exaltation, the Transfiguration further dramatizes the connection between Moses and the Son by having them appear together. High on a mountain and in the presence of three disciples, Christ radiates light: "His face did shine as the sunne" (Matthew xvii, 2); his "raiment did shine" (Mark ix, 3); and appearing "in glorie" (Luke ix, 31) with him are Moses and Elijah, a prophet whose ascension into Heaven likewise prefigures Christ's exaltation. In addition, a bright cloud (Matthew xvii, 5) appears from which the Father speaks. When he descends from the mountain, Christ resumes his previous state of humiliation, the appearance of a man.

Another parallel with Moses' transformation includes the reference to tents or tabernacles which the disciples wish to erect (Mark ix, 5). The site of the Transfiguration is thereby likened to the dwelling tent where Moses appeared radiant. Essential to an understanding of the Transfiguration is Christ's instruction to his disciples: that he "would suffer" at the hands of the people and that the vision of his exaltation should not be told until after he has risen from the dead (Matthew xvii, 9). By this instruction Christ implies that the Transfiguration looks forward to the humiliation of his Passion and Death and the exaltation of his Resurrection. In fact, his exalted appearance at the Transfiguration resembles his glorified state after the Resurrection. Other images he uses, or implies, include descent and ascent, darkness and light, concealment and disclosure — the very same images describing both Moses and the God of the Old Testament.

Interrelated typologically, the lives of Moses and Christ enact the cycle of humiliation and exaltation in Biblical history. In *Paradise Lost* their lives are also viewed as temporal manifestations of an eternal verity: the Father's announcement of the "begetting" of the Son (V, 603–11). This, of course, is one of the most controversial passages in the epic. Denis Saurat, for example, states that the Son is hereby created.[4] But Maurice Kelley believes the Son, who existed before the angels, is proclaimed and appointed ruler and king.[5] As such, he is to be exalted. William B. Hunter, Jr. argues that the Father is revealing to the angels that the Son will eventually become incarnate. Here begotten "metaphorically," the Son will "actually" assume manhood during a temporal ministry.[6] The angels also learn that following his humiliation the incarnate Son will ascend to be exalted at the right hand of the Father.

As Saurat, Kelley, Hunter, and others explain this episode of Book

V, their comments are related, in one way or another, to the revelation in Book III of the Son's eventual Incarnation, a humiliation that will result in exaltation. While the resemblances between these two episodes are clear-cut, the differences cannot be overlooked. Despite the arrangement of books in the epic, the begetting and exaltation of the Son in Book V precede the disclosure in Book III of his eventual Incarnation. In the former instance (Book V) there is an actual begetting; in the latter (Book III) a begetting is prophesied. In Book V the Father announces and presents *the Son begotten as an angel.* This begetting does not mean that the Son's divine nature is being created. It means simply that the Son in the presence of the angels has assumed their nature and form. To refute Satan's view that the angels have been degraded by the kingship of a recently begotten angel, Abdiel interprets the Father's intention:

> How provident he is, how far from thought
> To make us less, bent rather to exalt
> Our happy state under one Head more near
> United.
>
>   .   .   .   .
>
> *Or all Angelic Nature join'd in one,*
> *Equal to him begotten Son,* by whom
> As by his Word the mighty Father made
> All things, ev'n thee, and all the Spirits of Heav'n
> By him created in thir bright degrees,
> Crown'd them with Glory, and to thir Glory nam'd
> Thrones, Dominations, Princedoms, Virtues, Powers,
> Essential Powers, nor by his Reign obscur'd,
> But more illustrious made, *since he the Head*
> *One of our number thus reduc't becomes,*
> *His Laws our Laws, all honor to him done*
> *Returns our own.*   (V, 828–45, my italics)

Subject to the limitations of this lesser nature, the Son is humiliated, but the angelic nature is exalted because it has been assumed by the deity. In this way, too, the deity has chosen to manifest himself more fully to lesser creatures, and by governing the angels through someone who shares their nature, God is thus attentive to their dignity.

Such an interpretation of the begetting can resolve much of the critical controversy surrounding the episode. Reference to Saurat, Kelley, and Hunter, who typify the disparate range of interpretation, will demonstrate how this may be done. As Saurat argues, the Son is "created" at the begetting. But his divine nature is not being originated;

only an angelic nature and form are being assumed. In Kelley's view the Son's rulership over the angels is announced at the begetting, but this decree simply asserts that the Son continues to be God, even in his manifestation as an angel. In arguing that the Son is "metaphorically" begotten in Book V, thereby revealing to the angels his eventual Incarnation, Hunter perceives a connection between the events of eternity and time. But this connection is more fully affirmed by the recognition that the Son "really" becomes an angel in Book V, for the two begettings — the first in eternity, the second in time — show the continuing humiliation of the deity, first as an angel, then as a man.

In many ways the Incarnation of the Son is a temporal and earthly counterpart of his begetting as an angel. Striking resemblances between the two humiliations result from a comparison of Abdiel's comments in Book V and the Father's in Book III. In the two instances the Son's kingship is proclaimed. To Satan and the other angels, Abdiel asserts that the Son begotten as an angel is still their "rightful King" (V, 818); and in Book III the Father, prophesying the Incarnation of the Son, the events of the Paschal triduum, and the enthronement of the Incarnate Son at his right hand, proclaims him "Both God and Man, Son both of God and Man, / Anointed universal King" (III, 316–17). As Abdiel and the Father explain the two begettings, the Christology of *Paradise Lost* becomes more understandable. Their comments echo and adapt several scriptural passages, like Psalms ii and viii (both of which Milton paraphrased from the Hebrew), Hebrews i, 5, ii, 9, and Philippians ii, 6–9. These passages emphasize what has been called the kenotic Christology or humiliation of the Son — that he was made lower than angels but crowned with glory.[7] Though he assumed manhood, the Son is still God. He is to be exalted for two reasons: his divinity and his willingness to be humiliated by assuming a lesser nature. The former refers to his birthright, the latter to his merits.

Biblical passages describing the kenotic Christology emphasize the begetting of the Son as man. But in *Paradise Lost* Milton devises another begetting, the angelic manifestation of the Son. Though the canonical books of Scripture do not explicitly provide an analogue for such a begetting, the Apocrypha certainly do. In the New Testament Apocrypha, particularly the Ascension of the Prophet Isaiah, there is continual mention (chapters 6–10) of the Son's humiliation as a man and as an angel.[8] While he is in Heaven, Isaiah learns that the "Lord . . . shall descend in [man's] form" (viii, 26) and will become "like [man] in appearance," so that people on earth "will think that he is flesh and a man" (ix, 13). The Crucifixion is then foretold. Isaiah also hears the Father announce that the Son "shalt resemble the form of the angels" (x, 10). The angel guiding Isaiah through Heaven urges him to "attend . . . and behold" in order to "see the transformation of the Lord and his descent" (x, 18). Before that occurs he views the angels who "praised and extolled [the Son] . . . not yet . . . transformed into the form of the angels" (x, 19). Soon thereafter the Son "took the appearance of the angels" (x, 20) — later described as "the form of the angels" (x, 27) — and descended through their realm. During his descent some of the angels "did not praise him, for his appearance was like theirs" (x, 20). As an angel he arouses the "envy" of some of the beings whose nature and form he has assumed.

Despite the clear-cut parallels between the apocryphal Ascension of Isaiah and the begetting of the Son in *Paradise Lost*, including the envy of some angels after the transformation of the deity, I do not presume to have identified Milton's source material. In citing the parallel, I am simply suggesting that there is some tradition for the begetting and humiliation of the deity as an angel. In any case the episode in Book V of *Paradise Lost* enables Milton to make Satan's objection and protest against the Son's newly designated kingship more psychologically and dramatically plausible, while emphasizing the cause of Satan's downfall, pride. In the highest rank of angels in Heaven, Satan, then known as Lucifer, viewed his status as nearly godlike. Even after his downfall, in an oration to the fallen angels, he claims to be their ruler for a number of reasons, including what he calls "just right and the fixt Laws of Heav'n" (I, 18). This assertion recalls his previous status as their leader in Heaven, which he views, at least publicly, as a virtual birthright. From Satan's perspective in Book V, the "begetting" of the Son as an angel and the designation of his kingship are acts of usurpation and tyranny. Satan argues that he, in effect, has been deposed, that the other angels have suffered degradation because of the command to worship a recently begotten angel, and that a war of liberation must be initiated and pursued. Satan adduces many reasons for the rebellion, but the real cause is his sense of injured pride.

Although Abdiel explains the deity's intention in undergoing humiliation — "bent rather to exalt / Our happy state under One Head more near / United" (V, 829–31) — Satan persists in his argument for rebellion. The word "bent" has several meanings. Abdiel states that God's "bent" (that is, inclination or intention) is to "exalt" the angels, not to demean them as Satan had argued. He explains that this begetting of the Son provides a manifestation of the deity similar to the angelic nature, more understandable to the angels, and more accessible to them for unification under the deity:

> all Angelic Nature join'd in one,
> Equal to him begotten Son, by whom
> As by his Word the mighty Father made
> All things, ev'n thee, and all the Spirits of Heav'n. (V, 834–837)

And "since he the Head / One of our number thus reduc't becomes" (V, 842–43), the begetting of the Son represents a humiliation of the deity ("thus reduc't") that serves, in effect, to "exalt" the angelic nature it has chosen to assume. The word "bent" becomes synonymous with "reduc't," and these words or their synonyms are also used to describe the mystery of the Incarnation in Milton's poetry. In the incomplete poem entitled "The Passion," the Son is described as having "entered" the "Poor fleshly Tabernacle" by "stooping his regal head" (15–17). In *On the Morning of Christ's Nativity* the Savior, likened to "the mighty Pan," is "kindly come to live . . . below" (89–90). As Abdiel explains how and why the Son was begotten as an angel, his view parallels God the Father's commentary in Book III on the begetting of the Incarnate Son among mankind. Having earlier assumed an angelic nature, the Son will undergo further humiliation by "descending to assume / Man's Nature" (III, 303–04). Whether the mystery of the Incarnation is described as a bending, reducing, stooping, living below, or descending, the effect on mankind, like the effect of the Son's humiliation among the angels, is to exalt the lesser nature assumed by God.

After the Son is transformed into an angel, Satan refuses to acknowledge that all angels, including himself, have been exalted by the deity who shares their nature. In his soliloquy in Book IV, Satan recalls the angelic hierarchies in Heaven and his former status as governor of the angels, the status in which he gloried and which he declines to relinquish. In Book V, though, the deity in the form of an angel is proclaimed king, and Satan, who had governed the angels, is obliged for the first time to pay homage to a being who shares his nature and form. As Abdiel explains, moreover, the lesser angels over whom Satan had presided have acquired greater dignity: "Equal to him begotten Son" (V, 835). What Satan publicly construes as tyranny, Abdiel explains as the humiliation of the deity and the exaltation of the angelic nature. As Abdiel further comments, Satan is tyrannizing the angels by his continuing insistence on governing them and by his refusal to acknowledge the kingship of the Son. In the regions of the North, as Abdiel asserts,

Satan is enthroned: "In place thyself so high above thy / Peers" (V, 812). The epic narrator makes virtually the same comment in describing the rebellion of Satan and the disloyal angels: "With all his Host / Of Rebel Angels, by whose aid aspiring / To set himself in Glory above his Peers" (I, 37–39).

After the begetting of the Son as an angel, the previous hierarchical arrangement of angels, though still observed, is less important than their unity in and with the Son. The humiliation he experienced in laying aside divinity to become an angel provides a model whereby angels who have presided in the hierarchy should be willing to forego their status and degree. In so doing, they will be exalted, for the union of angelic and divine natures in the Son is but the prelude of the angels' final and full participation in the godhead, when "God shall be All in All" (III, 34). Refusal to imitate the Son's humiliation results in divine vengeance, like that directed against Satan in the War in Heaven. Rather than humble himself, Satan seeks to upgrade his previous status as governor to that of deity, an effort antithetical to the Son's self-abnegation. The War in Heaven provides continuing manifestation of the Son as an angel. This time the sceptre signifying his kingship when he was begotten as an angel becomes, as Abdiel says, an iron rod, a biblical image of God's wrath. The War in Heaven also shows the willingness of an angel, namely Michael, to relinquish governorship over his cohorts and to yield to the kingship of the Son begotten as an angel. Satan's disobedience and proud effort to elevate his governorship into kingship and godhead are contrasted with Michael's observance of the Son's preeminence:

> When the great Ensign of *Messiah* blaz'd
> Aloft by Angels borne, his Sign in Heav'n:
> Under whose Conduct *Michael* soon reduc'd
> His Army, circumfus'd on either Wing,
> Under thir Head imbodied all in one.   (VI, 775–79)

Milton positions the word "reduc'd," which Abdiel used earlier to describe the Son's humiliation, to promote a richness and ambiguity of meaning and association. Its Latinate meaning indicates that Michael places himself, and releads his angels, under the command of the Son.

Under the guise of a war against tyranny and a just attempt to redress the grievances of his followers, Satan conceals his efforts at self-exaltation. He argues, for instance, that if a recently begotten angel is divine, then the angelic nature has been and is deific. From this assumption he further asserts that the deity is tyrannical, for he has been arrogating dominion and authority over his peers, the angels, who are likewise divine. Having developed publicly the notion that the angelic nature must be divine, Satan underscores it by addressing the angels as "Gods."

In the begetting of the Son as an angel and the command to worship him, Satan perceives the enactment by the deity of the cycle of humiliation and exaltation, whereby the Son is extolled for his willingness to be humbled. He also perceives the resultant gratitude of lesser beings whose nature has been exalted by the Son's deed of self-sacrifice. As part of his mimicry of the deity, Satan will display a self-sacrificial attitude resembling that of the Son, though intended for a vastly different purpose. Satan seeks not to humble himself, but to use the pretense of humiliation. His aim is to elicit the praise of the fallen angels, to be exalted by them, and to acquire more regal distance from his peers.

Because he is implementing a strategy of deception initially with the angels and later with mankind, Satan must conceal his true nature and intent, whereas the Son first assumes the angelic nature and will later become man in order to disclose the godhead more fully to lesser beings. At times, Satan's imitation of the Son degenerates into vulgar burlesque—for example, when he "changes himself into the shape of a meaner Angel" (III, "The Argument") to converse with Uriel and when he later becomes, among other things, a cormorant (IV, 196), a lion (IV, 402), and a tiger (IV, 403). As he inhabits the serpent and comments on this act of degradation, there are striking contrasts between Satan's appearance to mankind and the manifestation of the deity as the Incarnate Son:

> Of foul descent! that I who erst contended
> With Gods to sit the highest, am now constrain'd
> Into a Beast, and mixt with bestial slime,
> This essence to incarnate and imbrute,
> That to the highth of Deity aspir'd;
> But what will not Ambition and Revenge
> Descend to? who aspires must down as low
> As high he soar'd, obnoxious first or last
> To basest things.   (IX, 163–71)

"Constrain'd" suggests that Satan, who is beset by the strongest passions throughout the epic, is virtually compelled by "Ambition and Revenge" to debase himself as he seeks to pursue his rebellion against God by deceiving and subverting mankind. In face-to-face combat with Satan during the War in Heaven, Abdiel recognizes that Satan is overpowered by, and enslaved to, the sinful passions of his fallen nature: "Thyself not free, but to thyself enthrall'd" (VI, 181). When, on the other hand, the Son tells the Father he will "this glory next to thee / Freely put off" (III, 239–40), his free choice, "meek aspect" (III, 266), and "Filial obedience" (III, 269) are respectively contrasted with Satan's "constrain'd" degradation, impassioned "Ambition and Revenge," and rebellious challenge to God.

In contrast to the Son's Incarnation, the degradation of imbruting extends beyond Satan to include the fallen angels, who reflect his sinful passions. In their appearance to mankind, they too are transmogrified and as "bestial Gods" (I, 435) are worshipped by pagans. Toward the end of the catalogue of pagan deities and in the description of the fallen angels' efforts to ascend to Earth, Milton alludes to the classical myth of the Titans' revolt. In these two instances he presents a version of the myth describing Titan or Ophion as the rightful ruler of Olympus, the ruler dispossessed of his status by the usurpers, Saturn and Jove. Titan is described as "Heav'n's first born" (I, 510); and the fallen angels, who have become pagan deities on Earth,

> some tradition . . . dispers'd
> Among the Heathen of thir purchase got,
> And Fabl'd how the Serpent, whom they call'd
> *Ophion* with *Eurynome*, the wide-
> Encroaching *Eve* perhaps, had first the rule
> Of high *Olympus*, thence by *Saturn* driv'n
> And *Ops*, ere yet *Dictaean Jove* was born.   (X, 578–84)

In this version of the genealogy of the gods, the serpent-shaped Ophion, to whom Satan is likened in *Paradise Lost*, first ruled Olympus. If he, assisted by the Titans, were restored to his rightful status, then an act of justice will have been performed. In a similar way Satan describes the Son's begetting as an act of usurpation and tyranny by a new angelic ruler who seeks to extort homage from his "equals" (V, 796). As Satan argues, "by Decree / Another now hath to himself ingross't / All Power" (V, 774–76).

What God the Father classifies as rebellion, Satan presents as a necessary and legitimate attempt to restore himself and the other "eclipst" angels (V, 776) to their rightful status. First, he is enthroned as a god at "the limits of the North" (V, 755) and later in Hell (II, 1–10), where he persuades the fallen angels that they cannot "fail to re-ascend / Self-rais'd, and repossess thir native seat" (I, 633–34). After having seduced mankind, he returns to Hell and again mounts his throne, expecting and encouraging the plaudits of the fallen angels. Addressing them as "Gods" (X, 502) and enjoining them to "up and enter now" (X, 503) toward deliverance, Satan appears to have fulfilled his promise. On the verge of triumph his pride is at its highest pitch. When the fallen angels do ascend to Earth, their bestial, even serpent-like, appearance as pagan deities indicates that they acknowledge the serpent Ophion as their ruler, that they are his "associate Powers" (X, 395), and that his rightful claim to godhead, as well as theirs, is the version of the myth of the gods they disseminate to the pagans whom they have deceived into false worship.

Before their ascent to Earth, the fallen angels view the transformation of Satan into a "monstrous Serpent" (X, 514) and then a "Dragon" (X, 529), while they themselves undergo transmogrification into serpents as a foreshadowing of their later appearance on Earth as "bestial Gods." The transition from Satan's seeming triumph to his actual debasement is an ironic reversal of the Son's enactment of the cycle of exaltation and humiliation. Concisely and effectively the epic narrator recounts Satan's decline from apparent preeminence: "A while he stood," then "down he fell" (X, 504, 513). Such a description likewise summarizes all of Satan's efforts at self-exaltation and the retributive consequence, forcible humiliation. Just as Satan was earlier "constrain'd / Into a Beast" by his own sinful passions of "Ambition and Revenge" (IX, 164–68), so also he is again compelled (this time from without) to assume the shape of a serpent: "A greater power / Now rul'd him, punisht in the shape he sinn'd, / According to his doom" (X, 515–17). Here the mention of "doom" echoes the "doom" (X, 172) or "curse" (X, 174) the Son pronounces in "Judgment" (X, 164) on the serpent:

> Upon thy Belly groveling thou shalt go,
> And dust shalt eat all the days of thy Life.
> Between Thee and the Woman I will put
> Enmity, and between thine and her Seed;
> Her Seed shall bruise thy head, thou bruise his heel.   (X, 177–81)

Having overheard the Son's pronouncement, Satan reports it to the fallen angels just after he has described his triumph over mankind — "successful beyond hope" (X, 463) — and immediately before his transmogrification into a "monstrous Serpent" and then a "Dragon." As reported by Satan, the Son's pronouncement highlights the contrast between the Son's Incarnation and Satan's transmogrification, because the human nature assumed by the godhead is to be exalted and elevated into Heaven, whereas the serpent form assumed by Satan and the fallen angels will be downtrodden.

In the Book of Revelation xii, 1–5, the woman clothed with the

sun, traditionally interpreted as the Virgin Mary, is about to be delivered of her child when she is threatened by a dragon. But "she broght
forthe a man childe, which shulde rule all nations with a rod of yron,"
the same image of divine retribution employed by Abdiel when he fore-
warned the fallen angels of the consequences of their rebellion: that the
"Iron Rod" will "bruise and break [their] disobedience" (V, 887–88).
These words dramatically foreshadow the role of the Son in the War in
Heaven, the curse that the woman's "seed shall bruise" the serpent's
head, and the epic narrator's comment that Satan and the fallen angels
will undergo annually a forcible transmogrification to "dash thir pride"
(X, 577). As the epic narrator also foresees, the "curse" or "doom" will
be fulfilled ultimately

> When *Jesus* son of Mary second *Eve*,
> [Will see] Satan fall like lightning down from Heav'n,
> Prince of the Air; then rising from his Grave
> Spoil'd Principalities and Powers, triumpht
> In open show, and with ascension bright
> Captivity led captive through the Air,
> The Realm itself of Satan long usurpt,
> Whom he shall tread at last under our feet.   (X, 183–90)

Several biblical passages are echoed here, including Psalm lxviii, 18,
Luke x, 18, Ephesians ii, 2, Colossians ii, 15, and Revelation xx. This
forecast or prophecy of the ultimate defeat of Satan is periodically iter-
ated throughout the epic — for instance, by the Son in III, 260–65, by
God the Father in X, 633–39, and again by Michael in XII, 451–65,
who includes it as part of Adam's vision into the future.

The prophecy's ultimate fulfillment, which is to be achieved at the
Second Coming and the Final Judgment (Revelation xx), is continually
foreshadowed in the action of *Paradise Lost*, notably by the victory of
the Son over Satan in the War in Heaven, the Son's triumphant ascen-
dancy afterwards, and Satan's punishment in the lake of fire in Book I —
called a "lake of fyre & brimstone" in Revelation xx, 10. In the War in
Heaven Satan's leadership, from the perspective of the fallen angels,
seems to carry them to the threshold of triumph, until they are deci-
sively expelled by the thunder and lightning of the Son. Thus, in Book X
when Satan transmogrified "down . . . fell / . . . prone" (513–14), his
posture resembles his prone appearance on the burning lake in Book I,
while it anticipates his coming decline when he will be trodden "at last
under . . . feet" (X, 190). In classical mythology Typhon, leader of the
Titans, is described as having scaled Olympus, but at the moment of his
seeming triumph, he is cast by Jove's lightning into Tartarus where he

lies outstretched in punishing confinement. As the defeat of Satan is envisioned, with the Son leading mankind triumphantly heavenward while he views Satan "fall like Lightning down from Heav'n" (X, 184), the classical myth recounting the battle between Jove and Typhon and numerous passages from Scripture are expertly fused. While the Savior and his redeemed multitude ascend together, their adversaries undergo an opposite downward plunge. Descent, darkness, forcible disclosure of his true nature and intent, and constrained humiliation characterize Satan's reenacted defeats in *Paradise Lost.*

Central to an understanding of the *agon* between the Son and Satan is the relationship between humiliation and exaltation and the imagery describing it. As I have suggested, the Son's humiliation and exaltation and Satan's parodic enactment are balanced and contrasted throughout the epic from numerous perspectives: time and eternity, history and prophecy, being and becoming. For angels and humanity alike, the Son is upheld as the model, witness, and judge of their participation in the cycle of humiliation and exaltation. Nowhere is this more clearly affirmed than by God the Father, who commends the Son: "Thy Humiliation shall exalt" (III, 313). Overheard by the angels, this affirmation is echoed in the aphoristic wisdom of the Gospels for all mankind to read: the humble shall be exalted. Indeed, the Christology of *Paradise Lost* is neither more nor less than a study of Milton's theology of humiliation.

Duquesne University

NOTES

1. Milton's poetry is quoted from *John Milton: Complete Poems and Major Prose,* ed. Merritt Y. Hughes (New York, 1957).

2. See, for example, John M. Steadman, *Milton's Epic Characters: Image and Idol* (Chapel Hill, N.C., 1968).

3. Scripture is quoted from *The Geneva Bible: A Facsimile of the 1560 Edition* (Madison, Wisc., 1969). I have modernized obsolete characters.

4. *Milton: Man and Thinker* (London, 1964), p. 98. The last section of the book, dealing with Robert Fludd and the Mortalists, is the only significant modification from the earlier edition (1925). Saurat amplifies his views in a review of Sir Herbert Grierson's *Milton and Wordsworth, Poets and Prophets: A Study of Their Reactions to Political Events* (London, 1937), *RES*, XIV (1938), 225–28.

5. *This Great Argument: A Study of Milton's "De Doctrina Christiana" as a Gloss upon "Paradise Lost"* (1941; rept. Gloucester, Mass., Peter Smith, 1962), pp. 94–105.

6. *Bright Essence: Studies in Milton's Theology,* ed. William B. Hunter, Jr., C. A.

Patrides, and J. H. Adamson (Salt Lake City, 1971), p. 123. An earlier version of the essay quoted here was published as "Milton on the Exaltation of the Son: The War in Heaven in *Paradise Lost*," *ELH*, XXXVI (1969), 215–31. In developing their views on the begetting of the Son, Saurat, Kelley, and Hunter allude at times to other interpretations, including those by David Masson, *Poetical Works of John Milton* (London, 1882), III, 363; Sir Herbert Grierson, *Milton and Wordsworth* (New York, 1937), p. 99; Arthur Sewell, *A Study in Milton's Christian Doctrine* (London, 1939), pp. 88–91; and Edmund Creeth, "The 'Begetting' and the Exaltation of the Son," *MLN*, LXXVI (1961), 696–700. They also refer to the passage in Milton's *De Doctrina* in which the begetting and exaltation of the Son are discussed (*The Works of John Milton*, ed. F. A. Patterson [New York, 1931–1938], XIV, 181). To my knowledge no critic has suggested, or even implied, the interpretation of *Paradise Lost*, V, 600 ff. that I will develop.

      7. Two excellent studies of Milton's concept of the Incarnation include William B. Hunter, Jr., "Milton on the Incarnation: Some More Heresies," *JHI*, XXI (1960), 349–69, reprinted in *Bright Essence*, pp. 131–48; and Michael Lieb, "Milton and the Kenotic Christology: Its Literary Bearing," *ELH*, XXXVII (1970), 342–60. For an excellent study of the satanic parody of the Incarnation, see Mother Mary Christopher Pecheux, "'O Foul Descent!': Satan and the Serpent Form," *SP*, LXII (1965), 188–96.

      8. All quotations are from Edward Hennecke, *New Testament Apocrypha*, ed. Wilhelm Schneemelcher and trans. R. McL. Wilson (Philadelphia, 1964), II, 651–61. I am grateful to Professor Michael Lieb for calling my attention to these chapters of the New Testament Apocrypha.

"IMPROV'D BY TRACT OF TIME": METAPHYSICS AND MEASUREMENT IN *PARADISE LOST*

Elizabeth Jane Wood

*P*ARADISE LOST has often been characterized as "spatial": it is said that space, the feeling of space, or the idea of space, dominates the poem.[1] Most critics concerned with the spatial aspect of the poem agree that Milton was influenced in one way or another by the intense interest in space generated by and, indeed, fundamental to, the philosophic-scientific revolution of the sixteenth and seventeenth centuries. Yet it was not simply space, or the notion of space, that commanded such interest; rather, there were pressing issues concerning the relation of space with time and motion through and for the sake of measurement. Interest in time and motion, although perhaps less striking, was no less intense. For instance, one primary motivation for Copernicus' astronomical pursuits was his desire to discover a solution to the problem of precession and, thereby, to provide the necessary information for development of a more accurate calendar.[2] This solution, of course, depended upon more accurate determinations of planetary and stellar motions. Moreover, increasingly precise measures of time were needed to meet the rapidly growing demands of navigation.[3] Assuming the revolution to have had its ground in such problems and issues, and assuming the influence of this revolution on Milton's thought, this essay examines the interdependent functioning of the notions of space, time, and motion in *Paradise Lost* as they are related, metaphorically, through the notion of measure. A few remarks concerning metaphor, as here conceived, will precede the examination.

I. A. Richards maintains that "the full use of language . . . takes its word, not as the repository of a single constant power but as a means by which the different powers it may exert in different situations are brought together."[4] An identification among a multiplicity of "powers" or senses of a word describes generally the kind of metaphorical function to be examined in this essay. The senses of a word or phrase which are active in a given metaphorical function, however, while being

43

transformed into one another (through "metaphorical identification"), retain their distinct significances. The metaphorical function, therefore, is implicitly paradoxical: the function "identifies" two or more senses of a word while, at the same time, relying on the differences among them to constitute the function. Without the presentation of these differences, the metaphor collapses into literal absurdity. For example, in a metaphorical function where the word "space" refers, in one of its senses, to time, the metaphor collapses if time loses those characteristics which distinguish it from space; or, as time is unequivocally identified with space, the metaphor constitutes a literal absurdity. Consequently, metaphorical functions of this type cannot be reduced to a set of literal statements.[5] In view of this, the present examination primarily describes relations among possible senses of words or phrases as these function within the general context of the poem.

In the opening invocation, the poet calls upon his muse to "say first what cause / Mov'd our Grand Parents . . . / . . . to fall off" (I, 28–30), and "Who first seduc'd them to that foul revolt?" (I, 33).[6] These questions are immediately and directly answered: "Th' infernal Serpent; hee it was" (I, 34)). The response, however, continues, elaborating the circumstantial details of the Satanic fall, until what appears to be a third question interposes: "what time his Pride / Had cast him out from Heav'n" (I, 36–37). Strictly speaking, the "what" of "what time" need not be comprehended as an interrogative adjective. Literally, it is purely descriptive, roughly equivalent to "at that time when" Satan's pride had cast him out. But several features of the context incline the reader to perceive "what time" as an indirect question. The passage opens with the two direct questions which appear not merely to be satisfied, but to be satisfied with absolute finality, in the accusation of Satan: "Hee it was" who caused their fall. These questions having been answered, the reader might expect another question to continue the forward movement of the poem. So, when "what time" appears, paralleling the syntax of "what cause" and separated from the preceding clause by a semicolon, it subtly fulfills the expectation. Moreover, even when the descriptive aspect of "what time" ("at that time when") is dominant, a reflective pause on the part of a reader aware of certain issues in seventeenth-century thought will automatically give rise to the question.

In particular, the controversy about the existence of time before the creation of the world comes to mind. It is significant that, in "The Argument" appended to the poem, Milton explains that "Heaven and Earth may be suppos'd as yet not made." His interest in the issue is indicated by his famous affirmation of "the elder state" in *The Christian Doctrine:*

It seems even probable, that the apostasy which caused the expulsion of so many thousands from heaven, took place before the foundations of this world were laid. Certainly there is no sufficient foundation for the common opinion, that motion and time (which is the measure of motion) could not . . . have existed before this world was made.[7]

This view was generally rejected by Milton's contemporaries, who subscribed to the belief that time began with the creation of this world.[8] Therefore, since the common opinion was that there was no time before the creation of the world, it seems reasonable to read "what time," within the contextual framework of the poem, as a genuine, problematical question.

Briefly, the metaphorical functioning of the "what" in "what time" focuses attention on the ontological status of time, on the existence and nature of the entity. The problem is also epistemological: how is one to comprehend a time that, presumably, predates the existence of the world in terms of which the very notion of the entity is founded? "What time," effectively, presents the reader with a concept which is immediately emptied of all content through the context in which it is presented. Herein lies the precision of the metaphorical function relating (by "metaphorical identification") the descriptive aspect of "what" with the interrogative aspect. Functioning metaphorically, "what time" introduces the oblique or indirect movement of sense that directs the reader's attention to the conceptualization of time in the context presented by the poem.

The poetic response to "what time," "Nine times the Space that measures Day and Night / To mortal men" (I, 50–51), fills the conceptual void into which the reader has fallen. But again, comprehension of the response relies on the perception of a rather complex, metaphorical function. Here the initial tendency, following "Hurl'd headlong" (I, 45), is to associate "Nine times the Space" with the Satanic fall and with the distance (that is, "space") of that fall. Then, when we get to "that measures Day and Night," we realize that the line refers to time — presumably, to the time it takes for Satan and his host to fall. The obvious allusion to classical accounts of a nine-day fall, such as the fall of the Titans in Hesiod's *Theogeny* (664–735), and the fact that the Satanic host is said to have fallen nine days in *Paradise Lost* (VI, 871), strengthen the sense of time in "Nine times the Space." Yet we cannot reduce the "space" of line 50 to a simple replacement metaphor for time. The metaphor here is more complex; it involves the relation of space and time through measure.

First, it is important to realize, "Nine times the Space" does not strictly describe Satan's *fall*. Continuing, we find that "hee with his horrid crew / Lay vanquisht, rolling in the fiery Gulf" (I, 51–52) nine times the space. Thus, Alastair Fowler claims that there are two distinct periods of nine days: one as Satan and crew fall, one as they lie vanquished in the fiery gulf.[9] Moreover, assuming that lying vanquished and "rolling" describe the same activity, when we perceive "Nine times the Space" in retrospect, the word "Space" resumes the sense of "distance" it had initially, only now this sense is modified by the *shape* implied by "rolling." "Space," therefore, while referring to time, retains its reference to the extended dimension or distance later expressed: "As from the Center thrice to th' utmost Pole" (I, 74). In addition, by suggestion, "falling" is loosely associated with "rolling."

The metaphorical functioning of "Nine times the Space" revitalizes the dead metaphor present in the commonplace phrase, "space of time." In ordinary usage the sense of genuine spatial expanse is lost and "space" becomes a synonym for "time." In Milton's line the relation between space and time, upon which the commonplace metaphor is founded, is reintroduced. We are confronted with a genuine spatial expanse that *measures* time. The fundamental measuring relation linking space with time appears even in the etymological origin of the word "temporal." In the words of H. K. Usener:

> The basic word τέμενος (*tempus*), *templum* signified nothing other than bisection, intersection: according to the terminology of later carpenters two crossing rafters or beams still constituted a templum; thence the signification of the space thus divided was a natural development; in *tempus* the quarter of the heavens (e.g. the east) passed into the time of day (e.g. morning) and thence into time in general.[10]

Thus, the awareness of space and the determination of motions through space are fundamental to the temporal concept. One referent of the word "Space" in line 50, then, appears to be that actual space, the visible heavens, in terms of which mortal men do in fact measure time. Satan and his followers *roll* nine times this space; their motions therefore are analogous to the motions of the heavenly spheres. In this manner, the elements required to form a concept of time and, perhaps, even to constitute the very existence of time, are presented in the universe of the poem.

But, in addition to space and motion, there is one further requirement for the conceptualization of time. The motions (and therefore, the spaces traversed) must be regular and repetitious. Since the motions of the heavens present these properties, the temporal concept is founded upon them. In *Paradise Lost*, regular, repetitious motion is introduced through the symbolic significance of the number nine. The importance of this number to the sense of the poem, therefore, depends not merely on the allusion to Hesiod or Dante, but on its significance in numerological thought. The repeated occurrence of the number itself, viewed in terms of the contexts in which it is presented, is sufficient to establish its general significance once the peculiar property of the number is recognized. The Pythagoreans considered nine to be a "circular" number because, when it is multiplied by any whole number, the sum of the digits of the product will also equal nine.[11] Thus, the number nine possesses the property that, multiplied, it repeats itself incessantly. It is probable that this property accounted for the identification of the stellar sphere, which was thought to exhibit perfectly regular, eternal repetition in its revolutionary motions, with the ninth sphere of the Pythagorean cosmological scheme.[12] In *Paradise Lost*, not only is Hell "ninefold" (II, 436) with gates "thrice threefold" (II, 645), but there are apparently three distinct nine-day periods. Chronologically, the first is the falling of the rebel angels from Heaven: "Nine days they fell" (VI, 871). Then there is the nine-day period spent rolling in the fiery gulf. Finally, there is the more complex span of nine days from Satan's first arrival on earth at noon up to the time that he seduces Eve at noon on the ninth day.[13] Each of the latter two instances, of course, represents a compounded repetition of his original fall.

Moreover, careful examination of the *motions* in the immediate context of each nine-day period reinforces the sense of circularity and the association of this with the heavenly motions. In the first instance, the rebel host falls beneath "the living Wheels" (VI, 846) of the Son's chariot as

> At once the Four spread out thir Starry wings
> With dreadful shade contiguous, and the Orbs
> Of his fierce Chariot roll'd, as with the sound
> Of torrent Floods, or of a numerous Host.   (VI, 827–30)

There is clearly a sense of the revolutionary motions of the night sky in these lines; and the rolling motion is transformed, through an aural image, into "torrent Floods" and "numerous Host" which undoubtedly recall the rebel host "o'erwhelm'd / With Floods and Whirlwinds of tempestuous fire" (I, 76–77) as it lay confounded in the fiery gulf.

The third, complex, nine-day period begins with a continuation of the same kind of rolling motions, but they have now been internalized by Satan. He arrives on Earth to begin "his dire attempt, which nigh the birth / Now rolling, boils in his tumultuous breast, / And like a devilish Engine back recoils / Upon himself" (IV, 15–18). "Rolling" and "tumultuous" again suggest the period of confusion spent in the fiery gulf. The recoiling motion manifests the sort of self-referential circularity that, as I hope to demonstrate, is characteristic of Satanic motion. But notice the parallel between Satan's awakening in Hell and his awakening here on Earth. In both instances he has traveled through Chaos and is awakened from the condition of obliviousness this involves into (and perhaps, by) an awareness of time: awakening in Hell, and, as Stanley Fish points out, in the present "now" of time, "the thought / Both of lost happiness and lasting pain / Torments him" (I, 54–56).[14] On Earth, now emphatically in the present, again his "conscience wakes despair / That slumber'd, wakes the bitter memory / Of what he was, what is, and what must be" (IV, 23–25; notice that the word "now" appears no fewer than seven times in the first thirty-one lines of Book IV, driving home the importance of the present moment of time). On both occasions, however, his vision fails to comprehend the significance of the present moment and, instead, substantiates the rotundity of Hell: "round he throws his baleful eyes" (I, 56) to view "A Dungeon horrible, on all sides round" (I, 61); and, arriving on Earth, he brings Hell "round about him" (IV, 21). As he turns his gaze "Sometimes towards Eden" and "Sometimes towards Heav'n" (IV, 27, 29), he is found "much revolving" (IV, 31). Finally, in this last nine-day period, Satan actually circles around the Earth much in the manner of a planet or star:

> The space of seven continu'd Nights he rode
> With darkness, thrice the Equinoctial Line
> He circl'd, four times cross'd the Car of Night
> From Pole to Pole, traversing each Colure.   (IX, 63–66)

In each instance, circling motions analogous to those of the visible heavens are explicitly or implicitly associated with the number nine and with the incessant repetition or permanence it signifies.

It has already been hinted that circularity, either physical or psychological, or both, is characteristic of Satanic motion in general. Satan's thoughts and actions consistently redound upon his own head, constituting a system of psycho-physical irony which, in the universe of the poem, represents the fallen condition. For example, recognizing (addressing) Hell for the first time, Satan claims that he brings "a mind not to be chang'd by Place or Time" (I, 253). But the truth of this self-imposed rigidity is fully realized when, although physically (literally) in Paradise, he finds that he "from Hell / One step no more than from himself can fly / By change of place" (IV, 21–23). The sense in which the "fixt mind" (I, 97; and see I, 560) of Satan constitutes a perpetually self-defeating disregard for significant (real) change, the potential given through time, is also demonstrated in Satan's original breach of the heavenly order of God: fearing an alteration in his own position as the result of an apparent alteration in the order of Heaven, Satan "could not bear / Through pride that sight, and thought himself impair'd" (V, 664–65). The thought, once more, is transformed into the actual circumstance when Satan, now fallen, finds "His lustre visibly impair'd" (IV, 850). Satan, of course, founds his revolt (which is a precedent in Heaven) upon the precedent of a change in Heaven's order; he resists, by revolt, the "new Laws" (V, 679) and "new minds" (V, 680) he believes to be implied by such change. Yet what is new in Heaven is the mentality of his revolt. Finally, at the height of self-deception in his seduction of Eve, the fallacious circularity of his arguments becomes manifest; he transforms himself into a serpent with "Circular base of rising folds, that tow'r'd / Fold above fold a surging Maze, his Head / . . . / Amidst his circling Spires, that on the grass / Floated redundant" (IX, 498–99, 502–03). As Mario A. DiCesare points out, this passage evokes the first description of Satan's appearance, "With Head up-lift above the wave" (I, 193).[15] In doing so, it also recalls and essentially repeats the motions of rolling in the fiery gulf.

In all of these instances of Satanic motion, as well as many others, there is an element reminiscent of St. Augustine's pronouncement that "the wicked walk in a circuit, not because their life (as they think) is to run circularly, but because their false doctrine runs round in a circular maze."[16] In *Paradise Lost*, not only Satan, but all those who follow him move in the rigidly prescribed circles of their own fallacious vision. The damned are "Immovable, infixt, and frozen round, / Periods of time" (II, 602–03); the fallen mankind of Michael's vision, oblivious to the lessons of history, repeats the errors which perpetuate its fallen condition. The "false doctrine" rejected by St. Augustine was that doctrine, implied by the Ptolemaic-Aristotelian cosmos with its emphasis on the absolutely uniform, rigidly perfect, eternal, circular motion of the celestial sphere, that time (being an aspect of the celestial motion) and history move according to a rigidly cyclical pattern.[17] The fatalistic view to which this doctrine partially gave rise is apparent in Augustine's denouncement of the circular pattern of men's lives.

But S. G. F. Brandon points out that "insofar as the cyclic concept of the temporal process, implicit in astrology, induced a sense of fatalism, as indeed it did, it was inspired rather by the notion that chance irrevocably associated each individual with some sidereal situation than by the thought of the undeviating cyclical movement of the stars in the course of time."[18] And this also appears to be borne out by the text of *Paradise Lost*. The celebrating angels, for example, perform a "mystical dance, which yonder starry Sphere / Of Planets and of fixt in all her Wheels / Resembles nearest" (V, 620–22; cf. III, 579ff. and V, 178ff.), and time is often described as "circling" (VI, 3; VII, 342; VII, 580), without any hint of fatalism. Nevertheless, where circularity is associated with Satanic motion, or where the perspective is decidedly Satanic, circular movement is imbued with overtones of fatalism. Consider, for example, Satan's argument against creation, that the angels were self-begot in a "birth mature," "when fatal course / Had circl'd his full Orb" (V, 861–62). This argument comprises not only the rationale for Satan's rejection of change ("We know no time when we were not as now"), but also reduces the significance of time to mere fate. Satan associates his existence with "fatal course," and his "fixt mind" assures that the association will be irrevocable. The idea that destiny is fixed appears as "Fate withstands" (II, 610) the attempt of the damned to reach the Lethe. More striking is the emblematic fatalism when Satan's appearance is likened to that of the Sun when it "In dim Eclipse disastrous twilight sheds / On half the Nations, and with fear of change / Perplexes Monarchs" (I, 597–99). Later in the poem, Satan assumes the role of monarch, perplexed by the apparent alteration in Heaven (that is, the rising of the Son/Sun; see V, 594ff.) and thinking himself "eclipst" (V, 776).[19]

The idea that destiny is fixed or that it is determined by the motions of the heavens obscures the proper regard for and true significance of time, subverting the potential for genuine change offered in time. Opposite the notion of fatalism, the idea was pervasive in the Renaissance that the temporal life determined the life in eternity and, therefore, that one needed to act at the present moment, while there is time.[20] The rebel angels' ironical response to Abdiel's advice that "pardon may be found in time besought" (V, 848) — "None seconded, as out of season judg'd" (V, 850) — exhibits the perversion of temporal awareness effected by Satanic influence. The awakening of Satan on the two occasions previously discussed — and especially the second, where there is an intense preoccupation with the "now" of time governed, it seems, by the opening instance: "now, / While time was" (IV, 5–6) — provides an example of the Satanic misjudgment of time. Recalling his past and recognizing his present state, Satan, although in Paradise, fatalistically conditions his future: "what must be" (IV, 25). Therefore, he resumes his revolutionary motion.

Linked to the fatalism associated with the Satanic awareness of time is a disregard for the importance of time as lived duration. Satan, briefly wavering from the oblivious rigidity of his fixed mind, recalls the occasion that precipitated his fall: "I sdein'd subjection, and thought one step higher / Would set me highest, and in a moment quit / The debt immense of endless gratitude" (IV, 50–52). The word "moment" here functions as a complex metaphor. The dominant sense is temporal, indicating a very brief, even immeasurable, interval of time. Additionally, two other senses are active: the sense of a single movement, which is reinforced by "one step"; and the notion of "determining factor" or "decisive consideration" (that is, "moment" as the decisive factor in quitting the immense debt). Therefore, three senses of the word are brought into an interanimating apposition that constitutes metaphor. The ironical strain of truth which characterizes Satan's thought appears in the metaphor: the "moment" is indeed the determining factor in an enormous alteration in Satan's position, but the change is not in the direction that Satan intends. On the other hand, insofar as the "moment" is intended to quit the debt immense, it determines nothing; payment deferred, the debt remains intact. More important is the perversion of the need to act now, while there is time. The "moment," from the Satanic perspective, lacks the significance it should have as part of that lived duration which determines the life in eternity; although his disposition of the "moment" determines his future existence, Satan views the "moment" merely as a means to escape the conditions of that existence.

A similar lack of endurance is expressed in several other passages of the poem. In Chaos, for example—and it is important to realize that this is as much a psychological state as it is a place—contrary forces "Strive . . . for Maistry" (II, 899). On achieving this, each "rules a moment" only (II, 907). The motion of striving for mastery easily suggests the Satanic "moment," to which the inconstant and unenduring qualities of Chaotic rule are transferable. Again, the rebel angels are "gently rais'd" (I, 529) by Satan's "high words, that bore / Semblance of worth, not substance" (I, 528–29); and they are raised "All in a moment" (I, 544) to follow a banner that is insubstantial, "like a Meteor streaming to the wind" (I, 537).[21] The damned attempt to reach the Lethe, "with one small drop to lose / In sweet forgetfulness all pain and woe, / All in one

moment" (II, 607–09). Their "moment," precipitated by their inability
to endure, merely constitutes one step as they continue on their
"confus'd march forlorn" (II, 615).[22]

These transitory "moments" ultimately constitute a flight from
time and, indeed, from the conditions of being itself. They are countered in the creative "moment" of God:

> I can repair
> That detriment, if such it be to lose
> Self-lost, and in a moment will create
> Another World, out of one man a Race
> Of men innumerable, there to dwell,
> Not here, till by degrees of merit rais'd
> They open to themselves at length the way
> Up hither, under long obedience tri'd. (VII, 152–59)

In the creative act of God, the decisive moment is expanded to include
all of human history, restoring the fullest significance to the entire extent of time. The importance of time is shifted from that diminishing interval into which Satan had cast his lot, to lived duration, endurance,
the whole long stretch of time that is the history of mankind. Raphael
reiterates this emphasis on the extensional aspect of time when he explains, "Time may come when men / With Angels may participate" (V,
493–94), and "perhaps / Your bodies may at last turn all to spirit, / Improv'd by tract of time" (V, 496–98). Moreover, with this shift from that
succession of ultimately insignificant, diminishing moments to the full-
ness of lived duration, the sense of fatalism associated with the Satanic
awareness of time is removed: God proclaims, "No Decree of mine /
Concurring to necessitate his Fall, / Or touch with lightest moment of
impulse / His free Will" (X, 43–46). The same denial of fatalism is explicit in the reminder that "Sin, not time first wrought the change" (IX,
70) as Satan enters into Eden.

If time is absolved of fatalistic efficacy along with God, which it
must be if man's will is truly free, how is man to be "improv'd by tract of
time"? This question is answered in *Paradise Lost;* and the answer, in
part, relies upon the realization of time's proper significance for man.
Recalling the conception of time established in the opening paragraphs
of this essay, consider Raphael's explanation of the proper significance
of the visible heavens:

> Heav'n
> Is as the Book of God before thee set,
> Wherein to read his wond'rous Works, and learn
> His Seasons, Hours, or Days, or Months or Years. (VIII, 66–69)

Raphael does not specify any particular periods of time as being God's; the important point is that man views all times as His and therefore as significant. This view, the view of Adam and Eve as they

> Both turn'd, and under op'n Sky ador'd
> The God that made both Sky, Air, Earth and Heav'n
> Which they beheld, the Moon's resplendent Globe
> And starry Pole   (IV, 721-24)

presents a sharp contrast to the "fatal course" invoked by Satan, denying creation. Moreover, the idea that "Heav'n" — the visible, physical heavens — "Is as the Book of God" indicates that man might be "Improv'd by tract of time" by reading the works and learning the times exhibited in the visible, physical universe.

The visible universe is placed before man "to know / In measure what the mind may well contain" (VII, 127-28). "Measure," however, not only bounds excess (V, 639); as number, it is the very language through which this visible universe of space, time, and motion is comprehensible. The heavens "move / Thir Starry dance in numbers that compute / Days, months, and years" (III, 579-81). And, as Raphael explains, "Time, though in Eternity, appli'd / To motion, measures all things durable / By present, past, and future" (V, 580-81). The importance of time, then, is that it is the measure of all things which *endure* — that is, all things which continue to exist through time. Time, when applied to motion or change, measures and makes comprehensible all things created by God.

Now there is another way of viewing this significance of time in *Paradise Lost*, and it is by far the most important for understanding the poem's justification of God's ways to man. Man does not readily comprehend all things created by God, so time is given in creation to enable him to learn. Time is the intermediary between angelic and human reason and, it seems, between the corresponding levels of existence. According to Raphael, reason is "Discursive or intuitive" (V, 488), meaning that it either requires time or is immediate. In addition, and this is the important ontological point of the poem, "discourse / Is oftest yours [man's]; the latter most is ours [the angels'], / Differing but in degree, of kind the same" (V, 488-90). The difference between angelic and human understanding thus reduces to the difference in the time required for comprehension. In his *Dialogue Concerning the Two Chief World Systems*, Galileo expresses a very similar idea; it is worth quoting at length:

The way in which God knows the infinite propositions of which we know some few is exceedingly more excellent than ours. Our method proceeds with reasoning by steps from one conclusion to another, while His is one of simple intuition. We, for example, in order to win a knowledge of some properties of the circle (which has an infinity of them), begin with one of the simplest, and taking this for the definition of circle, proceed by reasoning to another property, and from this to a third, and then a fourth, and so on; but the Divine intellect, by a simple apprehension of the circle's essence, knows without time-consuming reasoning all the infinity of its properties. Next, all these properties are in effect virtually included in the definitions of all things; and ultimately, through being infinite, are perhaps but one in their essence and in the Divine mind. Nor is all the above entirely unknown to the human mind either, but it is clouded with deep and thick mists, which become partly dispersed and when we master some conclusions and get them so firmly established and so readily in our possession that we can run over them very rapidly. . . . Now these advances, which our intellect makes laboriously and step by step, run through the Divine mind like light in an instant; which is the same as saying that everything is always present to it.[23]

Galileo's distinction between divine reason and human reason, like Raphael's between angelic and human reason, is one of degree. For both, the difference is constituted by time. Human understanding requires time whereas angelic or divine understanding requires, respectively, little time or none at all. Now Satan exhibits an almost complete lack of understanding of the conditions of his existence. This lack is demonstrated by his argument against his own creation, as well as by the whole notion that he can assume a place equal to God's. By closing his mind to the significance of time and place and change, he insures that his ignorance be perpetual. To repair this detriment, God creates (almost by way of providing a demonstration to counter Satan's denial of creation) a visible world of time and space and motion — a world of visible works through which He reveals Himself — and that "Race of time" (XII, 554), mankind, to endure and comprehend it.

The stress that Raphael places on the distinction between angelic and human reason — that it is one of degree and not of kind — is crucial. It implies a denial of the radical distinction of kind that St. Augustine imposed between the temporal and the eternal. He viewed time and eternity as two mutually exclusive realms, so that it was impossible to conceive any participation of one within the other. But Milton allows Raphael to suggest, when "lik'ning spiritual to corporal forms" (V, 573), that Earth might be "but the shadow of Heav'n, and things therein / Each to other like, more than on Earth is thought" (V, 575–76). Here the radical ontological distinction between the temporal world and the eternal is being challenged. Then, although almost as an afterthought, he asserts that time is *in* eternity (V, 580). Raphael again speaks of time in eternity (insofar as eternity is equated with Heaven) when he explains, "For wee have also our Ev'ning and our Mourn, / Wee ours for change delectable, not need" (V, 628–29). By making the distinction one of degree rather than of kind, Raphael avoids the difficulty that St. Augustine failed to solve—that is, if time and eternity are mutually exclusive, how can temporal existence have any significance for God, and how, if time has no significance for God, can He determine eternally a finite period of creation? This problem does not arise when eternity is simply that which endures all time.[24] Conversely, because the difference is one of degree, Raphael is able to answer Adam's questions by "measuring things in Heav'n by things on Earth" (VI, 893).

The final metaphor that I shall consider in this essay involves time in its capacity as measure and, so, time in relation to space and motion. This metaphor also gives some insight into the nature of the "fortunate fall" as it appears to be conceived in *Paradise Lost.* In the final book of the poem, as Michael descends with Adam from that height of speculation, he says, "The hour precise / Exacts our parting hence" (XII, 589–90), indicating, simply, that the time of the expulsion of Adam and Eve from the Garden is fixed. Yet, an earlier metaphorical function involving the word "exacts" needs to be recalled. After linking himself with Eve in the transgression of God's command, Adam addresses Eve thus:

> *Eve*, now I see thou are exact of taste,
> And elegant, of Sapience no small part,
> Since to each meaning savor we apply,
> And Palate call judicious; I the praise
> Yield thee, so well this day thou hast purvey'd.   (IX, 1017–21)

The apparent sense of the opening line is that he now sees Eve to be "accomplished," "finished," or "perfected" in matters of taste, that is, with regard to discrimination in such matters, hence "elegant," etc. And there is at least the hint of a pun, suggesting that he sees her to be exactly to *his* taste. But, as we are explicitly reminded in the lines above, *Adam* is not deceived (IX, 998); thus, his saying that Eve is "exact"of taste cannot be considered a mere case of mistaken judgment; although there is a mistake in judgment involved, Adam does not really see Eve as improved by the fruit, and no longer can she be regarded as "accomplisht *Eve*"(IV, 660).

Instead, since we are aware that "savor" has been applied to the meanings in this instance, we can allow the word "exact" to signify in its literal or verbal sense as well, so that the line implies that Eve is "thrown out" or "driven out" from taste, and hence unaccomplished or lacking discrimination in such matters. But the circular logic governing the sense of the term "exact" demands that the motion of "driving" or "forcing out from" be joined with that of "bringing to perfection." I believe that this logic applies in the later instance as well. Not only does the "hour precise" demand the departure of Adam and Eve from Eden, but the move to "fitter soil" (XI, 98) must be viewed as a motion toward that time of perfect union when "Earth will be chang'd to Heav'n and Heav'n to Earth" (VII, 160).

Milton's use of "exact" in relation to "the hour precise" once again indicates his concern with time and measurement, motion and space. Moreover, this concern cannot be dissociated from the philosophic-scientific revolution of the sixteenth and seventeenth centuries. Augustine's insistence on a radical difference between time and eternity entailed that man could only contemplate the eternal by withdrawing from his existence in the universe of daily life, by withdrawing from participation in the motions and times around him.[25] Conversely, in *Paradise Lost*, because the visible universe "is as the Book of God," motion and change, not permanence, are associated with perfection and precision. The motions of time, the visible heavens, constitute a continuous and progressive revelation of God, accommodating man's continuous and progressive capacity for comprehension. This notion could only arise in an age when man could contemplate the motions of the visible heavens, and all the vagancies they present, without the fear of some dire change; it could only arise in an age when man could gaze upon the visible heavens in awe of their majesty and see "mazes intricate, / Eccentric, intervolv'd, yet regular / Then most, when most irregular they seem: /And in thir motions harmony Divine" (V, 622–25). Finally, through the universe presented in *Paradise Lost*, we should recognize its author as a man who saw that the discipline and virtue in mankind need not "be confined and cloyed, with repetition of that which is prescribed,"[26] a man who could look back upon that long stretch of human history "with a view to improving our wisdom and our morals" and say, "This is the way to live in all the epochs of history, Gentlemen, and to be a contemporary of time itself."[27]

Stanford University

NOTES

1. Marjorie Hope Nicolson, for example, claims that "Beyond the universe of man — even the vastly expanded universe of the telescope which Milton himself had beheld — there stretched in his imagination space, and it is *space* which dominates *Paradise Lost*."

In "Milton and the Telescope," *ELH*, II (1935), 21; see also Nicolson's *The Breaking of the Circle* (Evanston, Ill., 1950), pp. 164–66; Isabel McCaffrey, *"Paradise Lost" as "Myth"* (Cambridge, Mass., 1959), pp. 51, 53, 76–77; and Jackson I. Cope, *The Metaphoric Structure of "Paradise Lost"* (Baltimore, 1962), pp. 34, 51, 60, 68. Several critics have considered the significance of time in the poem, most notably Rosalie L. Colie, "Time and Eternity: Paradox and Structure in *Paradise Lost*," *JWCI*, XXIII (1960), 127–38; Laurence Stapleton, "Perspectives of Time in *Paradise Lost*," *PQ*, XLV (1966), 734–48; Ricardo J. Quinones, "Milton," in his *The Renaissance Discovery of Time* (Cambridge, Mass., 1972), pp. 444–93; and Edward William Tayler, *"Paradise Lost*: From Shadows to Truth," in his *Milton's Poetry: Its Development in Time* (Pittsburgh, Pa., 1979), pp. 60–104. Finally, see Joseph H. Summers, "'Grateful Vicissitude' in *Paradise Lost*," *PMLA*, *LXIX* (1954), 251–64, for an account of motion or movement in the poem.

2. See Thomas S. Kuhn, *The Copernican Revolution* (Cambridge, Mass., 1957), pp. 11–12, 270–71.

3. See Seth G. Atwood, "The Development of the Pendulum as a Device for Regulating Clocks prior to the 18th Century," in *The Study of Time II*, ed. J. T. Fraser and Nathaniel Lawrence (New York, 1975), pp. 424–25; also Alexander Koyré, "An Experiment in Measurement," in his *Metaphysics and Measurement* (London, 1968), pp. 89–117.

4. *The Philosophy of Rhetoric* (New York, 1936), p. 85.

5. See Douglas Berggren, "The Use and Abuse of Metaphor," *Review of Metaphysics*, XVI (1962–63), 237–58, 450–72.

6. All references to *Paradise Lost* and to Milton's prose are to the text of Merritt Y. Hughes, ed., *John Milton: Complete Poems and Major Prose* (New York, 1957). Hereafter, "Hughes."

7. Hughes, pp. 978–79.

8. Arnold Williams, *The Common Expositor* (Chapel Hill, N.C., 1948), pp. 40–43.

9. See, for example, John Carey and Alastair Fowler, eds., *The Poems of John Milton* (London, 1968), pp. 441–44.

10. Quoted by Ernst Cassirer in *The Philosophy of Symbolic Forms*, II: "Mythological Thought," trans. Ralph Manheim (New Haven, Conn., 1955), p. 107.

11. See Vincent Foster Hopper, *Medieval Number Symbolism*, Columbia University Series in English and Comparative Literature, No. 132 (New York, 1938), p. 102. The procedure, sometimes called "mystical addition," is performed as follows: $9 \times 51 = 459$, $4 + 5 + 9 = 18, 1 + 8 = 9$. This procedure will produce nine in the multiplication of nine by any number. See also Galbraith Miller Crump's account of the significance of the number nine in *Paradise Lost* in *The Mystical Design of "Paradise Lost"* (Lewisburg, Pa., 1975), pp. 82–84.

12. See S. K. Heninger, Jr., *Touches of Sweet Harmony* (San Marino, Cal., 1974), pp. 180–82.

13. Albert R. Cirillo, "Noon-Midnight and the Temporal Structure of *Paradise Lost*," *ELH*, XXIX (1962), 376–77.

14. *Surprised by Sin* (Berkeley, Cal., 1971), pp. 32–33.

15. "Advent'rous Song: The Texture of Milton's Epic," in *Language and Style in Milton*, ed. Ronald David Emma and John T. Shawcross (New York, 1967), p. 16.

16. *The City of God*, trans. John Healey (New York, 1945), I, 356 (bk. 12, ch. 13). See Tayler, *Milton's Poetry*, pp. 8–17, for a discussion of the cyclic notion of time and its persistence through the Renaissance.

17. Piero E. Ariotti, "The Concept of Time in Late Antiquity," *International Philosophical Quarterly*, XII (1972), 526–52.

18. *History, Time and Deity* (New York, 1965), p. 96.

19. See J. B. Broadbent, "Links Between Poetry and Prose in Milton," *ES*, XXXVII (1956), 53.

20. Heninger, *Sweet Harmony*, p. 227; see also Mother Mary Christopher Pecheux, "Milton and *Kairos*," *Milton Studies*, XII, ed. James D. Simmonds (Pittsburgh, Pa., 1979), pp. 197–211, and Herman Hausheer, "St. Augustine's Conception of Time," *Philosophical Review*, XLVI (1937), 509–10.

21. The meteor, of course is the least durable and has the most irregular motion of all heavenly bodies.

22. Except for the specific difference in time, that is, "evil hour" (IX, 780) as opposed to "moment," the action of Eve as "her rash hand . . . / Forth reaching to the Fruit, she pluck'd, she eat" (IX, 780–81) resembles the "moment"of Satan. It is momentary, impulsive, and motivated by the thought of rising out of her present level of existence. The resulting "fruitless hours" (IX, 1188) and "vain contest" (IX, 1189) similarly resemble the Satanic regard for time.

23. *Dialogue*, trans. Stillman Drake, 2nd ed. (Berkeley, Cal., 1967), pp. 103–04. For discussion of Galileo's *Dialogue* as a possible source for astronomical references in *Paradise Lost* see Allan H. Gilbert, "Milton and Galileo," *SP*, XIX (1922), 152–85. Other relevant discussions of the astronomy and possible sources of the astronomical ideas in the poem include Grant McColley, "The Astronomy of *Paradise Lost*," *SP*, XXXIV (1937), 209–47, and "Milton's Dialogue on Astronomy: The Principal Immediate Sources," *PMLA*, LII (1937), 728–62; and J. H. Adamson, "Kepler and Milton," *MLN*, LXXIV (1959), 683–85.

24. Hausheer, "St. Augustine," p. 511.

25. Hausheer, "St. Augustine," pp. 508–09; also, John F. Callahan, *Four Views of Time in Ancient Philosophy* (New York, 1968), pp. 184–87; and St. Augustine, *Confessions*, bk. 11, ch. 11.

26. *The Reason of Church Government Urged Against Prelaty*, in Hughes, p. 643.

27. *Learning Makes Men Happier Then Does Innocence*, in Hughes, p. 625.

"AS THE RABBINES EXPOUND": MILTON, GENESIS, AND THE RABBIS

Cheryl H. Fresch

W HEN HARRIS FRANCIS FLETCHER published his pioneering studies fifty years ago, he intended to point the way to the major source of Milton's Hebrew learning, the Buxtorf Bible.[1] In *Milton's Rabbinical Readings*, Fletcher argued that Milton's writings reveal his debt to the rabbinical commentaries that Hebrew Bible supplies, which include those of Ben Gerson, Ibn Ezra, Kimchi, and Rashi. Fletcher especially stressed Milton's use of Rashi's commentary on Genesis in Books VII through IX of *Paradise Lost*. Although as recently as 1975 a book-length study of Milton's Hebraism opened by announcing that "the question of Milton's knowledge of Hebrew and usage of Buxtorf's Rabbinical Bible is no longer controversial,[2] such a fiat could hardly settle the dispute that has developed since 1930. For the past fifty years, many scholars have questioned, and some have rejected, the route Fletcher laid out for those seeking to study Milton's Hebraism.

Leonard Mendelsohn, who, unlike so many Milton scholars, reads Milton "from a perspective centered in a knowledge of rabbinic writings,"[3] is among the most recent scholars to speak on the persistent controversy surrounding Fletcher's thesis. Opening his 1978 article, Mendelsohn sets forth the views of the major disputants:

At present the major positions lie somewhere in or among three categories: (1) that Milton could and did read Rashi, Ibn Ezra, Kimchi, and Ben Gershon among other rabbinic commentaries, and much of the Talmud as well; (2) that he might have read these commentaries, but it is unlikely, and we have no significant proof that he did so; (3) that he probably read none of this material, since he was able to derive everything which might be attributed to it from concordances, thesauri and dictionaries, from Christian commentators and other secondary sources, as well as from his own independent intelligence. (p. 125)

Following George N. Conklin, whom he identifies as "spokesman for the third position," Mendelsohn strengthens that position by moving beyond Conklin's study of thirty years ago which demonstrated "that Milton could have taken from other sources much of what Fletcher says is from the rabbis."[4] Mendelsohn's meticulous and expert study of Milton's rabbinical references in *Pro Populo* permits him to conclude "that Milton either could not or at the very least did not read the Talmud. He also did not avail himself of the rabbinic commentators, neither those who elucidate the Gemora nor those who gloss the Bible, even though these sages would by and large have supported Milton's cause. To claim that he had read these materials would suggest a shoddiness quite uncharacteristic of John Milton."[5]

Although Mendelsohn does not refer to Samuel Stollman's article "Milton's Rabbinical Readings and Fletcher" (1972), the earlier study also very seriously attacked Fletcher's thesis. Stollman revealed that "almost half of Fletcher's rabbinical citations have been incorrectly translated and are therefore unrelated to his thesis. The remaining parallels can be traced either to the biblical lexicons, or to the extensive hexaemeral literature of the time, or can be explained as the result of Milton's rationalistic hermeneutics coinciding with the rationalistic tendency in the medieval Jewish commentators."[6] While undermining Fletcher's thesis, however, neither Mendelsohn nor Stollman denies the provocative presence of the connections between Milton's writings and the rabbis. To identify either the primary or the secondary source of those connections, though, may remain a goal that defies achievement. First, as Stollman warns, "the hexaemeral tradition is too ramified to permit identification of Milton's actual sources, whether rabbinical or Christian."[7] Furthermore, both Stollman and Mendelsohn suggest that Milton may have turned to intermediate sources such as "phrase books and lexicons and glossaries."[8] Finally, both critics acknowledge the possibility of Milton's raising questions similar to those the rabbis considered in studying the Bible and thinking through to the same kinds of answers. But if the fifty-year controversy about Milton's sources has left scholars without an answer to the question, "Where did Milton derive his information?",[9] it has nevertheless encouraged them to look more closely at that information. In an effort, not to identify Milton's "sources," but to consider the significance of those provocative resemblances between the rabbis' and Milton's treatments of the Genesis narrative, this paper therefore purposes to return to the rabbinic commentaries Fletcher so tantalizingly introduced to our attention fifty years ago.

Although Stollman and Mendelsohn have proved that Fletcher claimed too much for Milton's linguistic abilities, Fletcher did not exaggerate Rashi's enduring importance as a commentator on the Hebrew Bible. In his major study of the eleventh-century rabbi, Herman Hailperin writes:

We have long been accustomed to think of Rashi as one who was born to give light to the Jews only. It may be that he himself never thought of doing anything else. But it was an age in which all scholars, it seems, were looking for the light which Rashi gives. The interpretation of the Scriptures which he provided for the Jews was his great study of the historical-literal meaning of the Bible. It is not too much to say that Christians, scholars and all, felt the same demand.[10]

Such a demand certainly exerted control over the writings of the seventeenth-century Puritan poet, and, as Fletcher argued, Milton's elaborations of Genesis do sometimes repeat those found in Rashi's commentaries.

Genesis i, 19, for example, seems to argue that the birds were born from the waters, as were the fish, but because Genesis ii, 19, says "every fowl of the air" rose "out of the ground," the actual origin of the birds seems uncertain. Rashi's solution to this problem is as down-to-earth and logical as possible: "And *this statement* [Genesis ii, 19] comes (is repeated) *here* to point out that the fowls were created from the swamps; for above [Genesis i, 19] it is said that they were created from the waters and here it states that they were created from the earth."[11] Giving some attention to the chicken-egg controversy, Milton seems to follow Rashi, as Fletcher would have it, by combining the earth of Genesis ii, 19, with the waters of Genesis i, 19, so that the birds can rise from "the tepid Caves, and Fens and shores" (VII, 417).[12] Of course, as Stollman and Mendelsohn caution, the similarity here could indicate no more than the coinciding of Milton's "rationalistic hermeneutics . . . with the rationalistic tendency in the medieval Jewish commentators."[13] In other words, such a reading of Genesis could be reached by any thoughtful exegete concerned with the literal meaning of the Bible and faced with the challenge of explaining the apparent discrepancy between these two versions of the origin of the birds.

Fletcher tracked down a fair number of such similarities between Milton's Genesis story and Rashi's Genesis commentary as he built his case for Milton's reading of the Buxtorf Bible. When Milton describes the appearance of "the tender Grass, whose verdure clad" the earth (VII, 315), Fletcher argues that "the suggestion for this elaboration is contained in Rashi's commentary."[14] On Genesis i, 11, the rabbi writes, "Let it be filled and covered with a garment of *different* grasses."[15] When a divine "Guide" moves Adam into the Garden in *Paradise Lost* by first explaining "thy Mansion wants thee, *Adam*" (VIII, 298, 296), Fletcher finds what Genesis ii, 15, fails to supply by turning to Rashi: "The address to Adam by his guide, with its trace of persuasion, is not to be found in the text [Genesis ii, 15]. It is, however, directly indicated by

Rashi, who explained how it was that Adam was induced to enter the Garden. In his comment on the fifteenth verse of this chapter, the rabbi said: ' . . . By means of fine words he persuaded [Adam] to enter the Garden.'"[16] So too when Milton counts jealousy of a yet-unborn second woman as one of Eve's reasons for offering the forbidden fruit to Adam, Fletcher looks to Rashi's precedent in his gloss upon Genesis iii, 6: "*And she gave also to her husband* — so that she would not die while he lived and took another wife."[17] Acknowledging that the same explanation appears in *Josippon* and the *Zohar*, Fletcher does initially retreat enough to say that Rashi "may" have been Milton's source, but he later asserts that because of the Buxtorf Bible, Rashi's commentary, unlike the *Zohar* and *Josippon*, "can be definitely connected with Milton."[18] The notion of Satan's sexual jealousy of Adam and Eve, common to both *Paradise Lost* and Rashi's commentary, also figures importantly in Fletcher's argument. In his gloss on Genesis iii, 1, Rashi explains that the reference to the serpent's subtlety, which follows the reference in Genesis ii, 25, to the humans' unashamed nakedness, "informs you with what plan the serpent assailed them: he saw them naked and unashamed and he coveted her."[19] Concentrating upon the second and third Satanic soliloquies in Book IV, Fletcher claims that "Rashi's commentary also supplies the immediate cause for Satan's seduction of the human pair."[20]

In addition to the correspondences Fletcher discovered between Milton and Rashi are yet others. Extremely singular, for example, when *Paradise Lost* XI, 857–60, is compared with Rashi's remark on Genesis viii, 11, as well as with the treatment of the text in the Bible to which the blind poet most often turned,[21] is the kind of attention Milton gives to the dove sent forth from the ark. Milton writes,

> A Dove sent forth once and again to spy
> Green Tree or ground whereon his foot may light;
> The second time returning, in his Bill
> An olive leaf he brings, pacific sign.

Rashi had argued,

I am of the opinion that it (the dove) was a male and that therefore it (the text) speaks of it sometimes as masculine and sometimes as feminine, because *really* wherever יונה "dove" occurs in the Scripture it is spoken of as feminine, as (Song V. 12) "[His eyes] are like *those of* doves beside the water brooks, that are washing themselves (רוחעצת fem.) in milk"; (Ezek. VII. 16) "Like the doves of the valleys, all of them moaning (הומזת fem.)"; and as (Hos. VII. 11) "Like a silly (פותה fem.) dove."[22]

The Authorized version, however, identifies the dove as a female: "But the dove found no rest for the sole of her foot, and she returned"; "And the dove came in to him in the evening; and lo, in her mouth was an olive leaf" (Genesis viii, 9, 11).

When Milton's God creates Eve, "The Rib he form'd and fashion'd with his hands; / Under his forming hands a Creature grew" (VIII, 469–70). When Rashi elaborates upon Genesis ii, 22 ("And the rib, which the Lord God had taken from man, made he a woman," A.V.), he writes the following two-part explanation:

וֹיִבֶן AND HE FORMED (lit., He built) — as a structure, wide below and narrower above so that its weight should not strain the walls. . . .AND HE MADE THE RIB INTO A WOMAN — לְאִשָּׁה *means* that it should become a woman, like (Judg. VIII. 21) "and Gideon made it לְאֵפוֹד" *i.e.*, that it should become an ephod.[23]

In both interpretations the maker forms and fashions or builds, which closely adheres to the basic reading of Genesis ii, 22. The Geneva Bible gloss on "made," for example, is *Ebr buylt*. The object which he builds, however, is seen to assume its own life; that is, it grows or becomes, no longer remaining the passive object it had initially been. Throughout *Paradise Lost*, Milton develops this notion of the autonomous power of God's creatures to create both themselves and others. Even before the light is created, the Earth, purged by the Spirit of God, hangs "self-balanc't on her Centre" (VII, 242). Then, too, the first rain originates "from the Earth a dewy Mist" (VII, 333) without any provocation from God. The teeming earth herself simply exudes generative moisture. And most importantly, of course, the free-will of both angels and humans allows them to choose to become what they will.

The exegesis Rashi brings to Genesis i, 16 ("And God made two great lights; the greater light to rule the day, and the lesser light to rule the night: he made the stars also," A.V.) likewise recalls some points in Milton's presentation of the creation of the heavenly luminaries in *Paradise Lost* VII, 346–49, 370–84. The poet writes,

> And God made two great Lights, great for thir use
> To Man, the greater to have rule by Day,
> The less by Night altern: and made the Stars,
> And set them in the Firmament of Heav'n
>
> .   .   .   .
>
> First in his East the glorious Lamp was seen,
> Regent of Day, and all th' Horizon round

Invested with bright Rays, jocund to run
His Longitude through Heav'n's high road: the gray
Dawn, and the *Pleiades* before him danc'd
Shedding sweet influence: less bright the Moon,
But opposite in levell'd West was set
His mirror, with full face borrowing her Light
From him, for other light she needed none
In that aspect, and still that distance keeps
Till night, then in the East her turn she shines,
Revolv'd on Heav'n's great Axle, and her Reign
With thousand lesser Lights dividual holds,
With thousand thousand Stars, that then appear'd
Spangling the Hemisphere.

And Rashi:

THE GREAT LUMINARIES — They were created of equal size, but that of the moon was diminished because she complained and said, "It is impossible for two kings to make use of one crown." . . . AND THE STARS — Because He diminished the moon, He increased its *attendant* hosts to mollify It.[24]

Both the rabbi and the poet explain the stars as attendants upon the monarch of the night, the moon. The King James Version, by contrast, would seem to heighten the similarity between Rashi's and Milton's treatment of the verse.

Another not inconsequential association between Rashi's and Milton's readings of Genesis appears to take shape when the notion of sexual abstinence, which arises in Book X of the Christian epic, is considered in light of Rashi's response to Genesis iv, 19–25. The awkward gap separating the narrative about Lamech (Genesis iv, 19–24) and the announcement of the conception and birth of Seth (Genesis iv, 25) heightens the challenge to Rashi's exegetical skill. The eleventh-century rabbi eliminates the lacuna by explaining that Lamech's wives

had lived apart from him after they had born children, because God's decree had been issued that Cain's descendants should be exterminated after seven generations. They said, "Why should we bear children only to be destroyed? Soon the Flood will come and will sweep everyone away!" . . .AND ADAM KNEW — Lamech came to Adam Harishon, complaining about his wives. He (Adam) said to them: "Is it for you to be overparticular regarding God's decrees? You do your duty, and He will do His!" They replied to him: "First correct yourself: have you not lived apart from your wife these 130 years, ever since, through you, death was decreed as a punishment?" At once . . . "Adam knew his wife" [and] . . . "his love for her was now greater than before."[25]

Although the theme of sexual abstinence as a response to the penalty of death incurred by Adam and Eve is common to both Rashi's and Milton's elaborations upon Genesis, which itself hints at no such reaction, the variations between the poetic and rabbinic elaborations bring additional significance to the theme. In *Paradise Lost* the suggestion "to abstain / From Love's due Rites" (X, 993–94) comes from Eve. Recalling Lamech's wives, who did not wish to "bear children only to be destroyed," Milton's Eve suggests celibacy to avoid creating "a woeful Race" which would only be "devour'd / By Death at last" (X, 984, 980–81). In Rashi, however, Adam, not Eve, first shuns love, while in Milton, Adam, demonstrating a new command of the acumen with which he was originally endowed, explains that such abstinence, or the suicide which Eve has also proposed, would make impossible their revenge upon the Serpent:

> such acts
> Of contumacy will provoke the Highest
> To make death in us live: Then let us seek
> Some safer resolution, which methinks
> I have in view, calling to mind with heed
> Part of our Sentence, that thy Seed shall bruise
> The Serpent's head; piteous amends, unless
> Be meant, whom I conjecture, our grand Foe
> *Satan*, who in the Serpent hath contriv'd
> Against us this deceit: to crush his head
> Would be revenge indeed; which will be lost
> By death brought on ourselves, or childless days
> Resolv'd, as thou proposest; so our Foe
> Shall 'scape his punishment ordain'd, and wee
> Instead shall double ours upon our heads.   (X, 1026–40)

Milton's treatment of the sexual abstinence theme not only dovetails into and further develops the magnificent theme of love that figures so importantly throughout *Paradise Lost*, but it contributes some very bold, broad strokes to Milton's depiction of postlapsarian Adam and Eve. Hope glows over this scene. By firmly refuting Eve's faulty reasoning, Adam finally seems to have gained the self-assurance and self-esteem Raphael has tried to foster in him. Furthermore, Adam intellectually glimpses the truth that Milton will present in the final visual image of his great poem — from love will come humanity's eventual triumph:

> They hand in hand with wand'ring steps and slow,
> Through *Eden* took thir solitary way.   (XII, 648–9)

Rich as the sexual abstinence theme shared by both Milton and Rashi is, though, it cannot support any claim for Milton's having ever read Rashi. From at least two much more easily available sources the poet could have derived the material he needed. Both Calvin, in his *Commentaries on Genesis*, and Loredano, in his *Life of Adam*, develop the same motif.[26] Rashi would, of course, antedate both Christian writers and therefore might have been a source, especially for Calvin. But behind Rashi lies yet an earlier possible source for the sexual abstinence theme, and that source — the Midrash on Genesis, Genesis Rabbah — is directly and frequently mentioned by Rashi. Furthermore, seven of the nine motifs common to Rashi and Milton which have been surveyed in the previous pages also appear to draw Milton into some kind of association with the commentary offered in the Genesis Rabbah. That statistic comes close to the one Herman Hailperin derived when he considered Rashi's use of the Talmud and Midrash: "It is no exaggeration to say that two-thirds of his Pentateuch commentary has its source in Talmud and Midrash."[27]

As the eleventh-century rabbi makes clear in his remarks, the midrash on the very same verses anticipates the sexual abstinence theme he develops in response to Genesis iv, 19–25:

AND LAMECH SAID UNTO HIS WIVES, etc. (IV, 23ff). R. Jose b. R. Hanina said: He summoned them to their marital duties. Said they to him: "To-morrow a flood will come — are we to bear children for a curse?" . . . Said he [Lamech] to them [his wives]: "Come, let us go to Adam [and consult him]." So they went to him. He said to them: "Do you do your duty, while the Holy One, blessed be He, will do His." "Physician, physician, heal thine own limp!" retorted the other. "Have you kept apart from Eve a hundred and thirty years for any reason but that you might not beget children by her!" On hearing this, he [Adam] resumed his duty of begetting children, and forthwith, *And Adam knew his wife again* (Gen. IV, 25).[28]

Paradise Lost X, 1026–40, stresses, however, that the Adam who rejects Eve's suggestion of celibacy does so not primarily because he remembers it is their duty to "Increase and multiply," but because he thoughtfully considers the judgment against the serpent, whose head will someday be bruised by the seed of the woman. The anonymous midrash on Genesis iv, 1 ("And Adam knew Eve his wife; and she conceived, and bare Cain") therefore also seems to bear upon Milton's treatment of the sexual abstinence theme:

When Adam saw that his descendants were fated to be consigned to Gehenna, he engaged less is procreation. But when he saw that after twenty-six generations Israel would accept the Torah, he applied himself to producing descendants; hence *And Adam knew Eve his wife* (Gen. IV. 1). (p. 179)

Such a resemblance, however, can no more be offered as evidence of a direct link between Milton and Genesis Rabbah than can the similarity between Milton's and Rashi's views on the origins of the birds be offered as evidence of Milton's familiarity with that rabbi's commentary. A commonsensical approach dedicated to revealing the historical-literal meaning of Genesis could have led the rabbis and Milton to these same conclusions. Furthermore, as Calvin's *Commentaries* and Loredano's *Life of Adam* demonstrate, and as Stollman warned, "The hexaemeral tradition is too ramified to permit identification of Milton's actual sources."[29]

When Rashi develops his charming anecdote about God's mollifying the moon by giving her a following of stars, he again parenthetically acknowledges the importance of Genesis Rabbah. The midrash on Genesis i, 16, is attributed to Rabbi Aha, who is reported to have explained,

Imagine a king who had two governors, one ruling in the city and the other in a province. Said the king: "Since the former has humbled himself to rule in the city only, I decree that whenever he goes out, the city council and the people shall go out with him, and whenever he enters, the city council and the people shall enter with him. Thus did the Holy One, blessed be He, say: "Since the moon humbled itself to rule by night, I decree that when she comes forth, the stars shall come forth with her, and when she goes in [disappears], the stars shall go in with her." (pp. 43–44)

Similarly, Milton's handling of the Serpent's sexual jealousy, Eve's temptation of Adam, Adam's entrance into the Garden, and the plants' covering the ground recall the midrashim of Genesis Rabbah as firmly as they recall Rashi's commentaries. Furthermore, with three of these four motifs the midrashim not only supply explanations Rashi will adopt, but they offer other readings which also seem to surface in *Paradise Lost*. The eighteenth chapter of Genesis Rabbah, whose influence Rashi acknowledges in his commentary, does not significantly differ from Rashi in explaining Genesis ii, 25–iii, 1:

Now surely Scripture should have stated, *And the Lord God made for Adam and his wife garments of skin* (Gen. III, 21) [immediately after the former verse]? Said R. Joshua b. Karhah: It teaches you through what sin that wicked creature inveigled them, viz. because he saw them engaged in their natural functions, he [the serpent] conceived a passion for her. (p. 147)

But turning to the following chapter of Genesis Rabbah, one uncovers not only an earlier version of Rashi's gloss upon Genesis iii, 6, but some additional details that provocatively call to mind Eve's temptation of Adam in *Paradise Lost*.

SHE TOOK OF THE FRUIT THEREOF, AND DID EAT. R. Aibu said: She squeezed grapes and gave him. R. Simlai said: She came upon him with her answers all ready, saying to him: "What think you: that I will die and another Eve will be created for you? — *There is nothing new under the sun* (Eccl. I, 9). Or do you think that I will die while you remain alone? *He created it not a waste, He formed it to be inhabited*" (Isa. XLV. 18). The Rabbis said: She began weeping and crying over him. (p. 151)

Before she turns away from the tree (IX, 816–33), Milton's Eve certainly gives considerable thought to her approaching reunion with Adam; when "to him she haste[s]," like the Eve described in the Midrash, she too has "her answers all ready": "In her face excuse / Came Prologue, and Apology to prompt, / Which with bland words at will she thus addrest" (IX, 853–55). Of course, Milton's Eve does not simply mirror the Eve of the Genesis Rabbah.[30] Despite the selfishness and jealousy that undeniably and largely control her behavior, for example, Milton's Eve remains much too intelligent, graceful, and proud to sputter about another woman as does the termagant Rabbi Simlai describes. The forbidden fruit that Milton's Eve shares with Adam affects him, however, as if it were related to the grapes Rabbi Aibu identifies as the fruit: "As with new Wine intoxicated both," Adam and Eve "swim in mirth" (IX, 1008–09). As for the weeping and crying mentioned at the end of the rabbinic exegesis of Genesis iii, 6, Milton reserves such behavior for the reconciliation sequence, and he again presents a much more attractive woman than the hypocritical or perhaps merely frightened Eve described by the rabbis. Furthermore, the tears of the fallen, grief-stricken woman who implores, "Forsake me not thus, *Adam*" (X, 914) do not contribute to the seduction but rather the redemption of Adam.

Rashi's parenthetical reference to the sixteenth chapter of Genesis Rabbah after explaining that God "took him [Adam] with kind words and induced him to enter [the Garden]" reveals yet additional notions common to both Milton's account of the Genesis story and the Genesis Rabbah. Explaining Genesis ii, 15, Rabbi Nehemiah provided the gloss Rashi would adopt: "R. Nehemiah said: He persuaded him [to enter], as you read, *Take with you words, and return unto the Lord*" (Hosea xiv, 3, p. 130). Rabbi Nehemiah's exegesis of Genesis ii, 8, establishes the same explanation: "He persuaded him [to enter and eat thereof], like a

king who prepared a banquet and then invited guests" (p. 121). The "One
. . . of shape Divine" who "stood at [Adam's] Head a dream" therefore
would seem to have roots that reach back beyond Rashi's commentary:

> thy Mansion wants thee, *Adam*, rise,
> First Man, of Men innumerable ordain'd
> First Father, call'd by thee I come thy Guide
> To the Garden of bliss, thy seat prepar'd.   (VIII, 296–99)

As with so many other verses, however, the Genesis Rabbah presents alternative readings of Genesis ii, 15 and ii, 8. And although Rashi
chose not to accept Rabbi Judah's interpretation, Milton appears to
have settled upon a reading that recalls Rabbi Judah's, as well as Rabbi
Nehemiah's. The midrash on Genesis ii, 15 begins,

R. Judah and R. Nehemiah differed in their interpretations.
R. Judah said: He exalted him, as you read, *And the peoples shall take them, and
bring them to their place* (Isa. XIV, 2). (p. 130)

On Genesis ii, 8, Rabbi Judah again argued that "He exalted him, [WAY-
YASEM having the same meaning] as in the verse, *Thou shalt in any
wise set him* (tasim) *king over thee*" (Deuteronomy xvii, 15., p. 121).

In the seventeenth-century epic, both explanations figure in the
treatment of Adam's entrance into the Garden. Adam rises, or rather, is
raised — both physically and spiritually exalted — when he is escorted
into the Garden by the Guide who has explained, "I come thy Guide /
To the Garden of bliss, thy seat prepared":

> So saying, by the hand he took me rais'd,
> And over Fields and Waters, as in Air
> Smooth sliding without step, last led me up
> A woody Mountain; whose high top was plain. (VIII, 298–03)

Although Milton did not include the word *exaltation* in this sequence, it
is intriguing to notice that the word does appear to describe a very similar situation in Eve's recollection of the flying episode from her dream
of temptation:

> Forthwith up to the Clouds
> With him I flew, and underneath beheld
> The Earth outstretcht immense, a prospect wide
> And various: wond'ring at my flight and change
> To this high exaltation.   (V, 86–90)

Finally, even the Genesis Rabbah's brief remark on Genesis i, 11
("And God said, Let the earth bring forth grass, the herb yielding seed,

and the fruit tree yielding fruit after his kind, whose seed is in itself, upon the earth," A.V.), which has a focus different from that of Rashi's gloss, also brings to mind *Paradise Lost*. Rashi's figure of the grassy garment covering the earth ("Let it be filled and covered with a garment of *different* grasses") resembles Milton's description of the third day and the birth of the plants:

> He scarce had said, when the bare Earth, till then
> Desert and bare, unsightly, unadorn'd,
> Brought forth the tender Grass, whose verdure clad
> Her Universal Face with pleasant green.   (VII, 313–16)

But line 316 also carries an echo of the midrash attributed to Rabbi Joshua b. Levi in the Genesis Rabbah: "R. Joshua b. Levi said: When the rain descends it makes a face for the ground" (p. 110). The footnote reads, "By covering it with plant life, whereas formerly it was bare. This too is deduced from FACE."

A reading of the Genesis Rabbah not only reveals that much of the rabbinic influence upon Milton that Fletcher traced to Rashi can also be followed back to the Midrash Rabbah, the much earlier collection of rabbinic commentaries which developed over 1,500 years of Hebrew history (500 B.C.E.–1000 C.E.), but when the influence of additional midrashim (those not included in the two-thirds Rashi accepted into his own commentary) is also recognized in *Paradise Lost*, the importance Fletcher attributed to Rashi appears more dubious. Further weakening Fletcher's case, while simultaneously suggesting the importance of a more thorough reconsideration of the rabbinic influence upon *Paradise Lost*, however indirect that influence may be, is yet an additional group of thematic similarities between the Christian poem and the massive and monumental collection of diverse rabbinical commentary in the Midrash Rabbah. This cluster of material from the Genesis Rabbah elaborates upon points in the story of the fall of Adam and Eve that Rashi's commentary either passes over or only very abstractly considers. Herman Hailperin's remarks about all those midrashim Rashi chose not to incorporate into his commentaries would appear to describe the eleventh-century Hebrew's attitude about this cluster of earlier rabbinic interpretations: "There are cases when Rashi definitely rejects the *midrash*. If the biblical text cannot be brought into harmony with the *midrash*, Rashi declares that the midrashic interpretation is irreconcilable with the 'natural,' simple meaning."[31]

When Rashi develops the significance of God's choosing to build Eve from one of Adam's ribs (Genesis ii, 21), he refers to Exodus and the Talmud and makes no allusion to the Midrash Rabbah:

OF HIS RIBS— *The word means* of his sides, similar to (Ex. XXVI. 20) המשׁכָּן ולצלע "and for the second side of the tabernacle"; this has a bearing upon what they (the Sages) say, (Erub. 18a): They were created with two faces (*sides*).[32]

The earlier rabbis, however, had set forth an extended and enchanting explanation of the many alternatives God cautiously considered before he chose to borrow Adam's rib.

R. Joshua of Siknin said in R. Levi's name: WAYYIBEN is written, signifying that he considered well (*hithbonnen*) from what part to create her. Said He: 'I will not create her from [Adam's] head, lest she be swell-headed; nor from the eye, lest she be a coquette; nor from the ear, lest she be an eavesdropper; nor from the mouth, lest she be a gossip; nor from the heart, lest she be prone to jealousy; nor from the hand, lest she be light-fingered; nor from the foot, lest she be a gadabout; but from the modest part of man, for even when he stands naked, that part is covered.' And as He created each limb He ordered her, 'Be a modest woman.' Yet in spite of all this, *But ye have set at nought all my counsel, and would none of My reproof* (Prov. I, 25). I did not create her from the head, yet she is swell-headed, as it is written, *They walk with stretched-forth necks* (Isa. III, 16); nor from the eye, yet she is a coquette: *And wanton eyes* (*ib.*); nor from the ear, yet she is an eavesdropper: *Now Sarah listened in the tent door* (Gen. XVIII, 10); nor from the heart, yet she is prone to jealousy: *Rachael envied her sister* (*ib.* XXX, 1); nor from the hand, yet she is light-fingered: *And Rachael stole the teraphim* (*ib.* XXXI, 19); nor from the foot, yet she is a gadabout: *And Dinah went out*, etc. (*ib.* XXXIV, 1). (pp. 141–42)

Although Rashi may have assumed that this midrash "wander[ed] away into errancy and truancy,"[33] and therefore rejected it, Milton's poem reveals a similar spirit in its presentation of Eve. Milton humanizes prelapsarian Eve by gently touching her characterization with attributes like those the rabbis associated with such Old Testament daughters of Eve as Sarah, Rachael, Dinah, and the "daughters of Zion" described in Isaiah. It is of course because of the pride, the coquettishness, the eavesdropping, the jealousy, and the independence with which Milton has so enriched or complicated Eve that some readers have found her flawed. Others have responded that it is theologically impossible for her to be flawed or partly fallen; until she determines to eat the forbidden fruit she is "yet sinless" (IX, 659).[34] What both groups of critics would agree upon, though, is the undeniable humanness of Eve. She would perhaps seem more perfect if she did not respond so dangerously to her own reflection in the "Smooth Lake" IV, 459), if she did not yield herself to Adam "with coy submission, modest pride, / And sweet reluctant amorous delay" (IV, 310–11), if she did not admit to having eavesdropped upon the conversation between Adam and Michael (IX, 273–78), and if she did not at times seem jealous of

Adam's sexual superiority (IX, 273–89). Faced with a choice between the problem of adequately providing for the fall of an absolutely and rigidly perfect Eve and the problem of adequately maintaining the "yet sinless" state of a prelapsarian woman who so often resembles women born outside Paradise, Milton chose the latter.

Like Dinah, therefore, Eve is perhaps something of a gadabout. Nevertheless, the "first of women *Eve*" (IV, 409) doesn't sally forth alone merely to see other "daughters of the land" (Genesis xxxiv, 1), but to do some serious gardening, uninterrupted by the smiles, looks, and conversation she and Adam usually exchange while working. Ironically, though, Eve's fate anticipates Dinah's. As Dinah is "defiled" by Shechem the son of Hamor (Genesis xxxiv, 2), Eve returns to Adam "defac't, deflow'r'd" (IX, 901) by the Serpent. Milton takes great pains, however, to present Eve as more than just another headstrong, unwary, but beautiful woman like Dinah, and his extended treatment of the separation of Adam and Eve reveals an amazingly sensitive attention to the prelapsarian humanness of both our Grand Parents.

The dramatic necessity of getting Adam off the stage before the Serpent appears to Eve required the anonymous playwright of the Wakefield Corpus Christi Cycle to introduce the following exchange between Adam and Eve:

> ADAM. Eve, felow, abide me thore,
>   For I will go to viset more,
>   To se what trees that here been.
>   Here ar well moo then we have seen,
>   Gresys, and othere small floures,
>   That smell full swete, of seyr coloures.
> EVE. Gladly, sir, I will full faine.
>   When ye have sene theym, com agane.[35]

No such dramatic necessity demanded that the Jewish and Christian theologians who believed that Eve was alone when tempted explain the reason for her separation from Adam. Rashi's commentary, for example, offers no remark upon the separation, and no major Christian theologian had much more to say than did Calvin:

From these words ["And gave also unto her husband with her"], some conjecture that Adam was present when his wife was tempted and persuaded by the serpent, which is by no means credible. Yet it might be that he soon joined her, and that, even before the woman tasted the fruit of the tree, she related the conversation held with the serpent, and entangled him with the same fallacies by which she herself had been deceived. Others refer to . . . "with her," to the conjugal bed, which may be received. But because Moses simply relates that he ate the fruit taken from the hands of his wife, the opinion has been commonly received, that he was rather captivated with her allurements than persuaded by Satan's impostures.[36]

But while Calvin quickly moves away from simply insisting upon the separation to discussing the subsequent temptation of Adam, the rabbis of the Midrash Rabbah, like the Wakefield dramatist, thoughtfully pondered the separation and sought to explain why Eve was alone:

AND THE WOMAN SAID UNTO THE SERPENT: OF THE FRUIT OF THE TREES OF THE GARDEN WE MAY EAT (III, 2). Now where was Adam during this conversation? Abba Halfon b. Koriah said: He had engaged in his natural functions [intercourse] and then fallen asleep. The Rabbis said: He [God] took him and led him all around the world, telling him: 'Here is a place fit for planting [trees], here is a place fit for sowing [cereals].' (p. 149)

This midrash, like the one on Genesis ii, 21, apparently met with Rashi's disapproval, but its intent to explain why Eve was alone when the Serpent came upon her was shared not only by the Wakefield dramatist, but also by the poet of *Paradise Lost*. The woman who works alone among the flowers, trying to prop up their drooping heads, "mindless the while, / Herself, though fairest unsupported Flow'r, / From her best prop so far" (IX, 431–33), however, has not simply been abandoned by an exhausted husband or one off on a world tour or one out examining the local flora. Nor has she slipped away from home like the gadabout Dinah. Her reasons for wanting to work alone are neither illogical, wholly vain, nor unpersuasive (IX, 205–384). Further enhancing Eve's appeal during the separation sequence is Adam's failure to be "with such counsel nothing sway'd" (X, 1010), as he will be when she later suggests suicide or childlessness. Adam's emotions come to dominate his reasoning until he tells Eve to go, although Eve, despite her extended argument, remains "yet submiss" (IX, 377). What Milton has done to explain the separation of Adam and Eve remains unparalleled by any other treatment of Genesis — be that treatment a note, a commentary, a poem, a drama, a sermon, or a theological treatise.[37] The poetic elaboration of the separation in the ninth book of *Paradise Lost* presents a profoundly rich study of the emotionally charged encounter between Adam and Eve who, like the Wakefield Adam and Eve, determine to separate, while the rabbinical elaborations of the separation present a separation caused by happenstance. But what seems most remarkable is that the rabbis and the poet, who lacked the dramatic necessity that motivated the Wakefield poet, were attempting to answer a question few others even bothered to ask: "Where was Adam during Eve's temptation?"

Like Sarah, who was named, along with the gadabout Dinah, in the midrash on Genesis ii, 21, Eve also possesses enough ordinary humanness to be guilty of eavesdropping, although, as Carey and Fowler caution, this behavior hardly amounts to evidence of Eve's "moral deterioration."[38] This eavesdropping motif establishes another of several links between Raphael's visit to Adam and the three angels' visit to Abraham (Genesis xviii). Within the "Silvan Lodge" (V, 377) Eve, at Adam's request, prepares a noon meal to serve their angel guest, as Sarah will later work within the tent to prepare the meal Abraham orders for the three angels. But while Sarah, standing behind the tent door, will hear the angels announce God's blessing of a child to be born to Abraham and her, Eve, standing "behind" in a "shady nook" (IX, 277), hears Raphael convey God's warning of an "Enemy" who seeks to "ruin" Adam and her (IX, 274–75).

The eavesdropping episode during Raphael's visit develops more, though, than another analogy between that visit and the visit to Abraham recorded in Genesis xviii. Behind the eavesdropping in *Paradise Lost* lies more than Genesis xviii, 10 ("And Sarah heard it in the tent door, which was behind him") and more than the long midrash on Genesis ii, 21 linking Eve to such Old Testament women as Sarah. For Eve is not the only eavesdropper in Milton's epic. By eavesdropping, Satan hears the information he needs to wreck Paradise. Although very little has been said by scholars about Eve's eavesdropping, Grant McColley has examined the history of Satan's role as eavesdropper.

The motif of Satan's eavesdropping is not a common one in writings on Genesis. McColley explains that "in hexameral and related literature, we rarely meet the idea which Milton stressed here [IV, 393–595]." He posits, however, that the basic idea "probably reached Milton through the *Paradise* of Moses Bar Cepha . . . , [who wrote that, after] 'Eve had been formed from Adam's body, Adam instructed her concerning the precept in such a voice that could be heard; wherefore Satan heard perfectly *(exaudisse Satanum)* the words Adam spoke to his wife.'"[39]

Yet many centuries before the ninth-century Syrian Bishop wrote his treatise on Paradise, the rabbis whose teachings found their way into the Midrash Rabbah had touched upon the same theme:

AND THE MAN CALLED HIS WIFE'S NAME EVE—HAWWAH, i.e. life (III, 20). She was given to him for an adviser, but she played the eavesdropper like the serpent. [Another interpretation]: He showed her how many generations she had destroyed. R. Aha interpreted it: The serpent was thy [Eve's] serpent [i.e. seducer], and thou art Adam's serpent. (pp. 169–70)[40]

As was true with his response to Genesis ii, 21, Rashi's comment on Genesis iii, 20, is an implicit rejection of these midrashim: "Eve — חוה has the same sound as ח׳ה (and similar meaning 'life') — *she was so called* because she gives life (birth) to her children."[41] Furthermore, as was true with Milton's response to Genesis ii, 21, he again reveals the influence, indirectly received as it may have been, of the midrashim on this verse. When the repentant and reconciled Adam addresses Eve early in Book XI, he, like Rashi, expresses the basic reading of Genesis iii, 20 ("And Adam called his wife's name Eve; because she was the mother of all living"):

> Whence Hail to thee,
> *Eve* rightly call'd, Mother of all Mankind,
> Mother of all things living, since by thee
> Man is to live, and all things live for Man.　　　(158–61)

Yet the associations between Eve and the serpent that the midrashim on Genesis iii, 20, develop also surface in the epic. First, Rabbi Aha's midrash serves to explain Adam's earlier hateful epithet for Eve: "Out of my sight, thou Serpent, that name best / Befits thee with him leagu'd, thyself as false / And hateful" (X, 867–69). And second, dramatizing the first midrash on Genesis iii, 20, Milton also presents both Eve and Satan as eavesdroppers. Eve eavesdrops not only when she listens to the serpent's words of temptation (see n. 42), but also when she innocently listens in on the conversation between Raphael and Adam. Satan eavesdrops in the guise of prelapsarian lion and tiger and gains the information he needs when Adam discusses God's "one . . . easy charge" (IV, 421) to Eve and him. Furthermore, Milton makes certain that Satan's behavior is correctly understood by first remarking that as Satan changed his animal disguises, he moved "Nearer to view his prey, and unespi'd / To mark what of thir state he more might learn / By word or action markt" (IV, 399–401).

The second midrash on Genesis iii, 20, "He showed her how many generations she had destroyed," does not so directly show itself in *Paradise Lost* because the Eve who awakes from the bout of lustful lovemaking apparently understands, as does Adam, that they have brought death into the world. Certainly, by the time she suggests sexual abstinence to avoid sending "a woeful Race" (X, 984) to the grave, she seems fully to comprehend the direst consequences of her behavior. Nevertheless, even this midrash merits closer attention.

This second of the three midrashim on Genesis iii, 20 echoes the final sentence of the midrash on Genesis iii, 7:

AND THE EYES OF THEM BOTH WERE OPENED (III, 7). Were they then blind? R. Judan in the name of R. Johanan b. Zakkai, and R. Berekiah in the name of R. Akiba explained it by comparing them to a villager who was passing a glass-worker's shop and just when a basket full of goblets and cut-glass ware was in front of him he swung his staff round and broke them. Whereupon he [their owner] arose and seized him, saying to him, 'I know that I cannot obtain redress from you, but come and I will show you how much valuable stuff you have destroyed.' Thus He showed them how many generations they had destroyed. (p. 152)

The eleventh-century rabbi who "endeavored to search into the simple, natural, primary meaning of the scriptural materials"[42] not surprisingly avoided Rabbi Akiba's and Rabbi Johanan's figurative explanation:

Scripture speaks here with reference to intelligence (the mind's eye) and not with reference to *actual* seeing. . . . Even a blind person knows when he is naked! What then does "and they knew that they were naked" signify? One charge had been entrusted to them and *they now knew* they had stripped themselves of it.[43]

The explanation Rashi chose not to repeat nevertheless seems not at all inappropriate as a gloss on *Paradise Lost*, XI–XII. Although scholars have noted that other such visions (Ezekiel xl, Daniel x, *Aeneid* VI, *Faerie Queene*, III, iii) apparently influence Milton's treatment of Books XI and XII, none has included the midrashic understanding of "And the eyes of them both were opened."[44] The vision of history presented in Book XI to Adam's eyes, from which Michael "the Film remov'd / Which that false Fruit that promis'd clearer sight / Had bred" (412–14), and in Book XII to Adam's mind's eye, often almost overwhelms Adam by making him painfully aware of how many generations he and Eve have destroyed. The Christian view of history, of course, ends with the Second Coming and the eventual triumph of the godly, and Milton's Adam therefore descends the hill having seen more than the destruction and ruin that will follow from his act. Eve, too, though spared the series of grim, detailed visions Adam experiences, leaves Paradise with the sense of the "some great good" that is to come when "the Promis'd Seed shall all restore" (XII, 612, 623) what she and Adam have destroyed.

The "source" of Milton's knowledge of the rabbinic readings of Genesis has yet to be indisputably identified, and because of the repetition and imitation characteristic of all hexameral writings, that "source" may never be found, or accepted by most scholars. What has not eluded us, however, is the presence of the rabbinic influence in the Genesis narrative within *Paradise Lost*. That influence may have come down to Milton from innumerable and indirect sources, but it, often reinforced perhaps by Milton's own independent concern to establish the literal reading of the history of the first days, brings a unique flavor to his treatment of Genesis. One of the first to describe this flavor or style was Harold Fisch: "While the hexameral tradition represented by Du-Bartas, Pererius, and a host of Christian authorities early and late had emphasized the metahistorical region of theogony and eschatology, the Hebraic tradition had emphasized the quotidian, the concrete, and the historically visualizable aspects of the story."[45] As Fletcher argued, Milton does echo Rashi, but Rashi, more often than not, echoes the Midrash, and even without Rashi as an intermediary, Milton apparently found his way to those older rabbinic commentaries. Furthermore, from those rabbinic commentaries issued the kind of exposition and elaboration that served the poet's purposes as effectively as it had served the rabbis' purposes: the Midrash, "which is to bring heaven nearer to the congregation and then to lift man heavenward, approves itself in this profession on the one side as glorification of God and on the other as consolation to Israel."[46]

University of New Mexico

NOTES

1. *Milton's Semitic Studies and Some Manifestations of Them in His Poetry* (Chicago, 1926); *Milton's Rabbinical Readings* (Urbana, Ill., 1930).

2. Kitty Cohen, *The Throne and the Chariot: Studies in Milton's Hebraism* (The Hague, 1975), p. 2. Cohen makes no reference to Stollman's 1972 article (see n. 7 below). She only briefly touches upon the controversy surrounding Milton's abilities as a Hebrew scholar in the following remarks: "That Milton knew Hebrew well enough to read the Old Testament and its commentators in the original is now beyond dispute. His knowledge of Hebrew is felt on every page of his writings and pervades the style of his prose as well as his poetry. He certainly was a hebraist in the old sense, that is, a Hebrew scholar. If it is generally accepted that he had the use of a Rabbinical Bible, his indebtedness to other Hebrew sources has been seriously questioned. He probably had no access to early Midrashic and Talmudic literature and he did not read the Zohar" (p. 3).

3. "Milton and the Rabbis: A Later Inquiry," *SEL*, XVIII (1978), p. 125.

4. Ibid., pp. 125–26. George N. Conklin, *Biblical Criticism and Heresy in Milton* (New York, 1949).

5. Mendelsohn, "Milton and the Rabbis," p. 134.

6. In *Milton Studies*, IV, ed. James D. Simmonds (Pittsburgh, Pa., 1972), p. 196.

7. Ibid. Also see Frank Robbins, *The Hexaemeral Literature: A Study of the Greek and Latin Commentaries on Genesis* (Chicago, 1912): "Imitation is commoner in this branch of literature [hexaemeral writings] than in almost any other, and the majority of the Hexaemera are consequently lacking in originality" (p. 2).

8. Mendelsohn, "Milton and the Rabbis," p. 134. Cf. Stollman, "Milton's Rabbinical Readings," p. 196.

9. Mendelsohn, "Milton and the Rabbis," p. 134.

10. *Rashi and the Christian Scholars* (Pittsburgh, Pa., 1963), p. 11.

11. *Pentateuch with Targum Onkelos, Haphtaroth and Rashi's Commentary*, trans. and annotated by Rev. M. Rosenbaum and Dr. A. M. Silbermann, with A. Blashki and L. Joseph (New York, 1946), I, p. 11.

12. *John Milton, Complete Poems and Major Prose*, ed. Merritt Y. Hughes (New York, 1957). Subsequent parenthetical book and line references to *Paradise Lost* are to this edition. *Milton's Rabbinical Readings*, pp. 160–62.

13. Stollman, "Milton's Rabbinical Readings," p. 196.

14. Fletcher, *Milton's Rabbinical Readings*, p. 159.

15. *Pentateuch with . . . Rashi's Commentary*, I, p. 4.

16. Fletcher, *Milton's Rabbinical Readings*, p. 169. Also see *Pentateuch with . . . Rashi's Commentary*, I, p. 11.

17. Fletcher, *Milton's Rabbinical Readings*, pp. 206–07. Also see *Pentateuch with . . . Rashi's Commentary*, I, p. 13.

18. Fletcher, *Milton's Rabbinical Readings*, p. 206.

19. *Pentateuch with . . . Rashi's Commentary*, I, p. 12.

20. Fletcher, *Milton's Rabbinical Readings*, p. 181.

21. James Sims, *The Bible in Milton's Epics* (Gainesville, Fla., 1962), p. 4.

22. *Pentateuch with . . . Rashi's Commentary*, I, p. 35.

23. Ibid., I, p. 12.

24. Ibid., I, p. 5.

25. Ibid., I, p. 21.

26. *Commentaries on The First Book of Moses Called Genesis*, trans. Rev. John King (Edinburgh 1847), pp. 222–23. *The Life of Adam [L'Adamo]*, trans. Anon. 1659; facs. rept. ed. Roy Flannagan and John Arthos, Gainesville, Fla., 1967), pp. 72–74.

27. Hailperin, *Rashi and the Christian Scholars*, p. 83.

28. *Midrash Rabbah*, ed. Rabbi Dr. H. Freedman and Maurice Simon (London, 1939), I, p. 195. Subsequent parenthetical page references are to this text.

29. Stollman, "Milton's Rabbinical Readings," p. 196.

30. Cheryl H. Fresch, "The Hebraic Influence Upon the Creation of Eve in *Paradise Lost*," in *Milton Studies*, XIII, ed. James D. Simmonds (Pittsburgh, Pa., 1979), 181–99.

31. Hailperin, *Rashi and the Christian Scholars*, p. 37.

32. *Pentateuch with . . . Rashi's Commentaries*, I, p. 12.

33. Hailperin, *Rashi and the Christian Scholars*, p. 32.

34. Cheryl H. Fresch, "Milton's Eve and the Problem of the Additions to the Command," *Milton Quarterly*, XII (1978), 83–90.

35. *Medieval Drama*, ed. David Bevington (Boston, 1975), pp. 265–66.

36. *Commentaries on The First Book of Moses*, p. 151.

37. Cheryl H. Fresch, "Milton's Eve and the Theological Tradition," Diss. Cornell 1976.

38. *The Poems of John Milton* (London, 1968), p. 871.

39. *"Paradise Lost": An Account of Its Growth and Major Origins, with a Discussion of Milton's Use of Sources and Literary Patterns* (New York, 1963), p. 155.

40. The footnote in the most recent English translation of the Midrash Rabbah explains, "This is a play on 'hawwah', which is connected here with both (*hawweh*, sc. *da'ath*, an opinion), to show forth, i.e. state (an opinion), and *hiwya*, a serpent. — As the serpent had eavesdropped when God commanded Adam to refrain from the forbidden tree, so did she in turn listen to the serpent when he incited her to disobedience — and persuaded Adam accordingly."

41. *Pentateuch with . . . Rashi's Commentary*, I, p. 16.

42. Hailperin, *Rashi and the Christian Scholars*, p. 24.

43. *Pentateuch with . . . Rashi's Commentary*, I, p. 13.

44. Chapters XXV–XXIX of *Vita Adae et Evae* also develop this theme, as Adam relates to Seth the vision he had when the archangel Michael took him up into "the paradise of vision and of God's command (XXVIII. 3). Yet that Adam's knowledge of the future history is not so much a matter of his entering into God's paradise as it is a result of his eating the forbidden fruit: "Hearken, my son Seth, even to the rest of the secrets [and sacraments] that shall be, which were revealed to me, when I had eaten of the tree of the knowledge, and knew and perceived what will come to pass in this age" (XXIX. 1). "Books of Adam and Eve," ed. L. Wells in *Apocrypha and Pseudepigrapha of the Old Testament*, ed. R. H. Charles (Oxford, 1913).

45. "Hebraic Style and Motifs in *Paradise Lost*," in *Language and Style in Milton*, ed. Ronald David Emma and John T. Shawcross (New York, 1967), p. 41.

46. Hermann L. Strack, *Introduction to the Talmud and Midrash* (Cleveland and New York, 1959), p. 202.

MILTON AND THE MAKING OF
THE ENGLISH LANDSCAPE GARDEN

John Dixon Hunt

One man, one great man we had, on whom nor education nor custom could impose their prejudices; who, *on evil days though fallen, and with darkness and solitude compassed round*, judged that the mistaken and fantastic ornaments he had seen in gardens, were unworthy of the almighty hand that planted the delights of Paradise.

S O H O R A C E Walpole begins his celebration of Milton's contribution to "modern gardening."[1] What he offered by way of commentary upon Milton's role in the making of the English landscape garden has been taken over by later commentators without either much elaboration or skepticism.[2] Yet, as this essay will show, not only can Milton's influence upon later landscapists be much more precisely described and analyzed, but the poet's own debts to earlier (largely Italian) garden styles, ignored by Walpole as by modern landscape historians, can also be established; so that Milton's landscape of Paradise, looking backward as well as forward in gardening history, becomes an even more vital document than Walpole imagined.

Something of this double perspective can be appreciated in the gardens at Stowe in Buckinghamshire, where a bust of Milton, shown as figure 1, fills a niche in the Temple of British Worthies. Stowe was (and still is) a prime example of the English landscape garden; created for Sir Richard Temple, first Viscount Cobham, during the first half of the eighteenth century by a group of famous architects, like James Gibbs and John Vanbrugh, and garden designers, like Charles Bridgeman and William Kent, the gardens at Stowe realized Pope's prophecy for them, that they would "grow / A Work to wonder at."[3] And as well as being an inspiration and example to the landscape movement, Stowe, we are beginning to appreciate, is equally eloquent of eighteenth-century debts to Italy and to ideas of classical gardens. Exactly how Milton figures in the formal and ideological pattens of Stowe is complicated but crucial.

Figure 1. Bust of Milton by John Rysbrack, Temple of British Worthies, Stowe.
Photo: Peter Etches.

Milton's bust by John Rysbrack was originally one of eight installed at Gibbs' Building, a handsome pavilion, open on four sides to the garden's spaces.[4] These eight busts were moved to join eight new ones in Kent's Temple of British Worthies, erected in the mid 1730s (fig. 2). In contrast to Gibbs' Building this temple is a squat, rather *gothick* affair, with somewhat meager pediments over each niche; this design forms part of a larger, elaborately satirical message, which is announced through the juxtaposition of various other structures nearby. These are all situated in a valley known as the Elysian Fields, through which flow the waters of the River Styx, separating the rather diminished rhetoric of British Worthies from a fine and classical Temple of Ancient Virtue on the opposite hillside.[5] It is as if their separation insists that any comparison of ancient and modern worth must also take into account an unbridgeable divide in stylistic matters and in geography, for to reach one building from another the visitor must make a fairly lengthy detour; this detour itself probably enforces another idea, namely that Stowe and England are far from Tivoli and the classical ground of Italy. For the Temple of Ancient Virtue alludes by its shape to the so-called Temple of the Sybil at Tivoli, the ruins of which are reconstituted on this English ground to their full perfection.

As the visitor explored the Elysian Fields, probably beginning with the Temple of Ancient Virtue, their elaborate concoction of imagery and message gradually assumed its proper shape.[6] The literary analogy to this three-dimensional experience is probably Pope's *Dunciad*, where *Paradise Lost* plays such a crucial role, just as Rysbrack's bust of Milton does at Stowe. Indeed, Pope may well have participated in devising the scheme for the Elysian Fields, contributing above all an important strategy from his own satirical method. The classical past, in the form of Ancient Virtue's distinct allusion to an ancient Roman temple at Tivoli and in the form of four full-length statues of Lycurgus, Socrates, Homer, and Epaminondas which were once inside the building at Stowe, is contrasted with a ruinous Temple of Modern Virtue established a few yards away.[7] Since both the ruined temple of Modern Virtue and the reconstructed classical one of Ancient Virtue are "within a few Yards of a Parish-church," as William Gilpin noticed in 1747, the whole cluster is "designed to let us see the ruinous State of decayed modern Virtue."[8] Similarly, Pope had ridiculed the dunces by contrasting their *bêtises* with the rigors and splendors of classical games described by the epic poets.

It is at this point that the Temple of British Worthies across the little valley begins to assume significance. It is not in ruin, like Modern Vir-

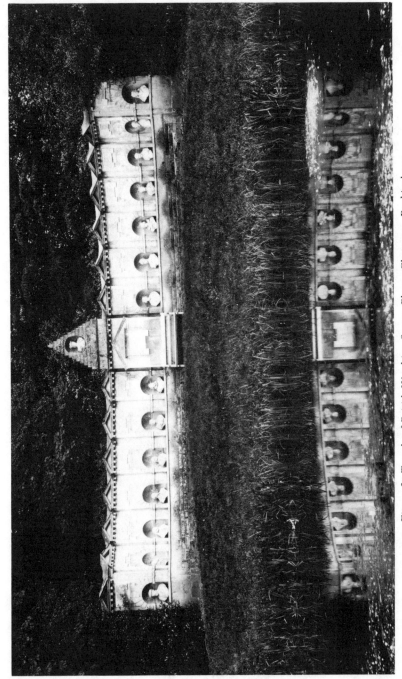

Figure 2. Temple of British Worthies, Stowe. Photo: Chapman, Buckingham.

tue, though those whom it commemorates are represented only in bust
and are accommodated in a not altogether very prepossessing structure.
Nor is the rationale of their choice immediately clear: Ancient Virtue's
full-length sculptures celebrated the greatest general, philosopher, poet
and lawgiver of the Greek world; but the selection of the others is less
explicable. Two modern sovereigns are represented, but Queen Anne,
for whom Lord Cobham had fought, is not one of them; she was, after
all, a Stuart. The patriot Queen Elizabeth is there, with her poet Shakespeare, and William III, supplanter of the Stuarts, with his philosopher
Locke. John Hampden, a local patriot from Aylesbury, is honoured because he had fought against the Stuarts and died for Parliament. Bacon
and Newton are there, doubtless because they sought to establish the intellectual basis of truth separate from that which priests wished to
teach — and perhaps at this junction we register that the lines from
Aeneid VI inscribed on the central block of the Temple wittily omit a
verse that mentions priests. It is perhaps here that John Milton takes his
place, for not only did he write the last great epic in the English language, but he worked for Oliver Cromwell and disliked priests. The
words inscribed above his niche testify to his "sublime and unbounded
genius [which] equald a subject that carried him beyond the limits of
the world." Milton's role here in the Temple of British Worthies, then,
parallels that of *Paradise Lost* in the literary spaces of the *Dunciad:* Milton and the other worthies serve to remind us of the estimable talents of
modern man, not perhaps comparable to the giants of classical times,
but appreciably superior to the rabble and rubble of so-called modern
virtue and thus a vindication of contemporary endeavours.

But beyond the *political* significance of Milton's inclusion among
Cobham's gallery of anti-Stuart worthies is the acknowledgment of his
decisive role in the English garden movement. Like Pope, whose bust
occupies a flanking niche in this same temple, Milton was a "patron"
and literary begetter of the idea of the landscape garden; in the words
of Joseph Warton's *Essay on the Genius and Writings of Mr. Pope:* "It
hence appears, that this enchanting art of modern gardening in which
this kingdom claims a preference over every nation in Europe, chiefly
owes its origin and its improvements to two great poets, *MILTON* and
POPE."[9] Warton goes on to list various of the famous landscape gardens
which he characterizes as "fine example of practical poetry." So Milton's
place among the British Worthies at Stowe declares his theoretic contribution to gardenist practice. His poetry served various succeeding
phases of the eighteenth-century landscape movement as inspiration
and justification; even as late as the picturesque vogue he could still be

read, as Stanley Koehler has shown,[10] for authoritative support of its
aesthetics. Relevant passages of *Paradise Lost*, especially Book IV, were
regularly and tendentiously ransacked for advice and retrospective
sanction of "informal" landscape designs. "His model of Eden," declared George Mason, "remains unimpeachable."[11] Walpole's is probably the most famous as well as the most fulsome declaration of Milton's
importance to landscape gardeners: "He seems with the prophetic eye
of taste . . . to have conceived, to have foreseen modern gardening; as
lord Bacon announced the discoveries since made by experimental philosophy";[12] Milton's conjunction with Bacon in the Temple of British
Worthies may even lie behind Walpole's emphasis there.

The first in the eighteenth century to invoke Milton's example was
significantly also the first to write systematically about the new gardening style — Stephen Switzer, nurseryman, seedsman, and garden de-
signer, whose *Ichnographia Rustica* praised the "noble and Majestic
. . . [and] Inimitable Description of Paradise by Mr. Milton."[13] Despite
that third adjective, it was precisely in their imitation of Milton's imagined landscape that eighteenth-century garden designers most acknowledged his influence upon their art.

Two general qualities of Milton's Paradise recommended themselves
to the landscape gardeners: first, its completeness, its all-inclusive repertoire of design elemenets — for, as Pope was also to emphasize (maybe
recalling Milton's "Earth hath this variety from Heaven"[14]) a garden's
paradisal image required the display of *all* possible variety of natural
forms; second, its condemnation of artifice:

> not nice Art
> In beds and curious Knots, but Nature boon
> Powrd forth profuse on Hill and Dale and Plaine.   (IV, 241–43)

Admittedly, the eighteenth-century appreciation of Milton's "natural"
landscape generally neglected the ambiguities of the passage — the invocation of an art term, *Lantskip*, for what is supposed to be a scene free
of art, and the link with "Hesperian Gardens fam'd of old, / Fortunate
Fields, and Groves and flourie Vales" (III, 568–69), which helps to intimate the ultimate unreality of such a scene. When Milton's artificial
emphases *were* singled out, it was by those who were themselves dissatisfied with "gardens deck'd with art's vain pomps": thus Joseph Warton
condemns the gardens at Stowe in his *Enthusiast: or, the Lover of Nature* of 1740 in much the same language as he expressed skepticism of
Milton's "Sapphire fountains . . . rolling over orient pearl."[15] But Warton's rejection of gardenist art at Stowe or in Paradise was radical and

somewhat exceptional; for long afterward the informality of Milton's landscape and its exciting range of natural features continued to offer themselves as an essential and aptly indigenous precedent for the English landscape gardenists. Indeed, Milton's "unimpeachable" model for an English garden was invoked so much by designers, commentators, and historians that by the 1790s it had become a commonplace theme, to be taken up in John Aikin's *Letters from a Father to his Son on various Topics*, where the sixth letter of the second volume discourses "On Milton's Garden of Eden as a supposed prototype of modern Gardening." Even in gardens which might have seemed totally dissimilar to Milton's prelapsarian landscape, like the popular and rather risqué Vauxhall Gardens, the poets' presence was acknowledged: his statue, in a listening posture, by Roubiliac, was installed in the "Rural Downs" section of the pleasure grounds, among the cypress, fir, yew, cedar, and tulip trees; significantly, Milton was associated, even here, with the most "natural" part of the gardens.[16] Obviously, then, in the century or so that followed the publication of *Paradise Lost* the formal aspects of many rural seats of various view were derived from Milton's descriptions. Three aspects in particular were influential: the handling of water, the relationship of garden to surrounding countryside, and the manipulation of natural features inside the garden.

The management of water in a landscape necessarily preoccupied garden theorists, and it is impossible here to quote them extensively. What is astonishing is their reiteration and elaboration of Milton's account of the waters of Paradise. Sometimes the debt is conscious, sometimes undeclared, though the workings of cultural osmosis must have given Milton's lines, reprinted on many occasions from Switzer to the *Lady's Magazine* of 1781 and 1789, a wide diffusion. Equally, one also has to admit with Walpole the astonishing percipience of Milton's vision of the manipulation of water in a perfect garden. Walpole cited the lines on the progress of the river "Southward through Eden" and under the "shaggie hill" to "exhibit Stourhead on a more magnificent scale."[7] But he might just as well have pointed to William Kent's Vale of Venus at Rousham in Oxfordshire: here descending waters emerge from a hillside into various "fresh Fountain[s]," from one of which a "mazie" channel runs under "pendant shades" to another part of the garden. Rousham also furnishes the example of a river flowing first in and then beyond the park, connecting the paradisal demesne with the world outside its scope and then "wandering many a famous Realme / And Country."[18] The particular satisfactions of "a Fair Stream or Current flowing through or neer your Garden," as John Worlidge put it in

Systema Horti-Culturae ten years after *Paradise Lost*, were often noted in works like Defoe's *Tour thro' . . . Great Britain.*[19] The diversification of water within a garden generally followed Milton's prescriptions: sometimes emerging from a "darksome passage" or "umbrageous Grots and Caves," sometimes murmuring in a cascade or expanded into a lake "That to the feigned bank with myrtle crowned, / Her crystal mirror holds." Addison's Leonora in *Spectator* 37 has contrived to include in her park all these versions of water — Grottoes, springs murmuring among pebbles and "collected into a beautiful Lake [which] empties itself by a little Rivulet which runs through a green Meadow." Since it was Addison who promoted the early landscape garden as well as *Paradise Lost*, the similarities are hardly accidental.

Water took its place, though, in a various landscape of hills, dales, and plains. Variety was, in fact, the self-proclaimed hallmark of the English gardenist, although, as we shall see, it was exactly by its variety that the Italian garden had impressed travelers like Evelyn the century before. The various characters which could be given to a garden and the sophisticated deployment of basic natural forms were themselves much elaborated in treatises — the debt to Milton often acknowledged, but the extent of the commentaries, alas, usually lacking the poet's economy. The *Daily Gazeteer* of 18 September 1735 reported that "all the Varieties of Nature are to be seen within" the grounds of Richmond Park — "Had *Milton* been living, his Description of Paradise . . . would, in great measure, have been thought to be drawn from the View of this Place." Much later, when the taste for landscaping spread to France, Milton's example was still acclaimed: the words, "A happi rural seat of different views" *[sic]* appeared as motto on the title page of the Marquis de Girardin's *De la Composition des paysages, ou les moyens d'embellir la nature autour des habitations, en joignant l'agréable à l'utile* of 1777.[20]

Among the famous formulations of the need for variety, the most eloquent and least tedious was certainly Pope's, in his *Epistle to Burlington* of 1731. In its succinct enunciation of landscape syntax may be heard distinct echoes of Milton's own version of "woodie Theatre," "Lawns, or level Downs," "palmie hilloc," and "flowrie . . . Valley":

> Consult the *Genius* of the *Place* in all,
> That tells the Waters or to rise, or fall,
> Or helps th'ambitious Hill the Heav'ns to scale,
> Or scoops in circling Theatres the Vale,
> Calls in the Country, catches opening Glades,
> Joins willing Woods, and varies Shades from Shades.[21]

Pope's own garden at Twickenham and those at Rousham and Stowe, which he delighted to visit and on which he probably advised his friends, all exemplify his own and, behind him, Milton's concern for careful modulation of contour and natural shapes. If this vision of a variegated, apparently "natural" landscape, sometimes almost indistinguishable from the "real" countryside around about, seems to us today merely the only obvious imagery for English landscape parks, it is in large part due to Milton's eloquent vision, whose realization transformed the "dead plains" of such French layouts as Hampton Court's—the phrase is Timothy Nourse's, yet we might as easily invoke Milton's "Subjected Plaine."[22] For why, asked Switzer, "instead of levelling Hills or filling up Dales, should [we not] think it more entertaining to be sometimes on the Precipice of a Hill viewing all round and under us, and at other times in a Bottom, viewing those goodly Hills and Theatres of Wood and Corn that are above us, and present themselves every where to our View?"[23]

By the second half of the eighteenth century the concept of an English garden, until then dotted with evidence of art like temples, sculpture, and inscriptions, was radically refined by "Capability" Brown. In his work, and less sensitively in that of his imitators, Milton's formal prescriptions seemed to be realized more sympathetically than ever before. A "sweet interchange / Of Hill and Vallie, Rivers, Woods and Plaines" (IX, 115–16) seems to signal Brown's characteristic sensibility for natural form and shape. To the anonymous author of *The Rise and Progress of the Present Taste*, "immortal Brown" subsumed many previous talents, among which Milton's sublime sense of nature's formal beauties is ranked among the first.[24] When to the lines from *Paradise Lost* was added the popularity of Milton's earlier poetry like *L'Allegro*, with its image of "Towers and Battlements . . . / Bosom'd high in Tufted trees," the poet's authority for sheer aesthetic delight, unattached to moral or political messages, was unchallenged. Repton frequently cited *L'Allegro* in support of what Sir Nikolaus Pevsner has called his "crazy visual singlemindedness,"[25] and some of his best work seems to have been executed, though this may simply be accidental, on sites like Blaise Castle, near Bristol, where rich woods and battlements enact Milton's imagery. Repton's affection for the poetry led him to adopt the "high lonely tower" of *Il Penseroso* as a distinctive element on his trade card.[26]

So far we have considered something of the extent to which Milton's authority lent its support to the aesthetics of the English landscape garden movement—quotations, in fact, could be infinitely extended, though we should soon be reduced to such an example as William Mason's *The English Garden* (Book I, lines 453ff.), where Milton's lines on Paradise are incorporated verbatim into Mason's turgid blank verse. But one other aspect of his presence in the eighteenth-century experience of landscape is worth considering very briefly: the invocation of his poetry to authenticate or constitute a scene. Quotations from *Il Penseroso*, for example, inscribed on buildings like the Hermitage at Hagley, defined their character by an easy appeal to already established literary experience; William Pitt prepared a design for a friend's garden and gave it the warranty of being based on Milton's Bower of Bliss.[27] Jonathan Richardson had argued in 1715 that "After having read Milton, one sees nature with better eyes than before, beauties appear, which else had been unregarded";[28] many landowners relied upon Miltonic allusions to, as it were, fake what their gardens could not achieve unaided. Equally the invocation of Milton could suggest economically to garden visitors a whole range of reactions—thus Henry Hoare could say, writing to his nephew who had visited Stourhead without his wife, "I hear you have been at Stourd. without the dame, so fear you saw undelighted all delight tho' you trod the enchanting paths of paradise."[29] More solemnly, the bluestocking Mrs. Chapone responded to the lake and "variegated hills" and "such a delicious green valley" at Taymouth that "even a Milton's pen, or a Salvator Rosa's pencil would fail to give you a complete idea of it."[30] Such invocations, dismally frequent among garden visitors and later picturesque tourists, allowed Milton or Rosa to save the writers the labor of their own descriptions. Mrs. Montague herself, no less inertly, exclaimed that "even Milton's images and descriptions fall short" of the gardens at Stowe.[31]

The prestige of Milton's Paradise among English gardenists depended upon the widely shared view that it was wonderfully ahead of its time: in 1777 Joseph Heely wrote that "Milton, though gardening still wore the same antiquated dress, seemed to dip into the just rules of the modern practise."[32] Such a view still persists, for B. Sprague Allen in his invaluable *Tides in English Taste* has this, in part, to say:

The garden which Milton has depicted with evident delight plainly has nothing in common with the formal garden of the period in which the epic was written. The waters of Eden neither rest in the unbroken calm of a long rectangular canal nor shoot upward from marble basins. . . . In a manuscript note Addison has remarked that 'Milton would never have been able . . . to have laid out his Paradise, had he not seen the . . . gardens of Italy'. This is perhaps true if Addison had in mind only the myrtles and palms, oranges, lemons, and grapes which struck Milton's imagination as they do any traveler from the bleaker North, but aside from their sumptuous, exotic vegetation it is impossible to discover anything that such grandly formal gardens as those of Lante or Caprarola could have contributed to Milton's conception of Eden.[33]

I propose to argue, in entire opposition to that view, that Milton's description and use of the Garden of Eden in *Paradise Lost* was derived directly from Italian examples, as Addison wisely perceived. For Milton was one of many seventeenth-century visitors to Italy who registered their admiration of Italian Renaissance gardens.[34] That this enthusiasm was not recognized by eighteenth-century commentators on garden history is, I suspect, a direct consequence of their need to justify the landscape garden as essentially an English creation.[35] Walpole was the most tendentious of such patriots, and after quoting from *Paradise Lost* in his *History of the Modern Taste in Gardening*, he asks his reader to

recollect that the author of this sublime vision had never seen a glimpse of anything like what he has imagined, that his favourite ancients had dropped not a hint of such divine scenery, and that the conceits in Italian gardens, and Theobalds and Nonsuch, were the brightest originals that his memory could furnish.[36]

What, of course, Walpole ignores is the enthusiasm for those Italian "originals" of the modern taste he champions; he forgets or chooses to forget that William Kent, the "hero" of his *History*, was simply the last of a long line of gardenists who drew upon a rich imagery of Italian gardens for their work in England. A modern critic like Sprague Allen is perpetuating the Walpolean thesis that the English landscape garden somehow sprang fully armed from the heads of Addison and Pope; for one thing, his reliance upon the word "formal" to describe a garden like the Villa Lante at Bagnaia, though widespread even among modern garden historians, is a largely nineteenth-century usage and simply misleading when applied to gardens Milton would have known. Furthermore, the language which Milton uses of his Paradise and which seemed so congenial to eighteenth-century taste proves to be exactly the same language Milton's contemporaries used when they wrote of their enthusiasms for Italian gardening. So that, when Sprague Allen writes that "Milton's description of Eden passed completely unnoticed in the seventeenth century,"[37] I suspect that he is actually pointing to the similarity between the poet's technical language in describing his Eden and the vocabulary invoked by other contemporary gardenists. John Evelyn, for example, praised the "variety" of Italian gardens,[38] just as the poet of *Paradise Lost* proclaims Eden's "various view"; that this "variety" was also the proclaimed hallmark of the landscape garden in the next century has not led its historians, then or now, to ask what continuities may be traced between the Italianate taste of Milton's age and the garden vision of Addison, Pope, or Kent.

Joseph Furtenbach's imaginary garden, published in *Architectura Civilis* (1628), crowds into little space a whole repertoire of garden elements, all of which can be shown to be derived from Italian examples.[39] But what is especially striking is that this variety includes what are generally termed "formal" and "informal" designs: both kinds of garden experience were deemed to be essential to a garden — in Signor Mattei's villa at Rome, patterned and geometrically designed plots are juxtaposed to "natural" areas around the house, while in the view of Cardinal Cesi's sculpture garden painted by Henrick van Cleef in 1548 it would be extremely difficult to say whether formal or informal would be the better label.[40] Even in gardens like those of the Villa Borghese (nowadays, of course, very much in the taste of the so-called *giardino inglese*) the regular rectangles which constituted the immediate garden near the villa were individually very varied and contained elements that the seventeenth-century English traveler considered as most wittily contrived naturalism.

One of Milton's difficulties with describing the Garden of Eden was that he had to communicate in terms that his readers could understand yet must shake off their expectations. The Italianate style of gardening exactly suited his purposes. By the time *Paradise Lost* was published in the Restoration, the modish new style was French, and Charles II was aping the grand gardens of his ally, Louis XIV, even trying to lure Louis's gardener, Le Nôtre, to England to remodel the grounds of some royal palaces. But before the *interregnum* the modish style had been Italian, and there is considerable evidence, I believe, for thinking that Italian garden ideologies survived into Restoration years as rivals to the French, for political as much as aesthetic reasons.[41] Milton, though he could not have *seen* the French style, might well have resented its political implications. What he could recall having seen in England before his blindness would have been a slow importation of Italian designs, slowly supplanting the small Tudor gardens of the sixteenth century.[42] The history of northern gardening in the seventeenth century, as far as it affects England, France, and Holland, is essentially the gradual absorption of Italianate ideas and their adaptation to local circumstances, so that for Milton to imply parallels between his Eden and Italian style would have made its scope seem novel yet at the same time comprehensible to his readers.

"Variety" was the hallmark of Italian styles as opposed both to the tightly packed, little Tudor gardens and to the pomp and circumstance of the French style, which was the extrapolation from Italian styles of a suitable garden art for an absolutist monarchy. The variety of Italian gardens was most eloquently illustrated at the Medici estate of Pratolino (fig. 3), where the difficulty, even absurdity, of labeling it formal or informal is immediately evident. Pratolino lay just off the road taken by all travelers, including Milton, who left Florence and headed north over the Appenines to Bologna. Evelyn was there and much delighted in the 1640s; its gardens still pleased William Kent over seventy years later.[43] At Pratolino there was an abundance of fresh fountains, many rills watering the garden, hillocks, dales, lawns, and level downs interspersed among bowers, groves, and grots or caves. The language used of its marvelous variety by English visitors was applied to an obviously more artificial world than the English landscape gardenists could have endorsed, even though they, too, invoked the same terminology. Here is Evelyn's account, in part, of his visit there:

'tis situate in a huge meadow like an amphitheater, ascending, having at the bottom a huge rock, with Water running in a small Chanell like a Cascade. . . . The Gardens delicious & full of fountaines; In the Grove sits Pan feeding his flock, the Water making a melodious sound through his pipe. . . . In another Grotto is Vulcan & his family, the walls richly composed of Coralls, Shells, Coper and Marble figures; with the huntings of Severall beasts, moving by force of water.[44]

The gamboling animals in Milton's paradise were often featured in grottoes, like that at another Medici villa, Castello, where the lifelike modeling and painting is further confused by the inclusion of real horns and tusks.[45] One even wonders whether the heraldic awkwardness of Milton's animals is not some legacy of the creations which frisked and sported, animated by hydraulic machinery, in some Italian grotto.

The "woody theatre" of Milton's Eden has its parallel in many Italian gardens. Certainly it is a term that adapts itself readily to many actual organizations of landscape: in the eighteenth century it could apply to Charles Bridgeman's umbrageous theater at Rousham or his Serliolike exedra at Claremont in Surrey; but equally it applies in the seventeenth century to theaters in the Boboli gardens, or to more modest layouts of water theaters, as at the Villa Celsa near Siena, or to larger hillsides formed into theaters as at the Villa Aldobrandini in Frascati.[46] The whole theatrical dimension of the Italian garden experience for Englishmen is a topic in itself: not only were many Italian gardens used for courtly entertainment and *intermezzi*, like the Palazzo Barberini where

Figure 3. Lunette of Pratolino by Giusto Utens, 1599. Museo Storico di Firenze.

Milton himself attended an opera, but whole gardens came to be shaped like theaters and visitors would respond to the excitements in the language of theater. But there was also the fact that Italian gardens, full of intricate and elaborate imagery, inscriptions, and iconography, were designed to work upon visitors like the memory theaters which Frances Yates has described;[47] the garden thus became a whole anthology of devices to recall us to ideas and memories we have stored and perhaps forgotten until we meet their images again along the paths and in the grottoes of a garden like the Villa d'Este (fig. 4). By a similar mode of operation the garden became, and was designed specifically to serve as, a *theatrum mundi,* offering to its visitor a whole anthology or *theater* or ideas articulated in garden terms, but otherwise just like those larger lessons of history and mythology that Michael provides for Adam — "His eye might there command wherever stood / City of old or modern fame" (XI, 385–86). Thus at the Villa d'Este a model of classical Rome was a central feature of the garden's message.[48]

The Villa d'Este, too, provides an example of a steeply sloping site where, like Milton's Eden, "murmuring waters fall / Down the slope hills" (IV, 260–61). If we are accustomed to think of Milton's water effects, after the eighteenth-century fashion, in "natural" terms, we must also register how well his language suits one of the most beautiful and much visited of Italian gardens, that of the Villa Lante at Bagnaia.[49] Here the various levels of the garden are watered and cooled in turn by diverse manipulations of one stream of water, sometimes in fountains, sometimes in curling channels, in modest jets or spread into pools presided over by river gods, whose presence recalls the nearby rivers which the garden could not contain. None of these devices appears in travelers' accounts as anything but a marvelous display of natural elements. Even the upper reaches of the water theaters at Aldobrandini, that seem to us today artificial or "formal," were called, and appreciated as, rural fountains.[50]

The steep sites of many Italian gardens, like those of the Villa Aldobrandini at Frascati and Villa d'Este at Tivoli, also parallel Milton's description of Satan's arrival at the Garden of Eden. They are all situated on the "champain head / Of a steep wilderness." At Tivoli the garden is partly concealed under the slope's "hairy sides / With thickets overgrown"; but at least on the side towards Rome the steep hillside forms a natural barrier, as Satan found in Eden, enclosing the garden from without, yet not blocking the view from within. Here again we have Milton's usage squaring with both seventeenth-century experience and later English landscape taste. The steep hillsides on which many

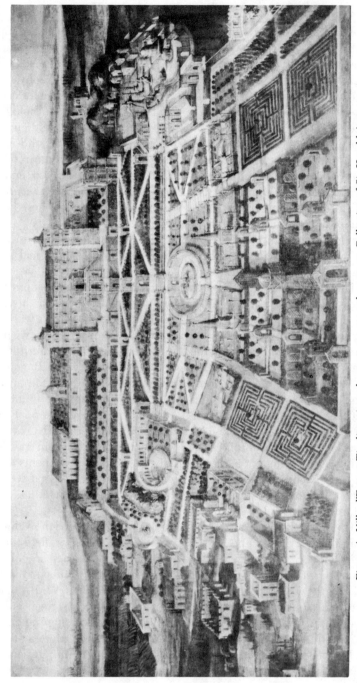

Figure 4. Villa d'Este at Tivoli, artist unknown, seventeenth century. Collection of Sir Harold Acton.

Italian villas were placed served, as the ha-ha would do in the land-scape garden, to deny access from the outside, while allowing those on the inside uninterrupted views beyond — "to our general sire gave pros-pect large / Into his nether empire neighbouring round" (IV, 144–45). Such was the situation of the Duke of Parma's garden on the Palatine Hill, where a steep rocky slope overlooks and separates the enclosure from the ruins of the Circo Massimo beneath.[51] It is a frequent experi-ence in Italy that a villa looks impenetrable as one approaches its hill-side ("those lofty shades his bower" [III, 733]), but once inside the visitor discovers "in wide landskip" (V, 142) the terrain he has recently traversed.

The walks and bowers inside an Italian garden, as at Pratolino, impressed English visitors not only by their variety, but by their spatial excitements and invitations. Milton's critics have always been im-pressed by his handling of the vast spaces of his poetic universe; it should also be emphasized how well he seems to have understood — what no small English garden could ever have taught him — the fashion in which Italian gardens involved their visitors in an often elaborate en-counter with forking paths and descents and ascents between different levels. The steep hill sites of many Italian gardens necessitated an often extensive series of ramps, terraces, and crisscrossing routes. Visitors, forced to turn either to the left or right, would be made conscious of missed alternatives: the Villa d'Este, as David Coffin has shown in his monograph,[52] exploited the site and its series of dividing ramps and staircases to realize within the garden the *topos* of the choice of Her-cules, who happened to be patron deity of the Estes and the town of Tivoli. One of the most eloquent testimonies to this general Italian garden experience is contained in a brief passage of Sir Henry Wotton's *Elements of Architecture*, which, considering his acquaintance with its author, we might expect Milton to have known. Wotton tells of

a *Garden* (for the maner perchance incomparable) into which the first *Accesse* was a high walke like a *Terrace*, from whence might bee taken a generall view of the whole *Plott* below but rather in a delightfull confusion, then with any plaine distinction of the pieces. From this the *Beholder* descending many steps, was afterwards conveyed againe, by severall *mountings* and *valings*, to various enter-tainments of his *sent*, and *sight:* which I shall not neede to describe (for that were poetical) let me onely note this, that every one of these diversities, was as if hee had beene *Magically* transported into a new Garden.[53]

These spatial excitements, capricious and full of inventions and the un-predictable, required of the visitor an answering delight in being ma-

nipulated by the garden. Milton's Eden is not the perplexing and potentially treacherous wild wood of *Comus;* as Northrop Frye reminded us,
nobody loses his way in Eden.[54] Nor did visitors to the Villa d'Este. But
in Eden and the Villa d'Este alike the choice of paths through a various
garden was a large part of its delight. Milton's freedom of choice for his
dramatis personae in larger matters is aptly echoed in the garden's un-
constrained layout of walks and alleys. The liberty to go wherever one
wishes contributes to its consistent character, and the poet seems always
to emphasize how his characters *use* its spaces.

Raphael's first visit to the garden takes him to "the blissful field,
through groves of myrrh, / And flowering odours, cassia, nard, and
balm" (V, 292–93). And, since it is an essential part of all three-
dimensional garden experience, his approach is watched by another:
"Him, through the spicy forest onward come, / Adam discerned, as in
the door he sat / Of his cool bower" (V, 298–300). Satan's first sight of
Adam and Eve in the garden is of their passing hand in hand towards a
clearing by a fresh fountain-side. His own exploration of the garden in
Book IX stresses how

> In bower and field he sought, where any tuft
> Of grove or garden-plot more pleasant lay,
> Their tendance or plantation for delight;
> By fountain or by shady rivulet
> He sought them both.   (IX, 417–21)

And, as Charlotte F. Otten has observed,[55] even Satan keeps to the paths
"among the groves, the fountains, and the flowers" (V, 126), like any
visitor in the alleys of the Villa Medici at Rome. Adam knows to trace
the route by which he can discover Eve at her solitary gardening:

> And forth to meet her went, the way she took
> That morn when first they parted.   (IX, 847–48)

As the moment of the Fall approaches, we are perhaps made more
aware of the labyrinthine layout of the external garden and of the circuitous maneuvres of Satan and the postlapsarian world to which his con-
duct leads. Eve's dream in Book V has hinted at this darker aspect of the
garden's intricate variety:

> I rose as at thy call, but found thee not;
> To find thee I directed then my walk;
> And on, methought, alone I passed through ways
> That brought me on a sudden to the tree.   (V, 48–51)

But the garden has always been, as Adam tells Raphael, a space of inviting and wondrous spaces where he seems correspondingly "freed from intricacies . . . / [and] perplexing thoughts" (VIII, 182–83). Adam's first experience of Eden is an intensified version of many travelers' accounts of their visits to fabulous Italian gardens — he shares their wonder with places of mythic potency ("whether true, / Or fancied so through expectation high / Of knowledge" [IX, 788–90]):

> About me round I saw
> Hill, dale, and shady woods, and sunny plains,
> And liquid lapse of murmuring streams; by these,
> Creatures that lived, and moved, and walked, or flew,
> Birds on the branches warbling.   (VIII, 261–65)

(Visitors at the Villa Borghese reported on the artificial birds that sang on the branches of trees and attracted real birds to sit beside them.)[56] Adam continues:

> While thus I called and strayed I knew not whither
> From where I first drew air, and first beheld
> This happy light, when answer none returned,
> On a green shady bank, profuse of flowers,
> Pensive I sat me down.   (VIII, 283–87)

God then acts as the *cicerone* of this paradise, and Adam's route through the garden is but a more potent version of Wotton's *mountings* and *valings* in another incomparable garden:

209588

> So saying, by the hand he took me, raised,
> And over fields and waters, as in air
> Smooth sliding without step, last led me up
> A woody mountain, whose high top was plain,
> A circuit wide, enclosed with goodliest trees
> Planted, with walks and bowers, that what I saw
> Of Earth before scarce pleasant seemed.   (VIII, 300–06)

There are other examples of search and exploration through the Garden of Eden. In all of them Milton displays what I believe he could nowhere have learned in old-fashioned Tudor gardens — a fine sense of gardenist space, where route, direction, and discovery play such a crucial role. But in Italian gardens and in imitations of them back in England he could have discovered this, as many of his contemporaries excitedly reported of their travels. Edmund Warcupp at Tivoli, for instance, tells how "in the descent into the first garden shews itself the

Colossus of Pegasus" or "[then] riseth an Island cut in the shape of a ship."[57] Another glimpse of these spatial invitations may be gathered from an account of how Sir Dudley Carleton's gift of a head of Jupiter to the Earl of Arundel was sited in the latter's "utmost garden, so opposite to the gallery doors, as being open, so soon as yu enter into the front Garden yu have the head in yor eie all the way."[58]

Milton shares other of his contemporaries' reactions to Italianate gardens. There is his sense, for example, that a garden must declare its owner, his prestige and family history — and it is of course endemic to Adam's and our response to Eden that it is "place by place where he voutsafed / Presence Divine" (XI, 318–19):

> All these with ceaseless praise his works behold
> Both day and night. How often, from the steep
> Of echoing hill or thicket, have we heard
> Celestial voices to the midnight air
>
> . . . .
>
> Singing their great Creator.   (IV, 679–84)

Among a garden's various plenitude, too, there must be room for much pleasant ambiguity. Having it both ways in a garden was not an exclusively Marvellian response, but was one shared by many visitors to Italian gardens where art and nature seemed to battle and mystify with their interchangeable modes — like the beasts in the Castello grotto, part sculpture, part real horn and tusk. But gardens themselves often played equally delightful tricks — out-of-doors seemed, as at the Villa Medici in Rome, but the extension of interior space — open-air corridors where "the roof / Of thickest covert was interwoven shade" (IV, 692–93). Especially in loggias, ambiguous areas between house and garden like Peruzzi's at the Farnesina in Rome,[59] the skills of architect and artist accentuated uncertainties: Taddeo Zuccari's decorations of the loggia at the Villa Giulia, also in Rome, make the plaster ceiling seem a trelliswork of flowers with clear sky beyond.

One last and important parallel between Milton's Eden and the seventeenth-century English experience of Italian gardens is a use of mythology. We have seen Adam react to Eden as if it were a fabulous place. Such a response became as much a cliché about elaborate Italian villas as did the idea that Milton's pen so exactly captured the beauties of such and such an English landscape garden. At Rome, for example, Fynes Moryson wrote that "the gardens without the wals are so rarely delightfull, as I should thinke the Hesperides were not to be compared with them; and they are adorned with statues, laberinths, fountains

. . . so as they seem as earthly Paradise."[60] Milton, too, must rely upon allusions to myth for persuading his readers of Eden's rare potential:

> Hesperian fables true,
> If true, here only. (IV, 250–51)

The Villa d'Este practiced the same conceits in its garden imagery. The dragon that once guarded the Hesperidean Gardens was defeated by Hercules, patron and namesake of Cardinal d'Este; now it protects the new pleasure house on the slopes of Tivoli, where we see it, as one might say, "involved in rising mists" (IX, 75) in the Fountain of the Dragon.[61] Whenever Milton announced some mythic parallel, like the wood-nymph vision of Eve departing from Adam in Book IX, we catch glimpses of a Renaissance idiom shared by Italian gardenists. Milton is, of course, often eager to insist on the postlapsarian resonance of some of his comparisons and to stress how the iconography of Renaissance gardens as well as of his own poetic similitudes ("Universal Pan, / Knit with the Graces and the Hours in dance" [IV, 266–67]) is the inevitable result of an original lapse from innocence. He can, however, and in his garden passages surely does, rely upon a knowledgeable and traveled reader, who may be counted upon to register that imagery encountered in Italianate gardens is specifically excluded from the poet's Eden even though invoked to help the reader understand it.

I am well aware that in canvassing these possible debts of Milton to his actual experience of Italianate gardens I ignore a whole range of literary sources and analogues, of travel literature, even of paintings (which have largely tempted Milton commentators in their search for antecedents or parallels).[62] But it seems to me that when a poet is obliged to depict even an impossibly perfect garden world, he will look at some stage to the contemporary art of gardening itself. If like Milton he is also a learned poet and the real gardens he bears in mind while inventing his own are the Italianate gardens of seventeenth-century Europe, he will discover that whole literary traditions, notably the *topos* of the *Locus amoenus*, were actually realized, were found contemporary, three-dimensional forms, in a country that was known to every traveler as the "Garden of the World." Milton acknowledges this clearly in *Paradise Regained*, where Italian gardens feature among the specific temptations of the city of Rome:

> thence in the midst
> Divided by a river, of whose banks
> On each side an Imperial city stood,

With Towers and Temples proudly elevate
On seven small hills, with Palaces adornd,
Porches and Theatres, Baths, Aqueducts,
Statues and Trophees, and Triumphal Arcs,
Gardens and Groves presented to his eyes.   (IV, 31–38)

Bedford College, University of London

NOTES

An earlier version of this essay was delivered as an illustrated talk at the annual dinner of
the Milton Society of America in Chicago in December, 1977. I was most grateful to the Society for providing me with an opportunity to organize my ideas on the topic. I am indebted subsequently to both Gordon Campbell and Douglas Chambers for their comments
and suggestions.

1. I. W. U. Chase, *Horace Walpole: Gardenist* (Princeton, N.J., 1943), p. 14.

2. For example, a standard European account, originally published in 1801, is Er-
cole Silva, *Dell' Arte de' Giardini Inglesi*, ed. Gianni Venturi (Milan, 1976), pp. 39–40; a
modern one is Edward Malins, *English Landscaping and Literature 1660–1840* (London,
1966), pp. 1–3.

3. *Epistles to Several Persons*, ed. F. W. Bateson (London, 1951), p. 143. For discussions of Stowe see Christopher Hussey, *English Gardens and Landscapes 1700–1750* (London, 1967), pp. 89–113, and Peter Willis, *Charles Bridgeman and the English Landscape
Garden* (London, 1977), pp. 106–27.

4. Illustrated in Willis, *Charles Bridgeman*, plate 135. Gibbs' Building was eventually moved to a distant part of the grounds and rechristened the Fane of Pastoral Poetry, on
the significance of which see my "Emblem and Expressionism in the Eighteenth-Century
Landscape Garden," *Eighteenth-Century Studies*, IV (1971), 294–317. On the various
buildings at Stowe see Michael Gibbon, "Stowe, Buckinghamshire: the house and garden
buildings and their designers. A catalogue," *Architectural History*, XX (1977), 31–44.

5. Illustrated in Willis, *Charles Bridgeman*, plate 153.

6. For my discussion of the "message" of the Elysian Fields I am indebted to a series
of articles in the Stowe School magazine, especially M. J. Gibbon, "The History of Stowe—
IX: Gilbert West's walk through the gardens in 1731," *The Stoic*, XXIV (1970), 57–64, and
G. B. Clarke, "The History of Stowe—X: Moral Gardening," *The Stoic*, XXIV (1970),
113–21.

7. Illustrated in Willis, *Charles Bridgeman*, plate 147b.

8. *A Dialogue upon the Gardens . . . at Stow* (1748; rpt. Augustan Reprint Society
176, Los Angeles, 1976), p. 21.

9. 2 vols. (1772), II, p. 243.

10. "Milton and the Art of Landscape," *Milton Studies*, VIII, ed. James A. Simmonds (Pittsburgh, 1977), p. 5 ff.

11. *An Essay on Design in Gardening* (1768), pp. 22–23.

12. Chase, *Horace Walpole: Gardenist*, pp. 14–15.

13. 3 vols. (1718), I, p. 344.

14. *Paradise Lost*, VI, 640. Cf. Pope, who invokes the variety of Paradise in his letter to Lord Bathurst, in *The Correspondence of Alexander Pope*, ed. George Sherburn, 5 vols. (Oxford, 1956), II, p. 14.

15. *The Enthusiast: or, the Lover of Nature* (1744), pp. 5–6 for Stowe; for Milton, see *The Adventurer*, CI (23 October 1753).

16. W. S. Scott, *Green Retreats: The Story of Vauxhall Gardens 1661–1859* (London, 1965), p. 48.

17. Chase, *Horace Walpole: Gardenist*, p. 15.

18. On Rousham see Hussey, *English Gardens*, pp. 147–53, and Willis, *Charles Bridgeman*, pp. 66–68 and passim.

19. *Systema Horti-Culturae: or, The Art of Gardening* (1677), p. 47. For Defoe, see the extracts in *The Genius of the Place: The English Landscape Garden 1620–1820*, ed. John Dixon Hunt and Peter Willis (London, 1976), pp. 166–76 and in the index under "Water."

20. Robert Berger has also pointed out to me the lengthy quotation from Milton used in the entry on "Jardin" in Diderot and D'Alembert, *Encyclopédie*, VIII (Neûchatel, 1765), p. 460.

21. *Epistles to Several Persons*, p. 142. On Pope's own garden consult Maynard Mack, *The Garden and the City* (London, 1969), and my own *The Figure in the Landscape* (Baltimore, 1976), ch. 2.

22. *Campania Foelix* (1700), p. 299.

23. *Ichnographia Rustica*, III, p. 47.

24. *The Rise and Progress of the Present Taste in . . . Gardens . . .* (1767; rpt. introd. John Harris, Newcastle Upon Tyne, 1970), p. 30.

25. *Studies in Art, Architecture and Design*, 2 vols. (New York, 1968), I, p. 140.

26. See my "Sense and Sensibility in the Landscape Designs of Humphry Repton," *Studies in Burke and his Time*, XIX (1978), 23 and plate 1.

27. On Hagley see Joseph Heely, *Letters on the Beauties of Hagley, Envil, and the Leasowes*, 2 vols. (1777), I, p. 193; on Pitt see B. Sprague Allen, *Tides in English Taste*, 2 vols. (Cambridge, Mass., 1937), II, p. 118.

28. *An Essay on the Theory of Painting* (1715), p. 14.

29. Quoted in Kenneth Woodbridge, *Landscape and Antiquity: Aspects of English Culture at Stourhead 1718–1838* (Oxford, 1970), p. 30.

30. Quoted in E. W. Manwaring, *Italian Landscape in Eighteenth-Century England* (New York, 1925), p. 174.

31. Quoted in Allen, *Tides in English Taste*, II, p. 175.

32. *Letters on the Beauties of Hagley*, I, pp. 29–31.

33. II, pp. 116–17. The Addison remark may be found in *The Spectator*, ed. D. F. Bond, 5 vols. (Oxford, 1965), III, p. 564.

34. For a survey of English visitors to Italian gardens see my "English Mirrors of Italian Gardens," *Country Life* 15 (September 1977).

35. I have argued this much more extensively in a paper read to the art history seminar at the Institute for Advanced Study, Princeton, in April 1978; a possible explanation for why Addison did not use his remark about the Italian inspiration for Milton's garden was his wish to promote English gardening's native sources and talent.

36. Chase, *Horace Walpole: Gardenist*, p. 16.

37. Allen, *Tides in English Taste*, II, p. 122.

38. *The Diary of John Evelyn*, ed. E. S. de Beer, 6 vols. (Oxford, 1955), II, p. 305 and passim.

39. Ilustrated in *Approaches to Marvell*, ed. C. A. Patrides (London, 1978), plate 15.12.

40. Illustrated ibid., plates 15.8 and 15.10. On the variety of forms in an Italian garden see Elizabeth MacDougall, "*Ars Hortulorum*: Sixteenth-Century Garden Iconography and Literary Theory in Italy," *The Italian Garden*, ed. David R. Coffin (Washington, D.C., 1972), pp. 41–52.

41. This, too, I have argued more thoroughly in the paper cited in note 35.

42. This hitherto neglected area of English garden history has been recently illuminated by Roy Strong, *The Renaissance Garden in England* (London, 1979).

43. The manuscript of Kent's journal is Bodleian Library MS. Rawl. D.1162; his brief mention of Pratolino occurs on p. 3.

44. *Diaries*, II, pp. 418–19.

45. See L. Chatelet-Lange, "The Grotto of the Unicorn and the Gardens of the Villa di Castello," *Art Bulletin*, L (1968), pp. 51–58. Roy Strong, *The Renaissance Garden*, pp. 73 ff. and passim has a discussion of *automata*.

46. Variously illustrated in Willis, *Charles Bridgeman;* Francesco Gurrieri and Judith Chatfield, *Boboli Gardens* (Florence, 1972); *Introduzione ai giardini del senese* (S. Quirico d'Orcia, Archivo Italiano dell'Arte dei Giardini, 1976); and C. L. Franck, *The Villas of Frascati* (London, 1966).

47. Frances Yates, *The Art of Memory* (London, 1966).

48. Illustrated in Roland Mushat Frye, *Milton's Imagery and the Visual Arts* (Princeton, 1978), plate 238. Frye's discussion appeared after I first gave this paper to the Milton Society in Chicago; we coincide on several points, but perhaps diverge most over what Frye calls Italian "formal" gardening which was "basically dissimilar to Milton's Garden" (p. 221). Both he (p. 226) and Hannah Disinger Demaray, "Milton's 'Perfect' Paradise and the Landscapes of Italy," *Milton Quarterly*, VIII (1974), p. 36, take up the matter of Milton's "woodie theatre," but neither treats it adequately. I have discussed some of the theoretical connections between gardens and theatres in "Theatres, Gardens, and Garden-Theatres," in *Essays and Studies*, ed. Inga-Stina Ewbank (London, 1980), pp. 95–118.

49. See Claudia Lazzaro-Bruno, "The Villa Lante at Bagnaia: An Allegory of Art and Nature," *Art Bulletin*, LIX (1977), 553–60.

50. Illustrated in Georgina Masson, *Italian Gardens* (London, 1966), p. 191.

51. Illustrated in *The Italian Garden* (see n. 40), opp. p. 78.

52. *The Villa D'Este at Tivoli* (Princeton, 1960).

53. *Elements of Architecture* (1624), pp. 109–10.

54. *Five Essays on Milton's Epics* (London, 1966), p. 32.

55. "'My Native Element': Milton's Paradise and English Gardens," *Milton Studies*, V, ed. James D. Simmonds (Pittsburgh, Pa., 1973), pp. 260–61. Otten is right, I think, to look to real gardens (p. 250), but she underestimates the European influence in England during the seventeenth-century.

56. John Raymond, *Il Mercurio Italico* (1648), pp. 94–95.

57. *Italy in its Originall Glory, Ruine and Revivall* (1660), pp. 309–11.

58. See M. F. S. Hervey, *Thomas Howard, Earl of Arundel* (Cambridge, Eng., 1921), pp. 101–02.

59. See C. L. Frommel, *Die Farnesina und Peruzzis architekonisches Frühwerk* (Berlin, 1961).

60. *An Itinerary*, 4 vols. (Glasgow, 1907), I, p. 239.

61. The dragon fountain, as it is today, is illustrated in *Approaches to Marvell*, plate 15.13; if, as Alistair Fowler suggests in his note to IX, 75 (*Paradise Lost* [London, 1971], the reference is "not a mist in the ordinary sense, but a fountain rising by capillary attraction," the force of my comparison is the stronger.

62. For example, John R. Knott, *Milton's Pastoral Vision* (Chicago, 1971), p. 49 and, of course, many other critics who have tackled this aspect of Milton's imagination.

MILTON'S INFLUENCE ON THOMSON: THE USES OF LANDSCAPE

David R. Anderson

M ILTON INFLUENCED Thomson in two distinct ways in *The Seasons*. There is, first, the challenge set by Milton's moral stature. *Paradise Lost* proved once and for all that an English poet could write a poem on the grand scale which would serve the interests of both art and morality, and it challenged every later English poet, whatever his theme, to do the same. That challenge tempered both Thomson's attitude toward landscape and his method of treating it.

In Book IV of *Paradise Lost* Satan breaks into the garden of Eden, perches on the Tree of Life and surveys God's paradise:

> Beneath him with new wonder now he views
> To all delight of human sense expos'd
> In narrow room Nature's whole wealth, yea more,
> A Heaven on Earth: for blissful Paradise
> Of God the Garden was, by him in the East
> Of *Eden* planted. (205–210)[1]

Here in the book which contains his most famous landscape poetry, Milton stops the narrative for a moral lesson which reverberates in *The Seasons*. Satan sat in the Tree of Life:

> yet not true Life
> Thereby regain'd, but sat devising Death
> To them who liv'd; nor on the virtue thought
> Of that life-giving Plant, but only us'd
> For prospect, what well us'd had been the pledge
> Of immortality. So little knows
> Any, but God alone, to value right
> The good before him, but perverts best things
> To worst abuse, or to thir meanest use. (196–204)

These lines make it clear that despite the evocative descriptions of Book IV, Milton does not delight in Eden's physical luxuriance for its own sake. Instead, landscape derives its importance from its direct link with God and the divine order. The poet of theodicy, Milton implies, espe-

107

cially the one who combines landscape painting with moral teaching, should be clear about the "virtue" of landscape. He commits an error (Milton would have called it a sin) who uses landscape "only . . . / For prospect."[2] Although the poet may draw the reader's attention to natural scenery in order to delight the senses, he should at the same time treat natural scenery as a "pledge" of its divine creator and orderer. For Thomson — who knew Milton's poetry intimately and felt deeply the weight of Milton's example — to describe landscape merely for delight, regardless of the need to instruct, would be to pervert "best things / To worst abuse" or, if that language seems too strong, to put landscape to its "meanest use."[3]

At first glance there is no compelling reason why Milton's condemnation of the corrupter of humankind should be taken as part of Thomson's poetics, yet a strong case can be made for the Miltonic influence here. Milton is "massively," as John Carey has said, "a moral phenomenon," a statement which is especially true with reference to the eighteenth-century view of Milton.[4] In *Spectator* 297 Addison speaks of Milton's "greatness of Soul," and regrets that the English language was inadequate to bear the weight of his "glorious Conceptions."[5] Even Johnson, despite the reservations he expressed in the *Life of Milton*, found unqualified praise for Milton's "Moral Sentiments," which "excel those of all other poets."[6] After Milton, every English writer of moral poetry had one great example to think of and to measure himself against. "Is not," Thomson asks in *Summer*,

> each great, each amiable muse
> Of classic ages in thy Milton met?
> A genius universal as his theme?   (1567–69)

Milton had written the great English epic, but more than that he had written an awesome moral poem, successfully fusing the two aims of poetry, *docere et delectare*, to teach and to delight. It was, after all, in his *Life of Milton* that Johnson had written, "Poetry is the art of uniting pleasure with truth, by calling imagination to the help of reason."[7] Thomson was fully aware of the standard set by Milton for a poet who, like himself, aspired to the moral strain. "Nothing," his Preface self-consciously declares,

can have a better influence towards the revival of poetry than the choosing of great and serious subjects, such as at once amuse the fancy, enlighten the head, and warm the heart. These give a weight and dignity to the poem.[8]

Elsewhere in his Preface, which singles out Milton by name as a moral poet, Thomson's concern for the moral quality of poetry in general, and implicitly for that of his own, reflects the influence of Milton's example:

Let poetry once more be restored to her ancient truth and purity; let her be inspired from Heaven, and in return her incense ascend thither; let her exchange her low, venal, trifling, subjects for such as are fair, useful, and magnificent; and let her execute these so as at once to please, instruct, surprise and astonish.[9] (p. 240)

Thomson felt Milton's influence in a second, more specifically literary way. Milton, who set so high a moral standard for Thomson, also supplied him with a method by which poetry could combine natural description with moral teaching: Milton taught Thomson to associate walking through nature with meditation upon it and led him from that meditation to praise of nature's God. Like almost every other minor eighteenth-century poet, Thomson often had his eye on the speaker of *Il Penseroso*, who frequented the "arched walks of twilight groves" together with "the Cherub Contemplation":

Poets have been passionately fond of retirement, and solitude. The wild romantic country was their delight. And they seem never to have been more happy, than when, lost in unfrequented fields, far from the little busy world, they were at leisure, to meditate, and sing the Works of Nature. (p. 241)

"To meditate, and sing the Works of Nature" describes precisely what Thomson does in *The Seasons*. His great exemplar not only in singing with a moral aim, but also in associating that song with meditative nature walks, was Milton. Thomson's purpose in *The Seasons* follows that of *Paradise Lost*, but he derives his method from *Il Penseroso*. The result is that, when Thomson wants to write explicitly moral passages in which description leads to meditation, and meditation to theodicy, he imitates Milton. The combination of solitude, quiet, landscape, meditation, and religious feeling which he found in *Il Penseroso* forms the ground upon which Thomson paints *The Seasons*.[10]

Before a close verbal comparison of *Il Penseroso* and *The Seasons* can be made, however, one document which stands between them demands attention. *Spectator* 425, by an unknown hand, combines in a curiously forward-looking way the method of *Il Penseroso*, the impulse towards moral teaching of *Paradise Lost*, and Thomson's metaphor of the seasons.[11] Printed fourteen years before *Winter* appeared, it is in many ways an embryonic version of the later work, reflecting its sources, adumbrating its style, and setting its tone. It shows how closely Milton, landscape, and meditative literature were associated in the early eighteenth century when Thomson was writing. Most of all, however, it shows how the combination of those three elements led to moralizing.

In this number, a gentleman writes to Mr. Spectator to describe a dream he has had. The writer describes himself walking in his garden at twilight one "cool still Evening" (p. 592), silently reciting a passage from *Il Penseroso*.[12] The writer has gone to his garden after "the Uneasiness of a hot sultry Day" (p. 592), just as the narrator of *Summer* vainly wishes to do:

> All-conquering heat, oh, intermit thy wrath!
> And on my throbbing temples potent thus
> Beam not so fierce! Incessant still you flow,
> And still another fervent flood succeeds,
> Poured on the head profuse. In vain I sigh,
> And restless turn, and look around for night:
> Night is far off.   (451–57)

Mr. Spectator's correspondent walks to a spot of "sweet Retirement" where he finds himself in a scene identical in nearly every detail to that in which Lyttleton finds himself in *Spring* as he walks through Hagley Park "Courting the Muse." Here is the correspondent's bower:

The Reflection of [the moon] in the Water, the Fanning of the Wind rustling on the Leaves, the Singing of the Thrush and Nightingale, and the Coolness of the Walks, all conspired to make me lay aside all displeasing Thoughts. (p. 593)

Thomson imagines Lyttleton sitting

>   beneath the shade
> Of solemn oaks, that tuft the swelling mounts
> Thrown graceful round by Nature's careless hand,
> And pensive listen to the various voice
> Of rural peace — the herds, the flocks, the birds,
> The hollow-whispering breeze, the plaint of rills,
> That, purling down amid the twisted roots
> Which creep around, their dewy murmurs shake
> On the soothed ear.   (*Spring*, 914–22)

The wind, the birds, the water in both scenes provide the setting for meditation and poetry. Of course, the principal reason why these settings are so familiar is that both draw upon the topos of the *locus amoenus;* what is important about the settings, however, is not so much the similarity between them as the fact that they are put to similar use: both provide contexts for meditation and for poetry.[13] In *The Spectator* the poetry comes from *Il Penseroso*, but in Thomson, naturally, it comes from the retired man himself:

> turning thence thy view, these graver thoughts
> The Muses charm — while, with sure taste refined,
> You draw the inspiring breath of ancient song,
> Till nobly rises emulous thy own.   (*Spring*, 932–35)

The correspondent finds the theme of the *Il Penseroso* lines "exquisitely suited to my present Wandrings of Thought" (p. 593) just as Lyttleton, abstracted by meditation from the scene he occupies, wanders in thought.

The quotation from *Il Penseroso* leads Mr. Spectator's correspondent to reflect upon "the sweet Vicissitudes of Night and Day, on the charming Disposition of the Seasons, and their Return again in a perpetual Circle" (p. 594). This notion of the cycle of the seasons, hardly a new one, is, of course, Thomson's governing metaphor. It is possible to illustrate allusions to it almost at will.

There is no coincidence in the fact that contemplation about the "perpetual Circle" leads the writer, as it so often leads Thomson, to moralizing:

Oh! said I, that I could from these my declining Years, return again to my first Spring of Youth and Vigour; but that alass! [sic] is impossible: All that remains within my Power, is to soften the Inconveniencies I feel, with an easy contented Mind, and the Enjoyment of such Delights as this Solitude affords me. (p. 594)

The writer in *Spectator* 425 puts his finger on the meditative elements of *Il Penseroso* that reappear in *The Seasons*. When the melancholy man pursues his walk, "Peace," "Quiet," "Leisure" all lead to "Contemplation." Stillness, Tranquility of Mind, and "sweet Retirement" all lead to reflection in the *Spectator*. And, in Thomson's *Spring*, "Contentment," "Pure Serenity," and silence induce "thought, and contemplation still."

Thus, even before the dream begins, *Spectator* 425 affords some striking parallels to *The Seasons*. Of these, the most important for this discussion is the presence of Milton. I have stressed the way Milton's attitude toward nature in *Paradise Lost* and his treatment of it in *Il Penseroso* reflected what Thomson sought from poetry: in the first case the urge, and in the second the opportunity, "to meditate, and sing the Works of Nature." Here, Milton's lines provide the setting, and the pageant of the seasons provides the context, for moralizing.

Mr. Spectator's correspondent now relates his dream. Briefly, four iconographical figures, Spring, Summer, Fall, and Winter, with their attendant months, parade through the garden. The last of these, Winter, is supported by Comus, "the God of Revels" (p. 596). The vision and the *Spectator* close with a moral observation on the fact that Comus appears, from the front, a picture of "Joy, Delight, and Satisfaction," while from the rear he seems bald, old, and deformed (p. 596). As with the introduction to the dream, numerous details of the dream itself look directly forward to *The Seasons*. Spring, for example, is accompanied by Mars, "who had long usurp'd a Place among the Attendants of the *Spring*" (p. 594). Mars makes way, however, for "a softer Appearance" who is Venus. The theme of love in spring is emphasized by May, who is

attended by *Cupid*, with his Bow strung, and in a Posture to let fly an Arrow: As he pass'd by methought I heard a confused Noise of soft Complaints, gentle Extasies, and tender Sighs of Lovers; Vows of Constancy, and as many Complainings of Perfidiousness. (p. 595)

Love in the vegetable, animal, and human worlds is of course the theme governing Thomson's treatment of *Spring*, "The Love Song of James Thomson," as Ralph Cohen calls it.[14] Lines 963–1073, in fact, describe the "charming agonies of love, / Whose misery delights" (1074–75) — merely an expansion of the *Spectator* passage.

Summer, with his train, brings excessive heat. August "seem'd almost to faint whilst for half the Steps he took the Dog-Star levell'd his Rays full at his Head" (p. 595). In *Summer* the Sun presides, driving the narrator into the shades and forcing him to view nature in his imagination:

> 'Tis raging noon; and, vertical, the Sun
> Darts on the head direct his forceful rays.
> O'er heaven and earth, far as the ranging eye
> Can sweep, a dazzling deluge reigns; and all
> From pole to pole is undistinguished blaze.   (432–36)

Autumn is accompanied by Plenty, Pomona, and Bacchus, with October "all soil'd with the Juice of Grapes, as if he had just come from the Wine-Press" (p. 596). Naturally enough, Thomson's *Autumn* focuses on harvest themes too, mentioning specifically "the brown October, drawn / Mature and perfect from his dark retreat / Of thirty years" (519–21); Phillips, "Pomona's bard!" (645); and

> The claret smooth, red as the lip we press
> In sparkling fancy while we drain the bowl,
> The mellow-tasted burgundy, and, quick
> As is the wit it gives, the gay champagne.   (703–06)[15]

The correspondent's dream, like Thomson's poem, uses the visual as a step to the moral when *Necessity*, "The Mother of Fate," accompanies Winter in his progress, or when Comus appears with "Joy, Delight, and Satisfaction" on his front and "Murder, Anger and Suspicion" on his back (p. 596).

Spectator 425, with its wealth of implicit and explicit allusion to Milton, connects England's first great poet of theodicy with one of his many lesser followers. Moral purpose, meditative tone, landscape setting—the main ingredients of *The Seasons*—all are derived from Milton. The fact that these elements should coalesce as early as 1712 in a popular publication demonstrates Milton's importance for the didactic treatment of landscape. Far from anachronistic, a poem that aimed to turn landscape to moral purpose was pointing a moral to which Augustan readers were prepared to respond.

Spectator 425 is a remarkably suggestive mixture of Miltonic and Thomsonian materials. A close comparison of *Il Penseroso* with sections of *The Seasons* will help to sort out some of these elements, to point out where Thomson leans on Milton and why he does so. Milton places his melancholy man in various postures during the course of the day his poem describes: Il Penseroso goes for a walk, sits by a fire and thinks about famous men, avoids the heat of the sun by seeking a cool forest grove, and reclines by a brook. All these activities Thomson describes in *The Seasons*, but in doing so he shifts the weight of the passage from description to theodicy.[16]

The invocation of Melancholy that begins at line 31 of *Il Penseroso* turns out to be an invitation to an evening walk. The narrator asks Melancholy to come "With ev'n step, and musing gait" and to join with her Peace, Quiet, Fast and, chiefly, Contemplation. Almost as an afterthought, he also asks her to bring Silence, in case the nightingale "will deign a Song, / In her sweetest, saddest plight, / Smoothing the rugged brow of night" (56–58). Il Penseroso never hears the nightingale, but he continues nevertheless to walk

> On the dry smooth-shaven Green,
> To behold the wand'ring Moon,
> Riding near her highest noon,
> Like one that had been led astray
> Through the Heav'n's wide pathless way.   (66–70)

Thomson, too, on a summer night's walk, looks up at the sky to watch the celestial activity. Miltonic echoes resound in his description of the scene as "sober Evening" (1648) takes its station, then yields to Night:

> not in her winter robe
> Of massy Stygian woof, but loose arrayed
> In mantle dun.   (*Summer*, 1685–87)

The "robe / Of massy Stygian woof" recalls Melancholy's "robe of dark-
est grain" (33) with a passing glance at *L'Allegro*'s "*Stygian* Cave
forlorn" (3). Thomson alludes, however, not only to Il Penseroso's language, but also to his actions:

> Sudden to heaven
> Thence weary vision turns; where, leading soft
> The silent hours of love, with purest ray
> Sweet Venus shines; and, from her genial rise,
> When daylight sickens, till it springs afresh,
> Unrivalled reigns, the fairest lamp of night.
>
> (*Summer*, 1693–98)

   What is of particular interest is the way Thomson concludes Milton's scene. Milton, of course, is moving toward that poignant moment
when the speaker dissolves into religious ecstasy in a cathedral. That act
is the culminating moment of *Il Penseroso*, since the poem focuses its account of the day's activities on the final dissolution. Thomson, whose
canvas is larger than Milton's, cannot wait for the end of *The Seasons* to
finish this scene. He must rely on periodic passages of emotional inten-
sity rather than dissolve all in one grand climax. Accordingly, where
Milton drops the evening walk and moves his poem indoors, Thomson
continues to gaze skyward. His gaze moves from Venus to a comet,
"kindly bent / To work the will of all-sustaining love" (1723–24). The
sight of the comet moves the narrator to a lengthy section in praise of
the new philosophy which enables humans to see and to understand
natural phenomena. This laudatory conclusion, not only to the evening's
walk but to *Summer* itself, evolves into explicit theodicy. Praising the
natural design which points to God, the narrator is

> intent to gaze
> Creation through; and, from that full complex
> Of never-ending wonders, to conceive
> Of the Sole Being right, who spoke the word,
> And Nature moved complete.   (1784–88)

As it should for a moral poet, the sight of the sky in all its beauty, variety, and order puts the Thomsonian narrator in mind of God.
   Milton takes Il Penseroso indoors, to "some still removed place":

> Where glowing Embers through the room,
> Teach light to counterfeit a gloom,
> Far from all resort of mirth,
> Save the Cricket on the hearth,

> Or the Bellman's drowsy charm,
> To bless the doors from nightly harm.   (79–84)

This room or, alternatively, "some high lonely Tow'r" (86), is the place where Il Penseroso can hold "high converse with the mighty dead" (*Winter*, 432). He thinks of Plato, Hermes Trismegistus, the Greek tragedians, and Chaucer. In keeping with his quiet, reclusive, meditative tone, Il Penseroso wants to hear the songs

> great Bards beside
> In sage and solemn tunes have sung,
> Of Tourneys and of Trophies hung,
> Of Forests, and enchantments drear,
> Where more is meant than meets the ear.   (116–20)

In *Winter* Thomson, too, retreats to a fire and old books. Instead of glowing embers "to counterfeit a gloom" he has a cheerful blaze "To cheer the gloom," but in other respects his retreat matches Il Penseroso's. Thomson also turns to "the mighty dead":

> Sages of ancient time, as gods revered,
> As gods beneficent, who blessed mankind
> With arts and arms, and humanized a world.
>
>   (*Winter*, 433–35)

The speaker sits "deep-musing" (437) as he hails Socrates, Solon, Lycurgus, and countless other ancient and modern heroes and patriots. Literary worthies, too, pass before him, from "Phoebus' self" (532) to Pope. Homer and Milton walk hand in hand in this procession. The impulse for solitude, silence and meditation, whose combination leads inevitably to praise of God, works for Thomson in a room just as it does in a landscape. The speaker moves from meditation to theodicy as naturally and inevitably as he would in a Claudian landscape or in Lyttleton's garden:

> Thus in some deep retirement would I pass
> The winter-glooms with friends of pliant soul,
> Or blithe or solemn, as the theme inspired:
> With them would search if nature's boundless frame
> Was called, late-rising, from the void of night,
> Or sprung eternal from the Eternal Mind;
> Its life, its laws, its progress, and its end.   (572–78)

The point of these lines is not merely that Thomson here, as elsewhere in *The Seasons*, draws on *Il Penseroso*. Indeed, it is more difficult to find a minor eighteenth-century poet who did not borrow from *Il*

Penseroso than to identify those who did. My point is that when Thomson makes his most significant raids on Milton, he does so just before a passage of explicit theodicy, for he associated the two in his mind. The lines quoted above preface Thomson's vindication of Divine Providence:

> Hence larger prospects of the beauteous whole
> Would gradual open on our opening minds;
> And each diffusive harmony unite
> In full perfection to the astonished eye.
> Then would we try to scan the moral world,
> Which, though to us it seems embroiled, moves on
> In higher order, fitted and impelled
> By Wisdom's finest hand, and issuing all
> In general good.   (*Winter*, 579–87)

Il Penseroso appears in one final view before Milton's transition to the concluding ecstasies of his poem. Like each of the other postures in which he finds himself, this one has its counterpart in Thomson, where, as we shall see, it serves as prelude to a passage of explicit theodicy. Here is Milton:

> And when the Sun begins to fling
> His flaring beams, me Goddess bring
> To arched walks of twilight groves,
> And shadows brown that *Sylvan* loves
> Of Pine or monumental Oak,
> Where the rude Axe with heaved stroke
> Was never heard the Nymphs to daunt,
> Or fright them from their hallow'd haunt.   (131–38)

In *Summer* the narrator's chief preoccupation is avoiding the sun's scorching rays, for the sun dominates that season just as Love dominates *Spring* and the harvest motif dominates *Autumn:*

> 'Tis raging noon; and, vertical, the Sun
> Darts on the head direct his forceful rays.
> O'er heaven and earth, far as the ranging eye
> Can sweep, a dazzling deluge reigns; and all
> From pole to pole is undistinguished blaze.   (432–36)

Not only the speaker, but all of the landscape suffers from the heat:

> Distressful nature pants.
> The very streams look languid from afar,
> Or, through the unsheltered glade, impatient seem
> To hurl into the covert of the grove.   (447–50)

Il Penseroso's progress from an unprotected glade to a cool, dark grove—suggested by the half-personified streams in Thomson—is copied by *Summer*'s narrator, who enters a grove where the atmosphere is redolent of Milton:

> Welcome, ye shades! ye bowery thickets, hail!
> Ye lofty pines! ye venerable oaks! (469–70)

The Miltonic echoes of this section are important because they show how Thomson used *Il Penseroso* to establish a meditative setting:

> Still let me pierce into the midnight depth
> Of yonder grove, of wildest largest growth,
> That, forming high in air a woodland choir,
> Nods o'er the mount beneath. At every step,
> Solemn and slow the shadows blacker fall,
> And all is awful listening gloom around. (516–21)

Thomson's woodland choir "forming high in air" recalls Milton's "arched walks"; his "wildest largest growth" is a weaker version of Milton's "monumental oak"; and his black shadows only deepen the shade of Milton's brown ones. Clearly, these properties are meant to suggest that "these are the haunts of meditation" (522).

Il Penseroso is led into his grove to meditate. Like Mr. Spectator's correspondent who, no doubt, was drawing on *Il Penseroso* for this detail, he falls into a dreamlike state:

> There in close covert by some Brook,
> Where no profaner eye may look,
> Hide me from Day's garish eye,
> While the Bee with Honied thigh,
> That at her flow'ry work doth sing,
> And the Waters murmuring
> With such consort as they keep,
> Entice the dewy-feather'd sleep. (139–46)

Thomson liked these lines so well that he paraphrased them:

> Beside the dewy border let me sit,
> All in the freshness of the humid air,
> There on that hollowed rock, grotesque and wild,
> An ample chair moss-lined, and over head
> By flowering umbrage shaded; where the bee
> Strays diligent, and with the extracted balm
> Of fragrant woodbine loads his little thigh. (*Summer*, 622–28)

The lines on the bee taken from *Il Penseroso* form part of the passage in which Thomson gradually works his way down from an emotional climax which began in his reaction to the landscape about him. Earlier, the setting has brought to his mind poets who have written with a moral purpose, the poets with whom he implicitly compares himself:

> These are the haunts of meditation, these
> The scenes where ancient bards the inspiring breath
> Ecstatic felt, and, from this world retired,
> Conversed with angels and immortal forms,
> On gracious errands bent.   (*Summer*, 522–26)[17]

Among the angels' "gracious errands" Thomson includes the duty of ministering to a certain kind of poet, of which kind Thomson clearly regards himself as an example: "The poet, who devoted gives / His muse to better themes" (531–32). Unlike Satan, who perverts "best things" to "thir meanest use," Thomson gives himself to "better things." Not a poet of description, but one of theodicy who uses description for a higher purpose, Thomson associates himself with the poets described in his Preface as "inspired by heaven." Recognizing him as a kindred soul, the angels invite Thomson "when musing midnight reigns or silent noon" (557) to sing "Of Nature . . . and Nature's God," an activity which is "A privilege bestow'd by us alone / On contemplation" (562–63). Thomson has traveled the full circle from his preface, which spoke of the poet "at leisure, to meditate, and sing the works of Nature" (p. 240).

Here, under Milton's shadow, all the elements of Thomson's poetics come together. He is a poet who has devoted his poetry to God. He performs his devotion by singing of God's presence in nature as proof of His Providence. Thomson, consciously or unconsciously, adopts a threefold response to landscape as a means to order his praise poetically: he walks in groves and glades; these inspire meditation which, in turn, leads up to God, who inspired the song in the first place. This use of landscape Thomson learned from Milton, who combined the idea of walking in nature with the idea that such walks inspired meditation, and then linked that meditation to holy things. However, as his frequent quotation, paraphrase, and allusion demonstrate, Thomson relied upon Milton for more than ideas: he also imitated his language in an attempt to recreate the setting and tone of *Il Penseroso*. All this was part of his larger effort in *The Seasons* to put landscape in a useful moral context by making it the basis of his theodicy.

Texas A & M University

NOTES

1. All quotations from Milton are from *John Milton: Complete Poems and Major Prose*, ed. Merritt Y. Hughes (New York, 1957).

2. Although Milton's narrator means that Satan used the tree as a lookout, he would have been as opposed to using the tree only to look at as he is to using it only to look from.

3. To corroborate the evidence of Thomson's knowledge of Milton presented in this essay, see Raymond Dexter Havens, *The Influence of Milton on English Poetry* (Cambridge, Mass., 1922), p. 121:

> Since nearly half of . . . [Thomson's] borrowings are from the minor poems, they reveal a close acquaintance, very unusual at the time, with the shorter as well as the longer works; and, as some of them occur in Thomson's juvenilia, it is clear that his familiarity with Milton dates from an early and impressionable stage.

4. *Milton* (New York, 1970), p. 147.

5. *The Spectator*, ed. Donald Bond (Oxford, 1965), III, 63. Further citations of the *Spectator* in the text will refer to this edition.

6. *Lives of the English Poets*, ed. George Birkbeck Hill (Oxford, 1905), I, 179. Johnson also quotes Addison's praise of Milton's "greatness of Soul," but he does so only to refute it. That refutation, however, is based upon theories of diction rather than upon any disagreement over Milton's moral value.

7. *Lives of the English Poets*, I, 170.

8. *James Thomson: Poetical Works*, ed. J. Logie Robertson (Oxford, 1908), p. 240. In quoting Thomson's 1726 preface to Winter, I shall be quoting from this edition. Page references will follow quotations in the text. My text for *The Seasons*, however, is the more recent *"The Seasons" and "The Castle of Indolence,"* ed. James Sambrook (Oxford, 1977). Unfortunately, Sambrook does not include the preface in his edition.

9. For a balanced discussion of the religious basis of Thomson's preface, see David Morris, *The Religious Sublime: Christian Poetry and Critical Tradition in 18th-Century England* (Lexington, Ky., 1972), p. 139.

10. In the case of Thomson, it seems to me, there can be no doubt that the tendency to associate walking in a landscape with meditation upon nature and meditation upon nature with an accession of religious feeling is due to the influence of Milton generally and of *Il Penseroso* specifically. It may well be, however, that eighteenth-century meditative landscape poetry in general ultimately derives from a broader tradition of religious meditation upon nature with its roots in the Old Testament and its greatest development among seventeenth-century English Protestants—the "meditation on the creatures." This meditative kind is discussed in Louis L. Martz, *The Paradise Within: Studies in Vaughan, Traherne, and Milton* (New Haven, Ct., 1964), pp. 17–31, 68–78, and 126–32, and in Barbara K. Lewalski, *Protestant Poetics and the Seventeenth-Century Religious Lyric* (Princeton, N.J., 1979), pp. 150–52, 162–65, and 172–73.

11. July 8, 1712. III, 592–97. Page references will follow quotations in the text. Bond notes (p. 597) that *Spectator* 425 is one of the papers signed "Z." It has been attributed to Pope, Parnell, and Budgell—never on conclusive grounds.

12. "Z" quotes *Il Penseroso* 61–72 and 147–54. See Bond, p. 593, for textual variants in the quotation.

13. The *locus amoenus* is defined and chronicled in Ernst R. Curtius, *European Literature and the Latin Middle Ages*, trans. Willard R. Trask (Princeton, N.J., 1953; rev. ed.,

1967), pp. 188–202, especially pp. 190–93 and 195–200. Curtius enumerates some of the genres in which the *locus amoenus* figures prominently after Virgil — pastoral poetry, erotic poetry, garden poetry. To this selective list I would add another sub-genre: moralized landscape poetry.

14. *The Unfolding of "The Seasons"* (Baltimore, 1970), p. 9.

15. These parallels, incidentally, demonstrate another tradition Thomson drew upon in *The Seasons:* the iconographical. Indeed, they merely confirm what can be demonstrated from landscape art, emblem books, or moral tracts: namely, that the visual artists and the poets had for centuries been using verbal and visual icons to talk about the progress of the seasons and nearly every other topic. One of the prime repositories of that tradition was *Paradise Lost*. See Jean Hagstrum, *The Sister Arts* (Chicago, 1958), pp. 17–28, 123–28, and 148. See also John Dixon Hunt, *The Figure in the Landscape* (Baltimore, 1976), pp. 107–11. Hunt briefly discusses *Spectator* 425 in his book.

16. Most of the Miltonic echoes I shall be discussing here have been noticed before by G. C. Macaulay, *James Thomson*, English Men of Letters Series (London, 1908), pp. 141–45; John E. Wells, "James Thomson and Milton," *MLN*, XXIV (1909), 60–61; or by Havens in Appendix A to *The Influence of Milton on English Poetry*. However, none of these lists of allusions puts Thomson's Miltonic echoes into a useful perspective.

17. These lines describe what happens in *Il Penseroso*, 151–54:

> And, as I wake, sweet music breathe
> Above, about, or underneath,
> Sent by some spirit to mortals good,
> Or th'unseen Genius of the wood.

Thomson's "ecstatic" curiously echoes Milton's "Dissolve me into ecstasies / And bring all heaven before mine eyes" (165–66). Even if Thomson is not alluding to Milton, the situation he describes is clearly Miltonic.

JOSEPH HALL AND
THE PROSE STYLE OF JOHN MILTON

Henry S. Limouze

J OHN MILTON'S battle against Joseph Hall, waged largely in two of Milton's early antiprelatical tracts, was stylistic as well as moral, political, religious, and philosophical. The traditional view has made it a later chapter in the seventeenth-century quarrel between *res* and *verba*, with an erratic but recognizably Ciceronian Milton taking on the "English Seneca." And Milton's few comments on language in these tracts seem to bear this out. In the *Apology against a Pamphlet*, he condemns the impure styles of university divinity students:

How few among them that know to write, or speak in a pure stile, much lesse to distinguish the *idea's*, and various kinds of stile: in Latine barbarous, and oft not without *solecisms*, declaming in rugged and miscellaneous geare blown together by the foure winds, and in their choice preferring the gay ranknesse of *Apuleius*, *Arnobius*, or any moderne fustianist, before the native *Latinisms* of *Cicero*.[1]

Similarly in *Of Reformation* (not addressed to Hall but written shortly before *Animadversions*) he accuses the Latin Fathers of cultivating styles marred by "the knotty Africanisms, the pamper'd metafors; the intricat, and involv'd sentences . . . besides the fantastick, and declamatory flashes; the crosse-jingling periods which cannot but disturb, and come thwart a setl'd devotion worse than the din of bells, and rattles" (568). But here the Fathers practice an annoying verbal luxuriance; the "setl'd devotion" of the Christian reader is more at home with "the sober, plain, and unaffected stile of the Scriptures." In terms of traditional positions in the quarrel over *res* and *verba*, we expect a Ciceronian to champion language, the repository of learning, the vehicle of international communication, and the form, texture, shape, and sound into which thought could be put artfully, expansively, and persuasively. Yet Milton is at once a lover of Cicero (and of Ciceronian expansiveness) and an enemy to verbal excess. Both of these attitudes are revealed in his famous comment on the style of his adversary:

I took it as my part the lesse to endure that my respected friends through their own unnecessary patience should thus lye at the mercy of a coy flurting stile; to

121

be girded with frumps and curtall gibes, by one who makes sentences by the Stat-
ute, as if all above three inches long were confiscat. (873)

Milton the Ciceronian naturally disliked Hall's cultivated brevity. But
cultivated brevity is as much an artificial rhetorical device as balance,
parallelism, isocolon, and the circular composition of the period which
are the Ciceronian's stock-in-trade. More fundamentally Milton is attacking any fixed rhetorical bag of tricks. The point of his last joke is
that Hall is obsessed with rigid outward measure: his brevity denies
freedom to expression; his statute-sentences are of a piece with his legal-
ism, his defense of a fixed liturgy, and his possession of a bishopric.

Stylistically the difference between Milton and Hall was never as
simple as the associations of "Ciceronian" (oratorical, copious, persuasive) and "Senecan" (plain, meditative, brief) may lead us to believe. In
many respects it was the reverse. In this essay I would like to discuss
more fully the stylistic implications of the quarrel, first by a selective
contrast of their persuasive strategies, and later by a more detailed examination of their individual styles. I will try to show that a case can be
made for their interaction which helps explain some of the difficult features of Milton's early prose style.

Contrary to Milton's implication, not all of Joseph Hall's sentences
are brief. In his earlier writings he did indeed cultivate the three-inch
sentence, and probably all his life he was a "tormenter of semicolons,"
but his style by the time of the Smectymnuan controversy tends to
greater looseness and freedom.[2] A long sentence like the following from
the *Humble Remonstrance* (which prompted the Smectymnuans' first
attack) is not uncommon, and it is worth quoting for several reasons:

Whiles the Orthodoxe part in this whole Realm, hath (to the praise of their patience) been quietly silent, as securely conscious of their own right, and innocence, how many furious and malignant spirits every where have burst forth into
sclanderous Libels, bitter Pasquines, railing Pamphlets? (under which more
Presses then one have groaned) wherein they have indeavoured, through the sides
of some misliked persons, to wound that sacred Government, which (by the
joynt-confession of all reformed Divines) derives it selfe from the times of the
blessed Apostles, without any interruption, (without the contradiction of any
one Congregation in the Christian world) unto this present age; Wherein, as no
doubt their lewd boldnesse hath been extremely offensive to your wisedomes,
and piety, so may it please you to check this daring, and mis-grounded insolence
of these Libellers, and by some speedy Declaration to let the world know, how
much you detest this their malicious, or ignorant presumption; and by some
needfull Act to put a present restraint upon the wilde and lawlesse courses of all
their factious combinations abroad, and enterprises of this kinde.[3]

This sentence as a whole illustrates perfectly the shape and some of the techniques of the "loose period," as described by Morris Croll.[4] Unlike the oratorical or Ciceronian period, of which the members point forward or back to a climactic point, the loose period at every point as it moves forward creates grammatical and intellectual possibility; in Croll's words it "moves straight onward everywhere from the point it has reached." There are some suspensions in this sentence which raise expectations of grammatical fulfillment, to be sure, but they are quite brief, and are not always fulfilled in comfortable ways (for example, the opening "whiles the Orthodoxe part" is not answered by the parallel we expect, "the furious and malignant part"). Balance is at once suggested and demolished when an adverbial phrase is echoed by a longer parenthesis: "without any interruption, (without the contradiction of any)." And Hall's connectives, finally, are used with the same looseness familiar to readers of Donne, Burton, and Browne. For example, the sentence is divided into three main sections, the second and third of which begin with the relative pronoun "wherein." The first "wherein" links two members whose length and independence vitiate the word's normally tight, binding function. But the second is weaker still, lacking even the specific meaning of the first: whatever "wherein" means here ("in which age," "wherefore," "for which reason") must be decided after the sentence is finished.

But if Hall's long loose period is typically anti-Ciceronian in appearance, it is not so in effect. It does not trace "the movements of a mind, discovering truth as it goes," in Croll's famous words. Rather Hall plays off his sentence's syntactically free development against a rigorously predetermined intellectual shape. The first two of the sentence's three parts (as described above) take the form of a large chiasmus, not of words but of ideas. In outline Hall moves from the "orthodoxe part . . . quietly silent," outward to the spiritual and grammatical disruptions of the pamphleteers; the second member reverses direction, moving from the pamphleteers back to their object, the ancient and unanimously approved church establishment. Another way of describing it is to say that the first two-thirds of the sentence form an intellectual circle, moving out from and back to a vision of Christian unity, personified by the "orthodoxe," characterized by "right, and innocence," and embodied by the "sacred Government" of the church.[5] The third section is different, because it directs the argument at the members of Parliament to whom the book was addressed. It is an oratorical call for action and deliberately assumes a more traditional oratorical form. But the first two parts do the main work of the sentence: they use a circular order to define a political and moral polarization, and to characterize through semantic argument the true nature of the opposing views.

Contrast with this a sentence from *Animadversions* in some respects similar to Hall's in appearance. Milton is responding to an attempt by his opponent to distinguish "popish bishops" from the enlightened English kind:

Since you would bind us to your jurisdiction by their Canon-law, since you would inforce upon us the old riffe-raffe of Sarum, and other monasticall reliques, since you live upon their unjust purchases, alleage their authorities, boast of their succession, walke in their steps, their pride, their titles, their covetousnesse, their persecuting of Gods people, since you disclaime their actions, and build their sepulchres, it is most just, that all their faults should be imputed to yee, and their iniquities visited upon yee. (730–31)

This is a familiar sort of oratorical period, in which the main clause ("it is most just") is withheld nearly until the end by a long series of dependent clauses. Thus, its organization is more formal than that of Hall's loose period. But beneath the surface of conventional rhetorical tricks (especially anaphora and syllepsis) its structure is also chiastic — "you . . . their . . . their . . . yee" — and it is this circle of pronouns that, like Hall's circle of ideas, does the work of the sentence. Milton's insight is into the network of reality behind a distorting veil of words, and his language consequently works to fuse "you" and "they" (Anglican and Roman) in a relationship that reveals the truth his opponent has attempted to disguise.

Yet despite its structural similarity to Hall's loose period and its apparently more traditionally oratorical construction, Milton's sentence is fundamentally different in purpose and effect. Hall's sentence outlines a clearly evaluated moral polarization that directly confronts the reader, whether he is a member of Parliament or not. When Hall suggests that "no doubt [the] lewd boldnesse [of the pamphleteers] hath been extremely offensive to your wisedomes, and piety," he combines an implied question ("you are offended, aren't you?") with its reassuring answer ("your wisdom and piety must prevent you from being on the wrong side"). The question and its answer, together with the preceding contrast of quiet orthodoxy and noisy error, serve to manipulate the reader, directing him firmly to take his position on the right side in a public conflict over policy and morality. Milton's sentence, by contrast, does not directly address the reader at all; the "you" Milton directly attacks is his opponent, and his sentence itself is a weapon wielded in a battle to which the reader is largely spectator.[6]

Where Hall brings his reader directly into his discourse by making him a kind of participant in its action, Milton subtly distances his reader, giving him the role of a judge without dictating his judgment. Hall's implied question, "No doubt you agree, don't you?" is comforting; Milton's "Do you agree?" is much simpler and much starker. To the extent that the reader has sympathized with Hall, has been persuaded by his manipulative rhetoric, and has agreed with his attempt to distinguish Anglican episcopacy from Roman prelacy, he is the individual ("you . . . yee") being attacked in Milton's sentence; the sentence is not reassuring but unsettling. The persuasive strategies of the two writers, then, appear to be opposed and complementary. A closer examination of certain of the techniques of each will show differences between them which reflect a fundamental division over issues of church membership, individual liberty and the nature of choice, issues central to their respective prose styles.

Because it is an underlying principle of order in a style which appears normally to cultivate asymmetry, Hall's use of circular patterns is an element of his rhetoric that deserves closer examination. An early and powerful example will serve by its obviousness to define the typical form and context. In a letter to the separatists Smith and Robinson (1609) he urges reconciliation through a variation of the well-known metaphor, "The church is our mother":

You could not do a greater injury to your mother than to flee from her. Say, she were poor, ragged, weak; say, she were deformed; yet she is not infectious: or, if she were, yet she is yours.[7]

The danger of an analogy rests in its ability to obscure differences even greater than the resemblances it exposes. Its beauty for the rhetorician has always been that the mental effort the auditor or reader must make to criticize a false analogy is always more arduous and less accessible than that required simply to perceive similarity. Hall's strategy here depends on this psychological truth, for his first sentence places the metaphor in a position which demands assent but at the same time clouds its moral implications. "Whose mother? What does she mean? Which church?" These are questions that Hall easily avoids. While he can hope for no immediate agreement from his intended (hostile) reader, he gives him no opportunity to raise an objection of any subtlety. Placing his reader in a position of weakness, Hall may more readily control his reaction. Specifically, he can now anticipate objections and thereby co-opt them; he can dull their individuality and edge by assimilating them into a fog of compromise. This is the job of the next, circular sentence, which appears to grant everything while granting nothing.

"Say she were poor, ragged, weak; say, she were deformed." The imagery here has specific contemporary reference. The "poor, ragged, weak" of the first member are familiar epithets applied in Anglican discussions of the *via media* to Puritan and separatist congregations;[8] their close juxtaposition with "deformed," which Puritans in turn tended to use to refer to Anglican and Roman excesses, forces a kind of amelioration of each. That is, the separatist reader who recognized and protested against the criticism of the first kind ("our church is not debased and ragged, but rather eschews a parade of worldly ceremonies and seeks its place in the heart of the believer") would naturally have assented to the second, the charge of deformity. Hall's strategy in juxtaposing the two is to make just such a distinction difficult. He identifies them both, through rhetorical parallel, as exaggerations of the same kind: "You say that the first charge is misdirected; acknowledge that the second may be too." If nothing else, this is a very active use of the *via media*. Hall's insinuations are particularly effective because they are directed not merely against Puritan principle but against all principle; the compromiser condemns all ideology because he pretends to be without it.

The implications of the compromise are made clearer as the circle rounds and returns. The two hypothetical situations paralleled earlier, the mother's poverty and deformity, are balanced temporarily: "yet she is not infectious." Hall appears to fall back on the moderate Anglican position that the ceremonious use of things indifferent would not tarnish the purity of inner worship: "The disease of the church will not infect you." But Hall was not content with halfway victories. Acknowledging in turn the possible inadequacy even of the moderate position — "or, if she were [infectious]" — he returns unexpectedly to his ultimate line of defense, the obedience of the individual due to the external church, "yet she is yours."

The closing of the circle is sudden and inexorable in its effect. Where the previous members had moved outward, revealing a speculative and even imaginative play of mind over possibilities (compressed only by the brevity of Hall's phrases), the conclusion severely circumscribes the freedom implied earlier and places all within the firm grasp of the possessive. "She is yours" becomes, when we translate the metaphor into the world of power, "you are hers," and Hall perhaps could not have explained in any clearer terms his conception of the church's mode of relation with the believer. It is doubtful that he would have wanted to. His early well-known liberalism, and in the later, more conservative work, his frequently equivocating rhetoric, have led to his being described as a moderate among the Anglicans, closer to the Bacon of *A Wise and Moderate Discourse* than to Laud.[9] It is true that he often appears to ask for and engage in the careful adjudication of differences and that he will even consider the possibility of moderate sorts of reform, admitting the excesses of individual priests and bishops. Nevertheless, his call for compromise is uncompromisingly asserted because in his view it is finally submission to the authority of the visible church, rather than the exercise of the individual conscience (how unlike Bacon) or the relation of conscience to Scripture, that is the measure of worth.[10]

At the center of this persuasive circle sits the metaphor itself, "the church is our mother," demanding childlike obedience to a particular worldly establishment as if differences of ideology did not exist. Of course, it was in Hall's interest to claim that they did not, and he continued to exploit the metaphor in later writings. It is one of the rhetorical moves Milton chose to highlight and criticize in *Animadversions:*

Wee acknowledge, and beleeve the Catholick reformed Church, and if any man be dispos'd to use a trope or figure, as Saint *Paul* once did in calling her the common Mother of us all let him doe as his owne rethorick shall perswade him. If therefore we must needs have a mother, and if the Catholick Church onely be, and must be she, let all Genealogie tell us if it can, what we must call the Church of *England*, unlesse we shall make every English Protestant a kind of poeticall *Bacchus*, to have two Mothers: but marke Readers, the crafty scope of these Prelates, they endeavour to impresse deeply into weak, and superstitious fancies the awfull notion of a mother, that hereby they might cheat them into a blind and implicite obedience to whatsoever they shall decree, or think fit. . . . Whatsoever they say she sayes, must be a deadly sin of disobedience not to beleeve. So that we . . . should now, if we be not betimes aware of these wily teachers, sink under the slavery of a Female notion, the cloudy conception of a demy-Iland mother. (727–28)

The prelates' general design, which was to redirect the energies of belief from the kind demonstrated at the beginning to the kind described at the end ("blind and implicite obedience") could not be more clearly traced. In particular Milton reveals his understanding of two interconnected stages: Hall's own trick, first, which is to use the conventional image for a rhetorical ploy in which it is both deliberately "cloudy" and commanding; and the prelates' larger plan, of which Hall's rhetoric is only a part, which is to replace obedience to the true church with obedience to *this* church. For Milton, episcopal self-pleading is directed finally at elevating a group of men to worldly power.

The style I have been discussing is by no means linked to a particular image, however, though it is often used for ends similar to the one above. Its later manifestations are usually less powerful and terse, but more open and relaxed, and therefore not as obviously pressuring. Here is another example from the *Humble Remonstrance:*

The wisedome of the ancient Grecians went so farre, as to forbid the removall of a well setled evill; But, if religion teach us better things, and tell us, that nothing morally evill, can be setled well: and being, however, setled, had the more need to be (after too long delay) removed; Yet right reason, and sound experience informe us, that things indifferent, or good, having been by continuance, and generall approbation well rooted in Church, or State; may not upon light grounds be pulled up.[11]

Stylistically this is an anti-Ciceronian loose period completely different from the abrupt curtness of the preceding example; yet it has a similar shape. The logical progression of statement, qualification, and return here is identical to that found in the preceding sentence, though the negatives are reversed. The movement appears to be dialectical. The initial thesis is stated in the first member, the qualifying antithesis in the second ("But, if religion . . . removed"), and the final synthesis in the third ("Yet right reason . . . informe us"). Yet the sentence is really a parody of dialectic, for while the first two clauses at least answer one another in specific terms (they deal with the question of removing evil), the final synthesis completely changes the issue, substituting merely the familiar vagueness, "things indifferent, or good." Hall thereby is able to move authority back again to "continuance, and generall approbation . . . in Church, or State." To be sure, the first clauses are not complete throwaways; their agreeable pieties serve some of the purposes of diversionary moves, drawing attention to irrelevant questions of history and philosophy and away from the crux to follow. The distinction Hall is attempting to make leaves open and undefined the central question — "what constitutes things indifferent, and how are they to be used?" — in a logical context that implicitly requires its being answered.

   This vagueness is something we have already seen in Hall's "cloudy conception of a demy-Iland mother," and Milton fully appreciated the varieties of its use in his opponent's works. Thus, we find him pointing out exactly Hall's move here when he describes the bishop as a schemer trying to delude his audience by "scattering among his periods ambiguous words, whose interpretation he will afterwards dispence according to his pleasure; laying before us universall propositions, and then thinks when he will to pinion them with a limitation" (694). Yet at the same time Hall's vagueness on central matters like indifferency and authority does not seem to have been something he took great pains to hide. How-

ever underhanded his dialectic may appear, in fact his refusal to specify
the nature of indifferency or the elements of the set of things indifferent
is part of his larger conscious intent. In a passage from an earlier work
Hall places one of his obscurer conceptions in an unusual and revealing
light:

Surely, as God is but one, and ever himself; so would he have his Church. There
may be threescore queens, and fourscore concubines, and virgins without number; but his Dove, his undefiled, is but one: and, though she may go in several
dresses and trimmings; yet, still and ever, the stuff is the same. Plainly, though
there may be varieties of circumstantial fashions in particular Churches; yet the
substance of the government is, and must ever be, the same.[12]

Here we have three brief circling movements which parallel one
another. The way in which the first two sentences move from plain
statement to apparent qualification only to return to a reassertion of the
initial point ("and, though . . . yet, still and ever") does not again need
explaining, although the particular method here differs from the cases
quoted above. Here it is the concept of "one," introduced at the beginning rather than at the end, that undergoes transformation and opens
itself up for something like the loading of value performed on "indifferency" earlier. The pattern is revealing because each succeeding version
of the circle is a slight variation on the first. The loose hyperbolic wit of
the "threescore queens . . . fourscore concubines . . . virgins without
number" in the first version cannot be directly translated into the
"dresses and trimmings" of the second, or the gray abstraction, "varieties of circumstantial fashions," in the third, without some loss. There is
even greater loss in the second member of each antithesis. The "Dove
. . . undefiled" and even the inelegant "stuff" of the first two clauses
are sufficiently vague to permit the reader to imagine, if he wishes, that
the church of multiplied forms and the church of integrated unity are
located in different realms. Hall might be distinguishing the external
church perceived and ruled by men from God's other temple in the soul
of each true believer. But his metaphors do not cut that deeply. He is
rather trying to give divine sanction to an exterior structure without
worrying about inner problems at all, and this forces him to retreat
from his interesting initial statement until, after two successive translations, he can be sure his reader has gotten it right: "Yet the substance *of
the government* is, and must ever be, the same" (emphasis added).
Thus, behind the flourish of three paralleled restatements of his idea,
there is a smaller, subtler movement in which the *unity* of Christ's beloved is eroded ultimately to the uni*form*ity (beyond a few "circum-

stantial fashions") of the "substance of the government." And in a work entitled *Episcopacy by Divine Right* that phrase included the hierarchy of bishops and priests.

What Milton must have found most irritating about Hall's style was not so much his automatic tendency to compromise, or even his deceitful vagueness, though these are important. Rather it was his apparent willingness to give up exactly as much of his ground as he needed to gain his point. The point, after all, lay not in the defense of an ideal, but in recruitment. If he could bring his reader to agree with him, he had won. In a general attack in the preface to *Animadversions,* Milton in turn defined very accurately Hall's characteristic way of proceeding:

Who can be a greater enemy to Mankind, who a more dangerous deceiver then he who defending a traditionall corruption uses no common Arts, but with a wily Stratagem of yeelding to the time a greater part of his cause, seeming to forgo all that mans invention hath done therein, and driven from much of his hold in Scripture, yet leaving it hanging by a twin'd threed, not from divine command, but from Apostolicall prudence or assent, as if he had the surety of some rouling trench, creeps up by this meanes to his relinquish't fortresse of divine authority againe. (663)

Masson pointed out that Milton referred here to Hall's apparent abandonment in the *Remonstrance* of the argument for the divine origin of bishops he had made in *Episcopacy by Divine Right*.[13] It is a measure of the fundamental relationship of style and content in Hall's work that Milton here is also offering a criticism of Hall's controversial style of thought, a style which shaped his sentences, his tracts, and his career. The "stratagem" Milton describes is a precise chart of Hall's circular rhetoric: the movement outward, relinquishing or weighing or qualifying or examining, followed by the inevitable return. What is more, the style of Milton's own sentence here imitates, almost too obviously, that of his opponent. The middle of the period is taken up with a long series of suspended participial modifiers ("yeelding . . . seeming . . . driven . . . leaving") which describes the "movement outward," the movement of qualification and meditation. After these the long-suspended predicate, "creeps up by this meanes," is even more inexorable in its closing than the circling return it describes. Milton's sentence traces Hall's style in a distorting mirror. It is a parody whose effect is not ridicule but exposure.

Except for a few deliberate parodies, Milton's stylistic relation to Hall could never be simple imitation. Exposure of even the most deceitful rhetorical practice is by itself too limited a purpose, its rewards too small. In developing an efficient and flexible prose style Milton paid much more attention to broader controversial and prophetic aims. As controversial works, his early prose tracts define a coherent view of religious discipline and prescribe a course of action, primarily by sorting out and clarifying perspectives on the many subsidiary questions raised in the debate about episcopacy. As prophetic works they envision and celebrate the possibility of a fully reformed society, in which subsidiary questions and the prose controversies they provoke will have vanished, and in which the only question will be the primary one, "do we serve God or Mammon?" Milton's early prose style is complex because it grows directly from the convergence of different and potentially conflicting motives.[14]

Yet when we remember that his attacks on Hall were almost the first pieces of prose English Milton wrote, we may begin to suspect that the bishop had at least a negative influence on his style. In part Milton's overall strategy was determined by his role of adversary. In criticizing Hall's arguments Milton resorted largely to redefining: exposing and correcting the "Remonstrant's" lies, turning the slanders of the "Modest Confutor" upon himself, purging and redeeming from the prelatical grasp the vocabulary of church government and worship. And all, even the most venomous accusation, was hurled at the opponent with the intent of instructing the reader: "For this my aime is, if I am forc't to be unpleasing to him whose fault it is, I shall not forget at the same time to be usefull in some thing to the stander by" (878–79).

Milton's wish simply "to be usefull" helps explain his stylistic practice. The traditional aims of Ciceronian rhetoric were to teach, to delight, and to move or persuade.[15] Joseph Hall, like his predecessors in the oratorical tradition, was most interested in the last of these. As we have seen, Hall often tries to move without teaching. But Milton rarely attempts to develop a purely persuasive argument. He often appears to want to teach without moving, and he cultivated a style whose purpose is to alienate the reader, to distance him from the passion and distortion at the center of the controversy in order to discourage his emotional identification with either side, to decrease the reader's susceptibility to sophistic flattery (his own and the remonstrant's), and to encourage his cooler exercise of choice. Needless to say, Milton's ultimate purpose was to win his audience to his side, but the victory he wanted was fundamentally different from Hall's: the bishop mainly wanted his audience's votes; perhaps prompted by his example, the younger Puritan insisted on having their minds.

The alienating distance Milton maintains in these early prose works is accomplished in a number of ways. Most simply (as in the sentence from *Animadversions* quoted earlier) he will address his opponent directly, leaving the reader out of the controversy. At other times he will address the reader directly but will preface his remarks with a theatrical gesture whereby he becomes a teacher addressing a pupil: "Trust this man, Readers, if you please, whose divinity would reconcile *England* with *Rome*" (671); "Wee see you are in choler, therefore till you coole a while wee turne us to the ingenious Reader. See how this *Remonstrant* . . ." (693); "Be not deceav'd, Reader, by men that would overawe your eares with big names" (945). These and other simple dramatic devices work firmly to place the reader outside the controversy which Milton simultaneously insists he understand and participate in.

More subtly, Milton controls his reader's distance from and relation to the controversy through a number of disruptive stylistic devices. The traditional oratorical period is generally long and intricately subordinate, yet almost always grammatically regular and unsurprising. Regularity is necessary for the sentence's patterns of clausal suspension and fulfillment to have their cumulative effect. Milton's sentences are likewise long and intricate, but they frequently violate rather than fulfill syntactic development and grammatical order. Specifically, Milton will join the typical pattern of suspensions and dependencies of a Ciceronian period with the looser linkages of anti-Ciceronian style, disrupting expectation and destroying the sense of finality and completeness the period strives to achieve.

For example, Milton often uses the trailing clause, a device of the loose style in which a new member of a sentence is subordinated to the final word or phrase of the preceding clause, not to its general idea or main word.[16] At one point in *Animadversions* he is attacking the Anglican insistence on a fixed liturgy and defending spontaneous prayer:

A Minister that cannot be trusted to pray in his own words without being chew'd to, and fescu'd to a formal injunction of his rote-lesson, should as little be trusted to Preach, besides the vain babble of praying over the same things immediatly againe, for there is a large difference in the repetition of some patheticall ejaculation rays'd out of the suddain earnestnesse and vigour of the inflam'd soul, (such as was that of *Christ* in the Garden) from the continual rehearsal of our dayly orisons, which if a man shall kneel down in a morning and say over, and presently in an other part of the Room kneel down again, and in other words ask but still for the same things as it were out of one Inventory, I cannot see how he will escape that heathenish Battologie of multiplying words which *Christ* himselfe that has the putting up of our Praiers told us would not be acceptable in heaven. (682)

Except for one awkward parenthetical intrusion ("besides the vaine babble"), the first half of this sentence is an ordinary period. The grammatical subject in the first words ("A Minister") is followed by a subordinate clause which parallels the predicate it has delayed, and the period closes with a subordinate clause joining two parallel prepositional phrases: "A Minister that cannot be trusted . . . should as little be trusted . . . for there is a large difference in . . . from . . ." But the sentence continues with a trailing clause ("which if a man shall kneel down") and in a surprising shift opens up a new main clause ("I cannot see how he will escape"), which is in turn followed and finally closed by a new trailing clause ("which *Christ* himselfe . . . told us . . .").

The technique and rhetorical effect of this sentence are typical in Milton's prose. The later members of the sentence introduce a new series of grammatical subjects — "orison," the antecedent of "which," is replaced successively by "a man," "I," "Battologie," and "Christ." Simultaneously there is a new momentum; each of the last five clauses is slightly longer than the one preceding it. Thus the later members destroy the hierarchy of subordination, the effect of cumulative rise and fall, and above all the unity, the sense of coherence that the oratorical period normally strives for. The sentence drains energy and directs our attention from the formal architecture of clausal balance and dependency to the surprising truths that can turn up within parentheses, "(such as was that of *Christ* in the Garden)," or doubly subordinated as an afterthought, "which *Christ* himselfe that has the putting up of our Praiers." In its exuberant growth it shatters the bonds of its own making, and perfectly illustrates the effect of "earnestnesse and vigour" on sentences as well as in Psalms.

Another way Milton has of introducing unsettling effects in his sentences is to distort the shape of the oratorical period from within by swelling one of its members disproportionately. In the following sentence he combines this with a pair of trailing clauses:

If others may chance to spend more time with you [the remonstrant] in canvassing later antiquity, I suppose it is not for that they ground themselves thereon; but that they endeavor by shewing the corruption, incertainties, and disagreements of those Volumes, and the easines of erring, or overslipping in such a boundlesse and vast search, if they may not convince those that are so strongly perswaded thereof; yet to free ingenuous minds from that over-awfull esteeme of those more ancient then trusty fathers whom custome and fond opinion, weake principles, and the neglect of sounder and superior knowledge hath exalted so high, as to have gain'd them a blind reverence: whose Books in bignesse, and number so endlesse, and immesurable, I cannot think that either God or nature, either divine, or humane wisdome did ever meane should bee a rule or reliance to us in the decision of any weighty, and positive Doctrine. (698–99)

As before, the trailing clauses drain energy from the earlier members, denying them the self-contained force of closure. But the cumulative force of the period had already been diminished considerably by its internal distention: the predicate, "endeavor," is separated from its infinitive complement, "to free ingenuous minds," by three lines of print. Again, if the sentence were trimmed of its internal interruption so that the word order moved naturally ("they endeavor to free ingenuous minds") and of the second trailing clause, it would have the shape and momentum of a perfect period. The long awkward separation between verb and infinitive serves, however, to clog the forward motion of the sentence, miring the reader in the "corruptions, incertainties, and disagreements" of the fathers, and so graphically illustrating the wisdom of Milton's avoiding them altogether.

It would be possible to multiply similar examples endlessly, and to show a variety of other disruptive, "alienating" techniques, like complex syntactic constructions, false parallels, and double negatives that require patient working out;[17] pages of sentences beginning with connectives ("for," "and," "wherefore," "wherein," etc.) which contribute to our sense of Milton's argument flowing "like currents in a mixed stream," but which weaken the smaller rhythms of individual sentences;[18] and several dramatic examples of anacoluthon (for example, 699, 702, 942), where the developing grammar of a sentence is simply abandoned before its completion, at times with great violence. These stylistic features, which I have called disruptive, all have the general effect of forcing a distance between the reader and the text, and of preventing the easy exchange of syntactic consolation for belief which operates in conventional rhetorical situations. One of a great orator's strongest arguments can be the beauty of his falling cadences, because the listener's desire to share an aesthetic experience will lead him to an easy assent. In developing a periodic structure in which the rhythms are broken and the cadences torn Milton at once encourages and frustrates identification. Further, as I have tried to show in my analyses, his stylistic intrusions often take on a meaningful shape of their own, and serve to clarify or at least reflect the content. Thus, while Milton seems to want his reader to stand off, he is at pains to make him understand. Milton's prose style is an attempt to present truth and seek agreement not on rhetoric's terms but on truth's. That is what makes it at the same time difficult and compelling.

The full range of strategies and effects available to Milton in his prose writing must await a definitive study. Nevertheless it is possible to suggest some ways in which the disruptive techniques I have pointed to serve larger aims and coherences, although I must quote Milton at some length in his discussion of a difficult issue. Prelates like Hall claimed that the existing establishment was necessary to insure a learned and adequately paid clergy, and they attacked the ignorance and poverty they felt Presbyterianism would lead to. Milton replies:

What would it avail us to have a hireling Clergy though never so learned? For such can have neither true wisdom nor grace, and then in vain do men trust in learning, where these be wanting. If in lesse noble and almost mechanik arts according to the difinitions of those Authors, he is not esteem'd to deserve the name of a compleat Architect, and excellent Painter, or the like, that beares not a generous mind above the peasantly regard of wages, and hire; much more must we thinke him a most imperfect, and incompleate Divine, who is so farre from being a contemner of filthy lucre; that his whole divinity is moulded and bred up in the beggarly, and brutish hopes of a fat Prebendary, Deanery, or Bishoprick, which poore and low pitch't desires, if they doe but mixe with those other heavenly intentions that draw a man to this study, it is justly expected that they should bring forth a baseborn issue of Divinity like that of those imperfect, and putrid creatures that receive a crawling life from two most unlike procreants the Sun, and mudde. And in matters of Religion, there is not anything more intollerable, then a learned foole, or a learned Hypocrite, the one is ever coopt up at his empty speculations, a sot, an ideot for any use that mankind can make of him, or else sowing the World with nice, and idle questions and with much toyle, and difficulty wading to his auditors up to the eyebrows in deep shallows that wet not the instep: a plaine unlearned man that lives well by that light which he has, is better, and wiser, and edifies others more towards a godly and happy life then he: The other is still using his sophisticated arts and bending all his studies how to make his insatiate avarice, & ambition seem pious, and orthodoxall by painting his lewd and deceitfull principles with a smooth, and glossy varnish in a doctrinall way to bring about his wickedest purposes. In stead of the great harme therefore that these men feare upon the dissolving of Prelates, what an ease, and happinesse will it be to us, when tempting rewards are taken away, that the cunningest and most dangerous mercenaries will cease of themselves to frequent the fold, whom otherwise scarce all the prayers of the faithfull could have kept back from devouring the flock? But a true Pastor of Christs sending hath this especiall mark, that for greatest labours, and greatest merits in the Church, he requires either nothing, if he could so subsist, or a very common and reasonable supply of humane necessaries: Wee cannot therefore doe better then to leave this care of ours to God, he can easily send labourers into his Harvest, that shall not cry, Give give, but be contented with a moderate and beseeming allowance; nor will he suffer true learning to be wanting, where true grace, and our obedience to him abounds: for if he give us to know him aright, and to practice this our knowledge in right establisht discipline, how much more will hee replenish us with all abilities in tongues and arts, that may conduce to his glory, and our good? (720–21)

In the broadest sense the passage moves from pondering a pair of false oppositions to focusing on a true one — the issue at the beginning and through most of the selection seems to be deciding between money and poverty, learning and ignorance. Specific values are assigned to specific things. But by the end these have been redefined in terms rather of God's learning versus man's. The question turns out to be not where the pastor's "treasures" are (in pursuing learning or not) but where his heart is. Peripheral issues are resolved by a movement toward the center of things. The opposition defined at the end of the passage is *the* final one.

What is important is that the false notions of worldly things that Milton purges out are *our* notions, or at least notions we have been encouraged temporarily to entertain. The author's biblical head-shaking over "filthy lucre" (1 Timothy iii, 3) is easy to share; it is more difficult to distinguish between vile cash and a "reasonable supply of humane necessaries." What appeared to be an easily discerned difference in kind (money is bad), becomes a more subtle matter of degree (some money is bad); perhaps there is no difference in appearance at all. As he will do in other writings Milton here points out a boundary line which he refrains from drawing clearly, leaving it to the understanding of each reader to complete.[19]

The presentation of alternatives early in the passage is carefully phrased, even at the expense of some awkwardness, to encourage a dichotomizing where dichotomies should not exist. The attack on the "Divine, who is . . . farre from being a contemner of filthy lucre," naturally suggests that the ideal is a divine who does condemn filthy lucre. The "especiall mark" of the "true Pastor" (notice how that language encourages us to expect the easiest of differentiating signs) is that "for greatest labours, and greatest merits in the Church, he requires either nothing, if he could so subsist, or a very common and reasonable supply of humane necessaries." We need not regard either of these suggestions of uncompromising opposition to material gain as a wholly ironic glance at impossible perfection. Milton certainly believed that the removal of "tempting rewards" would help improve the clergy by at least weeding out opportunists. Yet he also realized that poverty was neither a guarantee nor a requirement of virtue; he attacked monkish sloth as readily as he attacked prelatical avarice. The important thing is "greatest labours and greatest merits in the Church": if the pastor actually qualifies for this distinction, the ideal can readily give way to reality (even a Christian hero must eat); if he does not, the ideal that the pastor could subsist on nothing becomes meaningless, its fulfillment a pointless effort.

The oppositions of learning/ignorance and money/poverty are given impetus by the characteristic syntactic dislocations with which they are presented. The third sentence of the selection, "If in less noble and almost mechanik arts . . . ," is the first of two lengthy periods in which the dichotomizing tendency reaches its extreme point. The sentence begins with an intricate but fairly clear analogy and proceeds to contrast, in a straightforward periodic structure, the pastoral calling: "much more must we thinke him . . . who is so farre . . . that his whole divinity. . . ." Having apparently concluded the main clause, in which closure is reinforced by the alliterated *b*'s and the rhythmic listing, "Prebendary, Deanery, or Bishoprick," Milton appends a trailing clause: "which poor and low pitch't desires, if they doe but mixe . . . it is justly expected . . . issue of Divinity like that of . . . the Sun and mudde." By its length and complication the trailing clause takes over the syntactic movement of the sentence, achieving a life of its own at the expense of the earlier periodic stability, again with relevance to the meaning: the burgeoning growth of the appended clause mirrors the procreation and uncontrolled proliferation of the base offspring produced when "heavenly intentions" are coupled with the desire for ecclesiastical preferment.

The second syntactic dislocation occurs in the next sentence and is the more significant of the two. The initial clause divides for consideration two examples of the misuse of learning — the "learned fool" and the "learned Hypocrite." It is followed by the firmest attack on learning in the passage. As with "filthy lucre," we may understand in the abstract that not all learning, merely corrupted learning, is being criticized. But it is hard to see where the distinction, or Milton's appreciation of it, is given any expression at this stage. The "empty speculations" (with a pun perhaps on *speculum*), the "sowing the World with nice, and idle questions" (parodying the task of the true pastor, Proverbs xi, 18, Isaiah xxxii, 20, etc.), the "sophisticated arts" and "painting [of] . . . lewd and deceitful principles with a smooth, and glossy varnish in a doctrinall way": all these pressure the reader to devalue learning and even to identify it with corruption.

The tendency to identify learning and corruption is most encouraged by the unexpected interruption of the normal and preestablished order of the two character sketches ("the one . . . the other") with a portrait of the virtuous opposite of both our vicious preachers: "A plaine unlearned man that lives well by that light which he has, is better, wiser, and edifies others more towards a godly and happy life then he." Purposely placed at the end of the clause, "then he" may refer forward to the hypocrite or backward to the fool. The central position of the interruption places it syntactically in contrast to and apart from both of its neighbors, and the contrast is further emphasized stylistically: note the relative plainness and clarity bestowed by the absence of strong, particularly motional, verbs. "Sowing," "wading," "still using," "bending," and "painting" in the outer clauses, are a bustle of directionless activity; the plain man "lives well" and "edifies others," revealing a carefully worked-out priority of affections that contrasts with the fool's self-regarding "speculations" and the hypocrite's self-glorifying sophistry.

All this is to indicate the thorough and complex stylistic shape of the "interruption." Its effect in the perspective of the whole passage is to ratify the movement of denying learning altogether. From the very beginning the disturbing truth that a hireling clergy might have the advantage of learning was allowed to suggest that a learned clergy, committed to the more contemplative forms of pastoral action, would be necessarily hireling. At least, the easy movement from one to the other was not discouraged. "Unlearned is pure" is the corollary to "learned is corrupt"; the importance of the character sketch is that here, as never before, we are being asked to accept both evaluations. It is appropriate that immediately following this sentence the learning and money oppositions are nearly identified: when "tempting rewards" are taken away, the "cunningest" will cease to prey on the flock of Christ.

But of course "cunning" is not "learning"(though it readily uses learning), and not all money is temptation. If the "especiall mark" of the true pastor is that like everyone else he needs food, clothing and shelter (although presumably he does not worship them), the central characteristic of Christian learning is that it is Christian: "We cannot therefore doe better then to leave this care of ours to God." Once that is done, once the Christian moves to and decides the central question ("serve God or Mammon"), the other questions, the apparent either/or choices with which he has been surrounded, will resolve or vanish: "nor will he suffer true learning to be wanting, where true grace, and our obedience to him abounds." The pressure to devalue learning as in itself corrupt disappears. The change in the course of the passage is not simply that Milton draws a new distinction — "not all learning is corrupt; it can be good or bad depending on its use" — though this may be the most obvious message we take away. The change is more exactly that we are brought to understand which distinctions and divisions really matter. When we decide "to leave this care of ours to God," we are moving to a level of first principles next to which the simple either/or world of easily identified polarities (plain unlearned purity versus greedy learned corruption) seems trivial. That does not mean that simple purity and subtle corruption do not exist; but their characterizations are purposely placed in a situation allowing of facile moral identification precisely in order that the attempt at such identification may be transcended. The values we had thought to be out in the world are really to be found in us. Our choice, and the strength of our long-range commitment, will determine the worth of our possessions. "But seek ye first the kingdom of God and his righteousness, and all these things shall be added unto you" (Matthew vi, 33).

This is the rhetorical effect Milton's prose style is capable of having, an effect totally alien to Joseph Hall's heavy-handed manipulation and verbal fog. The tensions and disruptions created in a prose whose periodic substructure is in direct conflict with its rhetorical surface can result in a unique relationship: the reader is liberated from a nonpersuasive text to exercise choice at the very moment when the prose reformulates the choices available in a completely new and clarified context. To move from the strained and almost shattered Ciceronian periods of the center of our excerpt to the final loose Senecan sentence ("But a true Pastor . . ."), its members lying contiguously like the shards of a broken mirror, is to move from the temptation of an essentially easy wholeness of vision based on efforts of simple moral identification (as, in our reading, we engage in the parallel effort to apprehend and retain the wholeness of a sentence stretched by syntactic intrusion and asymmetry), to a truer and more complex wholeness next to which our previous coherences fall away. In refusing a traditional style Milton relinquished at least the last two of Cicero's three aims of teaching, delighting, and moving, together with their abuses. But in adopting a rhetoric of choice he created a style capable of dramatizing and effecting a progress of understanding, insight, vision.[20]

The criticisms which in various forms have been directed at the disorderliness of Milton's prose style all approach it with a set of assumptions Milton himself rejected. In style, as in church worship, he was resolute and consistent in his refusal to fix rigid evaluations on the habiliments of form and action. We saw this in our initial comparison of

Milton and Hall; it is arguably the central informing attitude of the prose, and it is what makes a simple description of "Milton's characteristic style" in the final sense impossible.

Wright State University

NOTES

1. *Complete Prose Works of John Milton*, ed. Don M. Wolfe et al. (New Haven, 1953), I, p. 934. All quotations from Milton's prose in this essay are taken from this edition. Page numbers will be cited in the text.

2. George Williamson, *The Senecan Amble: A Study in Prose Form from Bacon to Collier* (Chicago, 1951), p. 247, notes this change in Hall's style and comments that "Milton's appraisal is truer of the earlier Hall." Williamson discusses some of the stylistic aspects of the quarrel between Milton and Hall, pp. 209–14. A good general discussion, though it omits stylistic considerations, is that of Audrey Chew, "Joseph Hall and John Milton," *ELH*, XVII (1950), 274–95. Chew especially stresses the broad similarities in outlook of the two men, an important point which is weakened somewhat by the writer's frequent use of Hall's early works to determine views he may have held in 1641. T. F. Kinloch, *The Life and Works of Joseph Hall, 1574–1656* (London, 1951), notes that Hall's views changed between 1634 and 1638, when he was being promoted by Laud and the King; cf. ch. 6, passim, esp. pp. 153ff.

3. *An Humble Remonstrance to the High Court of Parliament* (London, 1640 [i.e., 1641]), pp. 6–8.

4. "The Baroque Style in Prose," in *Style, Rhetoric, and Rhythm: Essays by Morris W. Croll*, ed. J. Max Patrick, Robert O. Evans, et al. (Princeton, N.J., 1966), pp. 207–33.

5. In describing this and other sentences as "circular" I do not want to imply that they take the form of the "circular" or "rounded period" (from *circuitus*), periods whose movement rises to and falls from a climactic main clause at the center, surrounded by piled-up subordinate clauses. The circle is the best metaphor for a sentence which, beginning from a tentatively stated initial position, traces a movement outward of speculation and qualification and returns to a reaffirmation of the original position at the end. Both thought and style are usually involved. See Joan Webber's *Contrary Music: The Prose Style of John Donne* (Madison, Wisc., 1963), p. 34.

6. The idea of the prose tracts as missiles has been fruitfully developed by Joan Webber, *The Eloquent "I": Style and Self in Seventeenth-Century Prose* (Madison, Wisc., 1968), p. 204.

7. Joseph Hall, *Works*, ed. Peter Hall (Oxford, 1837), VI, p. 179.

8. See, for example, John Donne, *Essays in Divinity*, ed. Evelyn Simpson (Oxford, 1952), p. 51; *Complete Sermons*, ed. George R. Potter and Evelyn M. Simpson (Berkeley and Los Angeles, 1953), VI, p. 284; and "Holy Sonnet" #18 ("Show me dear Christ"). The subject is discussed by Sir Herbert J. C. Grierson, "John Donne and the 'Via Media,'" *PMLA*, XLIII (1948), 305–14.

9. Don M. Wolfe, introd., YP, I, pp. 28–33. Wolfe speaks of Hall's mastery of "the genius of compromise."

10. See Bacon's "A Wise and Moderate Discourse on Church Affairs," rptd. as "An Advertisement Touching the Controversies of the Church of England," in *The Works of Francis Bacon*, ed. James Spedding et al. (1861; rpt. Stuttgart-Bad Cannstatt, 1962), VIII, pp. 86–90. Elsewhere Hall comments on the need to defend order in the Church against the divisiveness of the schismatics, as in the *Apology against Brownists:* "Not so much the ceremonies are stood upon, as obedience. . . . What is commanded matters not so much, as by whom" (*Works*, X, p. 91). See also his *Letter to Mr. W. Struthers* (X, 116), and Archbishop Laud's *Speech Concerning Pretended Innovations in the Church* (London, 1637), pp. 53–54.

11. *An Humble Remonstrance*, p. 19.

12. *Episcopacy by Divine Right*, in *Works*, X, p. 242.

13. David Masson, *Life of Milton*, II, p. 258, as quoted in YP, I, p. 663 n.

14. In *The Politics of Milton's Prose Style*, Yale Studies in English 185 (New Haven, 1975), Keith W. Stavely emphasizes only one of these aspects, the prophetic. In his insistence on Milton's utopianism and his desire to contrast the poet's impractical reveries with the engaged radical writing he admires, Stavely overlooks an element of practical, even calculating realism with which Milton infuses his work, and which exists, astonishingly, even at the very center of some of his most visionary prose. This does not usually affect the accuracy of Stavely's description or the penetration of his best analyses.

15. See for example *De Oratore*, II, xxvii, 115; *Orator*, xxi, 69.

16. The trailing effect was described first by Croll, "The Baroque Style in Prose," p. 224. Stavely (*The Politics*, p. 8), first noted its importance in Milton.

17. This complexity has often received comment, mostly negative, as in K. G. Hamilton, "The Structure of Milton's Prose," in *Language and Style in Milton: A Symposium in Honor of the Tercentenary of "Paradise Lost,"* ed. Ronald David Emma and John T. Shawcross (New York, 1967), pp. 304–32. In the positive direction, Richard Weaver years ago pointed out the "heroic effort" certain sentences deliberately require of the reader: "Milton's Heroic Prose," in his *The Ethics of Rhetoric* (Chicago, 1953), pp. 143–63. The interpretive effort required by Milton's syntax is partly the subject of Stanley E. Fish, "'Reason' in *The Reason of Church Government*," in his *Self-Consuming Artifacts: The Experience of Seventeenth-Century Literature* (Berkeley and Los Angeles, 1972), pp. 265–302.

18. The phrase is J. Max Patrick's; Foreword to *Areopagitica*, *The Prose of John Milton* (New York, 1967), p. 253.

19. Another example is the boundary line Milton implies but never draws in *Areopagitica* between superstitious and papist books and all the others whose free publication Milton pleads for.

20. I have adapted the phrase "rhetoric of choice" from Leslie Brisman's *Milton's Poetry of Choice and its Romantic Heirs* (Ithaca, N.Y., 1973); see especially ch. 1. For further treatment of choice as an element of Milton's prose see my "Context and Method of Milton's Early English Prose," Diss. Johns Hopkins 1976, ch. 1.

COUPLING LOGIC AND
MILTON'S DOCTRINE OF DIVORCE

Lana Cable

W HEN MILTON'S *Doctrine and Discipline of Divorce* came out
on 1 August 1643, it caused an immediate sensation.[1] Copies
sold well enough to justify a second edition in six months, and soon after
that a scandalized public could hear Milton denounced in pulpit and
press as a purveyor of heresies and libertinism. As Milton himself makes
clear, it was not a reception to please him.[2] He had wanted to convince,
not to shock; if denied a consensus, he at least desired reasoned debate.
Not one of his attackers had deigned (or dared) to confront him directly
or to challenge his doctrine within what he considered the terms of rational argumentation. Yet that pamphleteering age was far from unaccustomed to radical arguments for reformation. Anticipation of the
millennium had stimulated the reforming zeal of numbers of English
preachers and polemicists, and if by 1643 their hopes (and Milton's with
them) had suffered disillusionment, certainly their habit of controversy
hadn't waned. Milton might even have expected his argument for reformation of divorce laws to gain a significant, though not major, percent-
age of sympathetic hearers. As Michael Fixler points out, most Puritans
"seem to have realized practically, as Milton did explicitly in his divorce
tracts, that social perfection was impossible for any to achieve in the
fallen condition of human nature. The establishment of the condition
for religious or spiritual perfectibility, which must take place within the
world, was not, however, impossible. If it were, the reality or validity
of the essential promise of Christ was at stake."[3] It was as a means toward establishing the condition for spiritual perfectibility that Milton
made his argument for divorce:

How can there els grow up a race of warrantable men, while the house and home
that breeds them, is troubl'd and disquieted under a bondage not of Gods constraining with a natureles constraint (if his most righteous judgements may be our
rule) but laid upon us imperiously in the worst and weakest ages of knowledge.[4]

Why, then, did Milton's argument so profoundly fail of its intended
aim? If, as Milton claimed, many of his detractors had not even read the

143

pamphlet, what was there about it which aroused such vehement opposition? Milton's own answer is that his readers dealt superficially with
him because they were afraid any deeper involvement might show them
the light:

Others . . . confess that wit and parts may do much to make that seem true
which is not . . . and thus thinking themselves discharg'd of the difficulty, love
not to wade furder into the fear of a convincement.[5]

I would suggest that there is in the aggressive rhetorical structure of *The
Doctrine and Discipline of Divorce* precisely that which puts his reader
in "fear of a convincement." Milton does not compose his tract as a carefully reasoned persuasion, classically aimed at winning the confidence
and ultimately the convictions of his audience. Rather, his strategy is to
marshal his arguments into tactical preparedness and then demonstrate, point by point, their prowess. To do this, he uproots and radically redefines common terms, ideas, and assumptions about marriage
and divorce. For example, Milton's central thesis may be baldly stated
as: "Christ's strict prohibition of divorce 'except it be for fornication'
means that a man may divorce for whatever reason he sees fit." On the
face of it, the thesis is startling and self-contradictory; and yet, once we
have thoroughly understood his tract, we can see how Milton makes this
thesis make sense. He constructs his argument upon the framework of a
distinctive pattern of logic which, on examination, proves consistent,
rational and even elegantly appropriate. The present study will show
how the rhetorical strategy operates.

If Milton's treatise antagonized even those who had not read it, one
reason may not be far to seek. His paradoxical thesis and the argument
with which he supports it are altogether no more daring or aggressive
than that part of the tract which even those most in "fear of a convincement" would have read — the title page.[6] Phrase by phrase, Milton leads
us in: "The Doctrine & Discipline of DIVORCE   Restor'd to the good
of both SEXES." The key word is "Restor'd." We do not even need to
know why restoration is being advocated to be cued to a critical first
principle governing the argument which follows. Divorce, it says, is
possessed of a true "doctrine," a right "discipline," an original perfection and correct practice which have fallen into abuse; and the purpose
of this tract is to "restore" that "doctrine and discipline" to its original,
unfallen state. And there is more. To any ordinary understanding, the
word "divorce" means the undoing or breaking of a bond — something
which could not occur unless a bond had been previously established,
and hence something which comes into being only secondarily, after

certain other acts have been performed. Yet the concept of divorce here seems to be granted full realization in the primal order of things. In fact, as the argument of the tract unfolds, we find that the concept of divorce has for Milton an existence prior to the order of things; it is, indeed, an operative principle upon which that very order depends.

But before getting too far ahead, let us return to the remainder of Milton's title, in which gradually our sense of what is to be discovered in the treatise becomes less and less abstract. Whereas the first few words have apparently limitless implications, the phrases which follow clarify and circumscribe the scope of the tract. The doctrine and discipline of divorce is to be "Restor'd to the good of both SEXES" (all mankind will benefit from it), "From the bondage of CANON LAW, and other mistakes" (the adversary, and the situation — "bondage" — are now identified and pejoratively labeled), "to the true meaning of Scripture" (now the authority, terms, and context for the argument are established), "in the Law and Gospel compar'd" (we can expect some sort of dialectic between the Old and New Testaments). The second sentence on the title page is even more explicit: "Wherein also are set down the bad consequences of abolishing or condemning of Sin, that which the Law of God allowes, and Christ abolisht not." This sentence is both a warning and a reassurance: if we fail to attend to the argument of the tract, evil will surely follow; but we may also rest secure in the promise that nothing irregular or contrary to the Scriptures is being advocated. Furthermore, we are reading an improved version of the argument: "Now the second time revised and much augmented, in Two BOOKS"; and as readers we share the document with the august "Parlament of *England* with the Assembly." From the pair of scriptural quotations at the bottom of the title page, we may gather that we are to receive fresh, inspired insights as well as established truths: "Every Scribe instructed to the Kingdom of Heav'n, is like the Maister of a house which bringeth out of his treasury things new and old"; and we are reminded of the wisdom and responsibility of reading with an open mind: "He that answereth a matter before he heareth it, it is folly and shame unto him."

By the time we have worked our way from the top of the title page to the bottom, our expectations about the tract have been carefully prepared. If initially we were struck by the curious attribution to divorce of primal beneficence, our perplexity is soon more or less allayed by the familiar trappings of polemical discourse: advantages to be gained, allusions to resources and authorities, a putative audience, and scriptural quotations. Unless exceptionally wary of "convincement," the reader may overlook the fact that, before the tract begins, the term "divorce" has already been used in a manner wholly unorthodox — used to suggest something proper and right in the original scheme, something which was once practiced freely and well but is now held in unjust captivity, something which in its pure and natural form is associated not with severence but with order and unity. In short, the word "divorce" has been used in such a way as to imply its opposite.[7]

I have suggested that we get a glimpse, in the first words of Milton's title page, of the rhetorical strategy which he employs throughout the tract. Milton's use of the word "divorce" derives not from commonly accepted practice, the criterion which ordinarily governs the application of words. Rather, his use of the word derives from his effort to find out the "truth" of divorce, as if the practice had an ideal form which we are obliged to discover. Such an obligation follows naturally from the contemporary Puritan assumption that all truth is contained in the Scriptures and wants only a fit reader to make it manifestly clear. Since "divorce" appears in Scripture, the truth of divorce must reside there as well, not as established by man, but as ordained by God. For Milton, such truth is organic, generative, and must be cultivated. Those who assume otherwise, those who rely (as we have done if we are disturbed by Milton's title) on the customary usage of terms like "divorce," align themselves with those pretenders to knowledge who would "cry-down the industry of free reasoning, . . . as if the womb of teeming Truth were to be closed up" (p. 224).

Milton's use of the word "divorce" to imply its opposite is just one version of a peculiar turn of logic that characterizes his own "industry of free reasoning" throughout the *Doctrine and Discipline of Divorce*. This same logic is the means whereby the words of Moses and the words of Christ, apparently contradictory, are finally reconciled, so that they no longer conflict but instead reveal themselves as obverse manifestations of a single truth, complementing each other to perfection. Furthermore, variations on this pattern of logic, whereby dichotomies and apparent opposites are joined to produce a transcendent whole, appear so frequently in the *Doctrine and Discipline of Divorce* that it becomes impossible to tell whether their recurrence is always part of an overt strategy. The tract is simply pervaded by a logic that finds — or creates, or compels — accord in the conjunction of seeming disparities. The specific details — the causes and consequences of this recurring pattern — vary considerably with each instance of it; but if we were to cast a symbolic paradigm for the logic of the *Doctrine and Discipline of Divorce*, we could do no better than refer to the dynamics of sexual union. Nor should we therefore be surprised by the terms in which Milton's adversary—he who neither accepts nor understands the logic of the tract—is dismissed:

And if none of these considerations with all their wait and gravity, can avail to the dispossessing him of his precious literalism, let some one or other entreat him but to read on in the same 19. of *Math.* till he come to that place that sayes, *Some make themselves Eunuchs for the kingdom of heavens sake.* And if then he please to make use of *Origens* knife, he may doe well to be his own carver. (p. 334)

If the opponent is true to his own practice and follows the text literally, his just doom will be a deliberate mutilation of his own nature, with the cause and consequence both antisexual and solitary.

Of the several means by which the adversary, who opposes divorce, gets associated with divisive and unprocreative thinking by Milton, who favors divorce, the most obvious is in the accretion of images of perverted or obstructed nature. Kester Svendsen has shown how imagery drawn from the natural sciences—astronomy, anatomy, and medicine—creates an inner structure (aside from traditional rules of rhetoric) for Milton's argument by way of accumulated scientific motifs:

Milton's fundamental comparison, carried all through the tract, amounts to this: canon-law impediments to divorce have created diseases in human society which result in a distortion of nature; Milton's proposals are remedies drawn from nature and natural law. The reasoning in canon law is described as indigestion, disorder of the humours, sores, blots, megrims, and the like. The law of nature is manifested in salves, medicines, and soothing treatments. Constantly expressed or implied is the comparison between truth as health and error as disease, with canon law a pollution, an unhelpful remedy, a producer of still further disease by force exerted against the bent of nature.[8]

The rhetorical structures of scientific metaphor "make the argument as well as support or embellish it." Yet Svendsen's study doesn't point out how often the natural science images are employed in a manner implicitly sexual, with those illustrating the adversary suggestive of perverted sexuality and sterility.

The allegory of Custom and Error in the address to Parliament is the first example of it. As Svendsen and others have noted, Custom and Error are figured as chronic intellectual indigestion, while virtue and conscience are wholesome and generative, related to "the womb of teeming Truth." But there are also sexual implications in the joining of Custom with Error:

To persue the Allegory, Custome being but a meer face, as Eccho is a meere voice, rests not in her unaccomplishment, untill by secret inclination, shee accorporat her self with error, who being a blind and Serpentine body without a head, willingly accepts what he wants, and supplies what her incompleatness went seeking. (p. 223)

The implications in depicting the "meer face" of Custom as female and the "blind and serpentine body" of Error as male are fairly obvious, but it is Custom's "incompleatness" that creates the subtler comment. The union of Custom and Error is a grotesque parody of the Anteros myth that Milton uses later to illustrate the nature of ideal love. Love and Anteros are mutually regenerative, hence each is spiritually incomplete without the other. As a result of mistaken alliances encountered on the long search for his complement, Love has been nearly destroyed; he is "undeifie'd and despoil'd of all his force: till finding *Anteros* at last, he kindles and repairs the almost faded ammunition of his Deity by the reflection of a coequal & *homogeneal* fire" (p. 255). This kind of mutual dependency is as spiritual union ought to be — two individuals uniting to create a higher being than they could have had separately. But stolid Custom interprets "incomplete" literally: she is lacking parts — specifically, a body — and her version of the search for love is to find another "incomplete" entity, a body that lacks a head. Instead of joining as complementary and mutually helpful individuals to form a higher spiritual union, or to become "deified," Custom and Error must join forces merely to make up a single physical body. Such is the process of plodding literalism, whose busy activity cannot transcend the flesh, and whose unregenerative, solitary physicality is capable of bringing forth only the products of a faulty digestion.

Hence it is, that Error supports Custome, Custome count'nances Error, . . . Who with the numerous and vulgar train of their followers, make it their chiefe designe to envie and cry-down the industry of free reasoning, under the terms of humor, and innovations; as if the womb of teeming Truth were to be clos'd up, if shee presume to bring forth ought, that sorts not with their unchew'd notions and suppositions. (pp. 223–24)

The point is not merely that Truth is generative while Custom and Error are dyspeptic, but that Custom and Error in their literalism *think* they have a complementary union which generates Truth, when in fact they have a cooperative solipsism which produces only excrement.

For Milton, falsehood characteristically is most insidious when it parodies truth, when its activities make it appear to the unpracticed eye as "the wholesome habit of soundnesse and good constitution; but is indeed no other, then that swoln visage of counterfeit knowledge . . . filling each estate of life and profession, with abject and servil principles; depressing the high and Heaven-born spirit of Man" (p. 223). The emphasis here should be not on "abject and servil," but on "principles." Milton is not simply stating that Custom has produced the wrong principles, but rather, that Custom is wrong when invoked *as* a principle. Indeed, it is wrong to assume that established principles of any kind can, in and of themselves, be adequate to the vital needs of the human spirit. The establishment of principles can at best be no more than half of the enterprise required to discover truth. It is the other half of that enterprise that Milton is concerned with bringing to his reader's attention. In the case of stated laws, the words of the law are merely the literal half; it is the spiritual half for which Milton argues.

Mark then, Judges and Lawgivers, and yee whose Office is to be our teachers, for I will utter now a doctrine, if ever any other, though neglected or not understood, yet of great and powerful importance to the governing of mankind. He who wisely would restrain the reasonable Soul of man within due bounds, must first himself know perfectly, how far the territory and dominion extends of just and honest liberty. As little must he offer to bind that which God hath loos'n'd, as to loos'n that which he hath bound. The ignorance and mistake of this high point, hath heapt up one huge half of all the misery that hath bin since *Adam.* (pp. 227–28)

Every enterprise must be twofold to be complete; it cannot justly aim at what it intends without giving generous consideration to the possibility of results it would not intend. The ambiguity in Milton's statement of "this high point" is surely deliberate. We are offered a principle, but one which cannot possibly be held by itself as a rule or explicit guideline. Its practical meaning is dependent wholly on the circumstances of the case. In a treatise on divorce, we can assume that man's binding and God's loosening — or man's loosening and God's binding — would refer primarily to the institutions of marriage and divorce. But it is impossible to tell which institution belongs to which agent or action. And yet, we are not wholly without direction. For, if by this time we can intuit (or guess) the probable answer "all," we have already more than half proven our fitness for the enterprise.

But this is not to suggest that Milton advocates anarchy — at least not in the terms we customarily think of. That, needless to say, would be the over-literal reading of "crabbed textuists." When the subject is marriage and divorce, the burden of proof would obviously have to depend not on the letter of the law but on the spirit of the individual case. Thus, an understanding of true marriage becomes indispensable, for by his own precept Milton cannot advocate divorce without a just regard for that "yoke of prudent and manly discipline." In the course of the argument, both marriage and divorce are redefined in terms which surpass customary usage in order to comprehend the spirit of Christian duty and service. For Milton, these are the only valid terms for making such definitions. Thus he approaches the conclusion of his address to the Parliament:

Yet when I remember the little that our Saviour could prevail about this doctrine of Charity against the crabbed textuists of his time, I make no wonder, but rest confident that who so preferrs either Matrimony, or other Ordinance before the good of man and the plain exigence of Charity, let him profess Papist, or Protestant, or what he will, he is no better then a Pharise, and understands not the Gospel: whom as a misinterpreter of Christ I openly protest against; and provoke him to the trial of this truth before all the world: and let him bethink him how he will solder up the shifting flaws of his ungirt permissions, his venial and unvenial dispenses, wherewith the Law of God pardoning and unpardoning hath bin shamefully branded, for want of heed in glossing, to have eluded and baffled out all Faith and chastity from the mariagebed of that holy seed, with politick and judicial adulteries. (p. 233)

The idea of marriage is by no means abandoned in its demystified status as "Matrimony, or other Ordinance." Even as Milton deflates its worldly authority, he reinvests the idea of marriage with higher meaning, establishing it as a locus of heavenly truth. By envisioning "that holy seed" which is "the Law of God" as engendered in "the mariagebed" of the Scriptures, Milton raises the idea of marriage to the highest level, while the patrons of matrimonial ordinance become cosmic adulterers. Thus emerges the paradigmatic union of disparities which enables attainment of a higher truth: to the ineffable workings of the Supreme Being, Milton ascribes precisely that copulative act which the pharisees idolize, and Milton himself debunks, as the prime end of marriage. This shift of meanings has been accomplished through a complicated syntactical maneuver. At first "the Law of God" seems to be implicated in the pharisaical practices of "pardoning and unpardoning," eluding and baffling. Then, after the word "mariagebed," the law of God is identified as "that holy seed" and thus made the victim of "politick and judicial adulteries." Because of the initially ambiguous status of "the Law of God," and because the qualities of "Faith and chastity" are ordinarily categorized among human virtues, it seems for a moment that the eluding and baffling is suffered by humans; hence "mariagebed" apparently refers to the corporal union of human marriage. But with the words "holy seed," all these terms must be reassigned godly, spiritual, or scriptural meanings. Nevertheless, since the image of engendering in a marriage bed remains, as an image, insistently human, the effect of the passage is not finally to dislocate our concept of marriage from a worldly, human sphere and reestablish it in a godly one. Rather, it is to evoke both spheres simultaneously — to say that unions of human with human, of the corporal with the spiritual, of man with God, and of the spirit of the Word with the letter of the Word — all, in their truest definition, are one. It is this union, sustained in delicate syntactic balance by the word "mariagebed," which is toppled by the "politick and judicial adulteries" of the pharisees. So, we have marriage and marriage: the matrimony of the modern pharisees is an idol which displaces both God and man, whereas matrimony truly defined is not only ordained by God but is of his essence.

Milton's striking investment of spiritual meanings with erotic imagery is not mere rhetorical sensationalism. Fundamental to the logic of *The Doctrine and Discipline of Divorce* is a belief in the essential unity of body and spirit. In giving precedence to the sufferers of mental as opposed to physical incompatibility, Milton is not devaluing the physical but rather showing the natural dependence in humans of physical powers on spiritual will:

As those Priests of old were not to be long in sorrow, or if they were, they could not rightly execute their function; so every true Christian in a higher order of Priesthood, is a person dedicate to joy and peace, offering himself a lively sacrifice of praise and thanksgiving . . . but in such a bosom affliction as this, crushing the very foundations of his inmost nature, when he shall be forc't to love against a possibility, and to use dissimulation against his soul in the perpetuall and ceaseles duties of a husband, doubtles his whole duty of serving God must needs be blurr'd and tainted with a sad unpreparedness and dejection of spirit, wherein God has no delight. (p. 259)

To undermine the spirit is to undermine the entire worldly office of the Christian. Yet there remains an apparent contradiction in Milton's argument for oneness of body and spirit. One may well ask why it is that this "bosom affliction," of such devastating spiritual import, should most commonly result in the wrongly married man seeking not spiritual counsel but seeking "to piece up his lost contentment by visiting the Stews, or stepping to his neighbor's bed" (p. 247). Milton repeatedly uses this consequence of "hardheartedness of undivorcing" to extend the canonists' culpability beyond the unhappiness of private individuals. Yet this extension of the argument seems to contaminate rather than arouse sympathy for the unhappy man.

One might argue that Milton is cloaking individual indiscretion in societal extensions of the evil, all merely to bully the opposition. But that is not so. When Milton's unhappy man resorts to sexual fulfillment of a spiritual yearning, his manifest duplicity is simply the logical consequence of that separation of body from spirit which the canonists in their literalism had begun. Indeed, even if the man does not openly violate his marriage vows, the consequences of his restraint by canon law differ only in outward appearance. By "suffering his useful life to waste away," he may keep up social forms, but "where love cannot be, there can be left of wedlock nothing, but the empty husk of an outside matrimony; as undelightfull and unpleasing to God, as any other kind of hypocrisie" (pp. 247, 256). The precedence which Milton gives the spiritual over the physical is inclusive, not exclusive; the body cannot finally contain the spirit, but neither can the spirit justly be forced to ignore the body. Separated from the spirit, the body's sexuality becomes something no longer whole or human: it deranges into a kind of combat, "so they be but found suitably weapon'd to the lest possibilitie of sensuall enjoyment" (p. 236); or a form of slavery, "to grind in the mill of an undelighted and servil copulation . . . forc't work . . . with such a yokefellow" (p. 258); it is a trap, "deceitfull bait . . . snare of misery . . . alluring ordinance" (p. 260); or akin to dealing with the devil, "superstitious and impossible performance of an ill-driv'n bargain" (p. 274). By contrast, sexuality enhanced with spiritual union is "that benevolent and intimate communion of body" (p. 263), "that comfortable portion" (p. 256), and "that mystery of joy and union" (p. 258).

Hence, the seeming contradiction — the apparent hypocrisy of the wrongly married man — turns out to be the protest of a victim and material witness to the more elusive but potent and causative hypocrisy of the canonists.

How the peace and perpetuall cohabitation of marriage can be kept, how that benevolent and intimate communion of body can be held with one that must be hated with a most operative hatred, must be forsak'n and yet continually dwelt with and accompanied, he who can distinguish, hath the gift of an affection very odly divided and contriv'd: while others both just and wise, and *Salomon* among the rest, if they may not hate and forsake as *Moses* enjoyns, and the Gospell imports, will find it impossible not to love otherwise than will sort with the love of God, whose jealousie brooks no corrivall. (pp. 263–64)

The canonists' affections are both unnatural ("divided") and artificial ("contriv'd") — idolatries doubly offensive to the spirit of unity that informs *The Doctrine and Discipline of Divorce*. Furthermore, the word "jealousy" subtly maintains another tension between the human and the divine, similar to that sustained by "mariagebed" in the earlier passage. That God is a "jealous" God is a trope of the Judeo-Christian tradition, but for him to be jealous in the context of explicitly sexual human relations requires once again our reassignment of spiritual meanings to the context, at the same time as we do not dispense with the physical meanings. It is the separating of physical love from spiritual love — the "operative hatred" of the spirit compelled by the enforced union of the body — which separates man from God, which makes an idol of the partner and the partnership, and which thus causes man in his literal faithfulness to commit spiritual adultery.

When Milton finally broaches the subject of Christ's actual words to the pharisees, he states a "solid rule" which resembles the "doctrine" or "high point" to which he had earlier referred the members of Parliament: "For this is a solid rule that every command giv'n with a reason, binds our obedience no otherwise then that reason holds" (p. 308). Here, as before, a professedly "solid rule" turns out to be no less than a sanction against what is usually meant by "solid rule": responsibility for the practical meaning of a given law is thrown from the letter of the law back onto the person or persons whom the law is intended to govern. Therefore, once more the principle looks at first as though it encourages anarchy; but in fact, it encourages a higher discipline than any rules could exact through literal obedience. It requires the understanding — man's reason — to interpret and apply the "reason" of the law. Every rule is thus a test of the interpreter: by his reading of the law, he judges himself. So it is that Christ's dealing with the pharisees becomes one more instance in *Doctrine and Discipline of Divorce* of an apparent contradiction which finally resolves into a higher truth. Christ, the messenger of charity and grace, seems uncharitably close-minded and even priggish in his dealing with the pharisees: "for it was seasonable that they should hear their own unbounded licence rebuk't, but not seasonable for them to hear a good mans requisite liberty explain'd. But us he hath taught better, if we have eares to hear. . . . Christ therfore mentions not here what *Moses* and the Law intended: for good men might know that by many other rules. . . . Only he acquaints them with what *Moses* by them was put to suffer" (pp. 307–08).

By granting the pharisees only that part of the law which pertained to their own ill behavior, Christ would seem to provide only negative and literal enforcement of the law, as if he were selfishly excluding them from any opportunity to see whatever light might support their reform. At the same time, so it seems, he insures their exclusion from the light by continually reminding them of their ignorance. But the key to

Christ's action, and its true justice, is in the words "if we have eares to hear." The entire case against the pharisees is based on the question of whether they have "eares to hear," whether they are "fit" for the truth; and the answer to that question is determined not by Christ but by the pharisees themselves. The relevant evidence is not their outward behavior, their record of licentiousness, but rather their demonstrated manner of interpreting the law. They are known to have "ill cited" the law, "suppressing the true cause for which *Moses* gave it, and extending it to every slight matter" (p. 307). They have proven themselves capable only of literal readings of the law, and abusive application of what they read. To the pharisees, any law is meaningful only as a license or a prohibition of explicitly enumerated acts, hence the law Christ gives them is explicitly prohibitive of the license they had taken. As Milton sees it, the pharisees were not without the opportunity to recover grace; they might at any time have demonstrated their fitness to receive the truth.

What if they had thus answered, Master if thou mean to make wedlock as insepa-rable as it was from the beginning, let it be made also a fit society, as God meant it, which we shall soon understand it ought to be, if thou recite the whole reason of the Law. Doubtles our Saviour had applauded their just answer. For then they had expounded this command of Paradise, even as *Moses* himself expounds it by his laws of divorce, that is, with due and wise regard had to the premises and reasons of the first command. (pp. 310–11)

They can receive the truth — they have "eares to hear" — only so far as they can expound the truth. The appropriateness of a given point of law to a given individual is determined not by any outside judge, not by God's omniscience, but by the individual's makeup and capacity, which are continually tested and revealed by his own response to his situation.

The operation of this system for law and truth, designed according to the "all-wise purpose of a *deliberating* God" (p. 309, my emphasis) is well illustrated in the exchange between Adam and God preceding the creation of Eve (*PL*, VIII, 363–451). By using his own rational powers, Adam must show his worthiness to receive a helpmate, even though it is a worthiness of which God is fully aware. In the exchange between God and Adam, it becomes apparent that it is not God, but Adam who needs to discover his worthiness *to himself;* his self-awareness is what enables him to be responsible for what he is to receive. Thus, on one level, we get the rather amusing image of a ratiocinative master artisan who enjoys an almost teasing exchange of professional viewpoint with his protégé; on another, we have the operation of an omniscient God:

> Thus farr to try thee, *Adam*, I was pleas'd,
> And finde thee knowing not of Beasts alone,
> Which thou hast rightly nam'd, but of thy self,
> Expressing well the spirit within thee free,
>
> . . . .
>
> I, ere thou spak'st,
> Knew it not good for Man to be alone,
> And no such companie as then thou saw'st
> Intended thee, for trial onely brought,
> To see how thou could'st judge of fit and meet. (VIII, 437–48)

Even when the delighted Adam receives his mate, the tone of a friendly competition between mutually respected colleagues remains in his converse with God. Adam's first words upon seeing this latest example of God's handiwork are congratulatory:

> This turn hath made amends; thou hast fulfill'd
> Thy words, Creator bounteous and benigne,
> Giver of all things faire, but fairest this
> Of all thy gifts.   (VIII, 491–94)

Milton's God not only permits but expects his creatures to be intellectually alert, ready to make a case for themselves and their needs. The only way men can demonstrate their worthiness of the truth is to show their ability rationally to perceive and "expound" the truth.

There we learn also *that the Law is good, if a man use it lawfully*. Out of doubt then there must be a certain good in this Law which *Moses* willingly allow'd; and there might be an unlawfull use made thereof by hypocrits; . . . Christ therfore mentions not here what *Moses* and the Law intended; for good men might know that by many other rules: and the scornful Pharises were not fit to be told, untill they could imploy that knowledge they had, lesse abusively. (p. 308)

To make the law work is to "use" it, to "imploy" knowledge of it as "intended" — not to "enforce" the law, or even to "apply" it. Just law operates from within, realizing its meaning not as a stricture imposed from the outside but as a function of the understanding. When the pharisees failed to perceive this difference — the difference between the inner and the outer, the spirit and the letter — they defined for themselves the kind of law that would be both applicable and understandable to them.

But Milton does not suppose that it is enough simply to have made of Christ's words an isolated law relevant only to a special group of people.[9] That would be a partial reading, and for Milton, the most obvious, literal reading that could still be consistent with Mosaic law. Therefore, as he had employed his "industry of free reasoning" to find out "the whole reason of the law" of wedlock, so he uses further enterprise to discover the "whole reason" behind Christ's allowance of divorce for fornication. As with virtually every other progression of logic in *The Doctrine and Discipline of Divorce*, the process with which Milton determines the true meaning of "fornication" involves reconciliation of seeming disparities by removing them to a higher level of meaning. Throughout the tract Milton has stated that "he who affirms adultery to be the highest breach, affirms the bed to be the highest of marriage"; yet paradoxically, Milton himself gathers every offense that constitutes such a breach under none other than the heading "fornication." Furthermore, an irreconcilable breach may conceivably be made by what objectively seems the mildest of offenses — something which in any context other than marriage would cause no difficulty: "considering also that many properties of nature, which the power of regeneration it self never alters, may cause dislike of conversing even between the most sanctifi'd . . . who were they disseverd would be straight friends in any other relation" (pp. 279–80). As no social institution is so intimate as marriage, so no relationship is so susceptible to the exigencies of individual temperament — or so needful therefore of charitable treatment. The effort to find Christ's just and true meaning accordingly becomes a test case for Milton's doctrine that in order to impose just restrictions, one must know first "how far the territory and dominion extends of just and honest liberty" (p. 227).

Implicit in that doctrine, as also in the doctrine of charity, is a recognition of the supremacy of the individual:

Let the statutes of God be turn'd over, be scann'd a new, and consider'd . . . with divine insight and benignity measur'd out to the proportion of each mind and spirit, each temper and disposition, created so different each from other, and yet by the skill of wise conducting, all to become uniform in vertue. (p. 230)

If the end of the law is perfection of virtue, then due consideration must be given to the circumstances which will most contribute to the individual's moral and spiritual progress toward that virtue. Therefore, Milton's understanding of what Christ meant by "fornication" begins with an allowance for individual requisites which might even seem at variance with the priorities he himself has already presented.

And out of question the cherfull help that may be in mariage toward sanctity of life, is the purest and so the noblest end of that contract: but if the particular of each person be consider'd, then of those three ends which God appointed, *that to him is greatest which is most necessary:* and mariage is then most brok'n to him, when he utterly wants the fruition of that which he most sought therin, *whether it were religious, civill, or corporall society.* (p. 269, my emphasis)

In light of Milton's own priorities, which expressly place "corporall society" last, this may seem an extraordinary statement. But in fact it is perfectly consistent, not only with his principle of "just and honest liberty," but with the "reason" of the statutes of God. Whatever their initial claims to priority, all corporal, civil, and even religious estates turn out to be merely temporal forms which must yield to the sanctity of the individual soul. As the qualities which make for a "meet help" to the soul can be known to no other, so the character of its disappointment can be known only to the individual soul. If there is marriage and marriage, there is also fornication and fornication. Milton spurns the definition that says sexual adultery or "fornication" is the highest breach of marriage, and instead argues that the highest breach of an individual marriage — whatever that breach may be — is "fornication." Indeed, of the infinite possible meanings this term "fornication" may comprehend, one of the least significant is actual sexual errancy:

For that fault committed argues not alwaies a hatred either natural or incidental against whom it is committed; neither does it inferre a disability of all future helpfulnes, or loyalty, or loving agreement, being once past, and pardon'd, where it can be pardon'd. (p. 331)

At the same time, even though adultery is a pardonable offense, it constitutes the one *pardonable* offense for which the injured party is nonetheless permitted to obtain a divorce — which explains Christ's allowance of "fornication" as an exception to the rule. Thus "fornication" is made simultaneously to stand for actual adultery, a "reconcilable" offense, and also for whatever else in good conscience a man "could not force himself to live with" (p. 331). So it is that the law of Moses and the law of Christ turn out to be the same law, only viewed from complementary angles:

Moses therfore permits divorce, but in cases only that have no hands to joyn, and more need separating than adultery. Christ forbids it, but in matters only that may accord, and those lesse then fornication. (pp. 331–32)

The law of Moses and the law of Christ are merely two manifestations of the same "reason," which is to protect the sanctity of the spirit and to aid the progress toward virtue of the individual soul.

In a tract made up of reconciled disparities and things defined as their opposites, it seems only appropriate that the essential idea of divorce should be cast in a new and unaccustomed light. In fact, Milton grants the idea of divorce the most unaccustomed light of all. Almost lost amid the welter of descriptives such as "the cure of an inveterate disease" and "some conscionable, and tender pitty" is the true intent of Milton's argument as stated in the Preface:

He therefore who by adventuring shall be so happy as with successe to light the way of such an expedient liberty and truth as this, shall restore the much wrong'd and over-sorrow'd state of matrimony, not onely to those mercifull and life-giving remedies of *Moses*, but, as much as may be, to that serene and blisfull condition it was in at the beginning. (pp. 239–40)

By what principle or power Milton would hope to restore marriage to its original unfallen state is not made clear until after his argument is well under way: he does it by finding the doctrine and discipline of divorce to exist prior to marriage, prior to man, prior to the world itself. It is this archetypal act of divorce which gives the highest sanction to the principles by which Milton argues:

And certainly those divine meditating words of finding out a meet and like help to man, have in them a consideration of more than the indefinite likeness of womanhood; nor are they to be made waste paper on . . . in not compelling together unmatchable societies, or if they meet through mischance, by all consequence to dis-joyn them, as God and nature signifies and lectures to us not onely by those recited decrees, but ev'n by the first and last of all his visible works; when by his divorcing command the world first rose out of Chaos, nor can be renew'd again out of confusion but by the separating of unmeet consorts. (pp. 272–73)

Not only does Milton make divorce God's original creative act in *The Doctrine and Discipline of Divorce*, but years later he reasserts its priority:

> Darkness profound
> Cover'd th' Abyss: but on the watrie calme
> His brooding wings the Spirit of God outspred,
> And vital vertue infus'd, and vital warmth
> Throughout the fluid Mass, but downward purg'd
> The black tartareous cold infernal dregs
> Adverse to life: then founded, then conglob'd
> Like things to like, the rest to several place
> Disparted, and between spun out the Air,
> And Earth self-ballanc't on her Center hung.
>   Let ther be Light, said God, and forthwith Light
> Ethereal, first of things, quintessence pure
> Sprung from the Deep.   (*PL*, VII, 233–45)

Light is granted, as in the Scriptures, precedence as the first of *things;* but contrary to the Scriptures, God's first *act* is made the separation of adverse elements. Thus the original act of creation is an act of disruption; out of apparent disunity emerges unity and order, and the paradigm for Milton's logic is realized once again.

Johns Hopkins University

NOTES

1. William Riley Parker's *Milton's Contemporary Reputation* (Columbus, Ohio, 1940) collects most of the contemporary allusions to the divorce tracts. These are amplified by J. Milton French in *The Life Records of John Milton*, 5 vols. (New Brunswick, N.J., 1949–1958), and Ernest Sirluck includes several more on pp. 142–43, 506, and Appendix C of volume II of *The Complete Prose Works of John Milton*, ed. Don M. Wolfe et. al. (New Haven, 1959), hereafter cited as YP.

2. In the Addresses to Parliament of *The Judgement of Martin Bucer* and *Tetrachordon*, and in *Colasterion*.

3. *Milton and the Kingdoms of God*, (Evanston, Ill., 1964), pp. 84–85.

4. *The Judgement of Martin Bucer*, YP, II, p. 431.

5. "To the Parliament," *Tetrachordon*, YP, II, p. 583.

6. All references are to the 1644 revised version, printed in YP, II. Page numbers of quotations will appear in the text.

7. In *The Fierce Equation* (The Hague, 1965), pp. 71–82, Thomas Kranidas includes the divorce tracts among those of Milton's prose works which use "definition by opposites," or "negatives," to achieve a "positive vision of unity." Although I have arrived independently at the use of similar terminology, nothing I say should be thought of as conflicting with the insights in Kranidas's excellent book.

8. *Milton and Science* (Cambridge, Mass., 1956), pp. 216–17.

9. Ernest Sirluck maintains that Milton's argument remains dependent on such a special interpretation of Christ's dictum until, in *Tetrachordon*, he elaborates the concept of natural law. See the Introduction to YP, II, pp. 145–58.

POEMS (1645): ON GROWING UP

Gale H. Carrithers, Jr.

THE ENGLISH poems in the order of Milton's presentation in *Poems* (1645), from *On the Morning of Christ's Nativity* to *Lycidas*, constitute a meaningful sequence. I mean a fictive sequence with a thematic coherence verging on the dramatic. Neither this thesis nor the quasi-drama of maturation I anatomize in what follows are totally new views, of course.[1] But I'm urging a higher degree of coherence in the whole sequence (which Milton could have given different members, or a different arrangement), and urging the fruitfulness of considering individual poems especially within that context. A (roughly) analogous argument might be made for the other series of poems in *Poems* (1645), those in Latin and Greek. That the two series taken together illuminate Milton as "rising poet" to be taken always seriously but not always solemnly Louis Martz has shown. But the argument for the classical sequence can be separate from this, as can elucidations of the historical Milton.

John Milton in these poems presents a self who by various steps and trials becomes a priestly poet in the priesthood of all believers, a sophisticated one who frames the whole sequence in a book with prominent date and urbane comment in Greek on the engraver's poor likeness of the poet.

He who hymns the infant God has scarcely met the problem of theodicy. He must first discover in himself and the world that divine justice is questionable or problematical, and then test the options. Don Parry Norford has commented that a descent to a contrasting world (and subsequent transcendence in a resurrection), a "night-sea journey . . . is central in Milton's poetry."[2] One thinks of the Incarnation in the beginning of this sequence and of Lycidas at its end. But the beginning, middle, and end of the sequence itself can repay our attention now with one emphasis, now another in terms of vocation (what shall I do?), medium or genre (how shall I do it?), and context (what importance have associates, and where is God among us?).

Individual poems in *Poems* (1645), have a great deal of history— long established generic forms, conventional poetics and thematics. But there's an internal sense in which these poems have little history. The past is present to the speakers in the first half of the sequence extensively but thinly, mainly as raw material, as a medium for current work. There is almost no thickness of interpersonality, almost no sense (until later in the sequence) of complexly human causality and vicissitude, and little "anxiety of influence."

This poet comes to history in these poems. We see — if not quite a drama — a serious entertainment of movement from ahistoric, youthful incompleteness to realized, adult self-hood. That has by the end entailed finding vocation, what we might more generally and in an Augustinian sense call his true love, and finding it implicated in history, a fallen world of persons and vicissitude.

I

> This is the Month, and this the happy morn
> Wherin the Son of Heav'ns eternal King,
> Of wedded Maid, and Virgin Mother born,
> Our great redemption from above did bring;
> For so the holy sages once did sing.[3]

It begins, the first poem of these "two books with single cover," as its author was later to begin the account of creation itself: an originating distinction now born in human consciousness, articulated as old wisdom differentiated by a new song. The old wisdom — from "holy sages" in this "nativity" ode, from Urania "with Eternal wisdom . . . In presence of th' Almightie Father" in *PL* VII, 9–11 — and new song are alike necessary causes but not sufficient causes of redemptive action. Apparently we must have divine help in conjunction with knowing and acting by song; song is to be understood as the form action takes here. Language may be fallen for Milton at twenty-one as in later life, but not so sundered from effective action and from truth as it was construed to be by later poets and antipoets.

We are presented in the Nativity ode, as in *PL* VII, with a "new acquist" not so much of knowledge or virtue as of consciousness — light out of dark, a new morn. There is a kind of history indicated by "sages once did sing" or "Father, pleas'd / with thy Celestial Song." But it tends to be the quasi history of myth: "sons of morning sung," "age of gold" (119, 135). The heaviest emphasis falls on *newness*. It is less Book VII's new creation of a human world between an angelic and a human fall than a new creation of the self in orientation toward the divine child — in keeping with biblical and prayer book invocations of new creations in Christ.[4]

This voice acknowledges "deadly forfeit" early in the poem but is

confident of "release," acknowledges mysteries of godhead in "light un-
sufferable" but finds them reassuringly "laid aside" and finally almost
domesticated to "Handmaid Lamp" and "order serviceable." This
young poet acknowledges that making "a present to the Infant God" always implies a new welcome, but such new sayings of the old redemptive truth come with relative ease. Similarly, would-be subverters of the
old-promised, new-recognized "meek-ey'd Peace" are acknowledged
through this poem; but they are more readily confounded or discounted
than in *Paradise Lost* (so vanity, sin, "Hell it self" in stanza XIV,
Dragon, oracles, Lemures, Baalim, brutish gods, Osiris and Typhon in
stanzas XVIII–XXV). "Nature" for this exuberant young poet in a new-
worldly Now of "holy song" appears "almost won / To think her part
was don," appears close to incorporation in a redemptive telos of
"Heav'n and Earth in happier union" (107). Hence there's decorum to
the jaunty assumption that the rising Sun of this friendly Nature, rising
from bed as the infant Son will eventually do, "pillows his chin upon an
Orient wave" (231). Fire and water and whatever they associate with
are apparently reconciled.[5]

The trouble is not that Milton's control falters here, or even in the
poem's extraordinary shifts of tense.[6] The informed and passionate
speaker is not unlike the New Testament wise virgins conjured up by the
last stanza's reference to "Handmaid Lamp," not without celebratory
spirit. True, in trying to make the known sacred history and recurring
stage of the Christian year into the existential now of a new creation in
Christ he does not maintain a steady and constant hold on the sacred
moment. The poet who relegates "Shepherds" a little too distantly to
"the Lawn . . . in a rustick row" (87), who rhymes "wisest Fate says
no. / This must not yet be so" a little too briskly, should be understood
as a speaker who is the appealing ingenue, whether chronologically
young or not. It may be granted that personhood in this poem —
whether of God, or of speaker, or of others — lacks thickness. John Milton wrote poems before this, and modern editors may choose to place
them first. He chooses to begin his book with this one, and seems to mean
more than 25 December 1629, when his impassioned speaker proclaims:

> But now begins; for from this happy day
> Th' old Dragon under ground
> In straiter limits bound,
> Not half so far casts his usurped sway.   (167–170)

The remainder of the English poems exhibit a deepening sense of losses
to be redeemed, of bitterness of crosses, of lesser straitness in the Drag-

on's limits than younger poet could have supposed or older poet and audience wished. Evasions of these trials are essayed but prove unsatisfactory; more of that shortly.

We are given versifications of Psalms cxiv and cxxxvi, schoolboy exercises with debts to other paraphrasers (as has long been noted). But seventeenth-century eyes and ears might well have noted some significant contrasts with the Authorized Version, and the Bishops' Bible as preserved in the Psaltery of the Book of Common Prayer (cited below as AV and BCP).

Milton's Nature in Psalm cxiv is more animate, even if in a quite conventionally pastoral way: only his sea that fled had "froth-becurled head"; only his Jordan recoils "as a faint host," only his skipping mountains are "huge-bellied."[7] More tellingly, he changes beginnings:

> When Israel came out of Egypt:
>   and the house of Jacob from among the strange
> people, [people of strange language, AV]
> Judah was his sanctuary:
>   and Israel his dominion. (BCP)

> When the blest seed of *Terah's* faithfull Son,
> After long toil their liberty had won,
> And past from *Pharian* fields to *Canaan* land,
> Led by the strength of the Almighties hand.

From a Hebraic emphasis on divine doings and arbitrary power amid disparate societies, we have been moved to a rather cozy universe. The miraculous God-the-child-Son of the Nativity ode, the infant Hercules, has here a counterpart God-the-Father: powerful in a variously animate, handsome, and pleasant world, paternally benign and reciprocally caring (albeit not prematurely so) for His generations of faithful. Only in this young poet's Jehovah do we find that quite this majestic explicability "ever was, and ay shall last."

The paraphrase of Psalm cxxxvi and *The Passion* are usefully considered together. What are we to make of his inclusion of *The Passion*, though "nothing satisfi'd with what was begun"? Milton presents us with a young poet who has not yet realized suffering in any depth, much less resolved it in costly struggle. He's a speaker who accordingly and not unbecomingly feels that the subject of the Crucifixion requires the existential removal to "holy vision . . . pensive transe . . . ecstatick fit." Once there (so to speak), he's lost, turning uncertainly from Jerusalem's towers to "Sepulchral rock . . . Or should I thence" to "Mountains wild." He asserts that "grief is easily beguil'd," then belies that unbelievable sentiment by contorting himself into a neo-Spenserian gaucherie out of the metaphysical literature of tears, about his groans and tears begetting echoes and rain as if "a race of mourners on som pregnant cloud."

Though six years earlier in Miltonic biographical time, it was only a page, a moment, earlier for us in this sequence that we were with cxxxvi, of all psalms. Though simplistic in terms of biblical explication, it's sensible here to consider the bloodthirsty and vindictive gloating of this paraphrased psalm as tribally/boyishly unaware of what's really involved in the deific execution of "the first-born of Egypt land." This paraphraser is more intrigued with the physics of divine action: "thunder-clasping hand," "[Red Sea] floods stood still like Walls of Glass," "larg-limb'd Og" subdued — all language supererogatory to BCP or AV. Almost ingenuously, too, he expands the BCP/AV refrain, "For his mercy endureth for ever," to "For his mercies ay endure / Ever faithfull, ever sure."

In terms of this essay's thesis, that we do well to read *Poems* (1645) as exploration toward theodicy and self-commitment in history, then we have in these first four a beginning. The god is born into the young poet's world, not without worshipful recognition. But his recognition of why that world should need the incarnate god scarcely extends beyond simple notice that there are enemies out there. Nor is there much sense that the interaction of God and world might be not just powerful or puzzling but mysterious; nor, again, that human interrelationship or intersubjectivity might compound the problem; nor that, among other consequences of that, song itself might be compromised. Compare the uncritical relationship to pastoralism in Psalm cxiv with the action in *Lycidas*. The next few poems reify preliminary discoveries.

II

On Time surprises by its curious distancing. *On* means both "about" time and, as if "set upon a clock case," script (rather than voice) affixed to a mechanical gauge of time. But is the distance lessened by the poet's personifying time? Not much. This personification is out there as an *other*. One might argue — as congenially to Renaissance Christianity as to Gabriel Marcel or José Ortega y Gasset — that the self and others are linked as mutual determinants. But that linkage seems obscured or attenuated here by the I's being quite a vague corporate "our . . . us . . . we" and the personified Time simply an Other, neatly vanquished.

The poems in the sequence begin to show provocative dichotomies.

In *The Passion*, commonplace glances at history ("once glorious towers . . . now sun," [40]) stand at odds with events transcending history.[8] *On Time* presents a more interrelated but largely static taxonomy of temporality opposed by eternity; so *Upon the Circumcision* with the redeemed and the unredeemed, and *At a Solemn Musick* with harmony and discord. But the differences claim attention too.

That vanquishment of Time as alien Other is orthodox, though distant. So too the notions of "meerly mortal dross" and "earthy grossness quit"—however impersonal. But this orthodox speaker remains somewhat childlike. He fancies dress-up ("attir'd with Stars"). He could be vengeful ("sit, / Triumphing over"); he lumps together as bogeymen the existentially incommensurable "Death, and chance, and thee O Time." Eternity's "individual kiss; / And Joy shall overtake Us *as a flood*" (my emphasis); the imagery betokens a kind of regressive hearkening toward lost maternal plenitude.

Yet again there is ambivalence: the "Time" of line 4, whose (not *maw* but) "*womb* devours." No doubt we should not make too much of that because poem and sequence alike go on to other things (leaving the image of swallowing womb for Belial in *PL* II and Satan in *PL* X). This poem artfully gives a somewhat mixed bearing toward life, which may be associated with adolescence but can persist indefinitely.

Upon the Circumcision, next, though relatively labored in syntax, diction, cadence—and listlessly conventional in imagery—claims some attention by its position after the Nativity ode and *Passion*, on the way toward but existentially far from *Lycidas*. The Feast of the Circumcision is to the Christian year somewhat as the poem is to the symbolic "year" of the poetic speaker's life. The joy at the birth of the god into a needy, anticipating world is once more acknowledged and the dénouement of a penitential Lent and culminating Easter are lightly prefigured: with a stronger sense of infidelity to "that great Cov'nant," and with the circumcision as micro-Passion. The Passion has been domesticated, but at a critical cost in scale; the last three lines acknowledge that.

This speaker's uneasy stand in pseudo-canzone involves other problems. Less established than epic bard or Miltonic deity, he merely asserts just law and exceeding love. And even if "that great Cov'nant which we still transgress" has been "intirely satisfi'd," what do we do the rest of the Christian year, or even tomorrow? The question has yet to be faced, and with it the cost of whatever "seals obedience" in the speaker and the sweepingly included remainder of us. This speaker may know important things common to all—our fallibility and deathwardness, say, our constitution as creatures of symbol, even—but does he know enough about what divides us?

At a Solemn Musick suggests that he knows a great deal about divisions and — in the perennial metaphor that has already enriched the Nativity ode and (in composition though not in sequence) the Ludlow *Mask* — discord. Some celebratory poetry draws its energy from the opposition between noticing the subject and neglecting to notice. *At a Solemn Musick* draws power from opposition to adversaries by no means so inchoate as entropy.

The many adjectives point to menacing opposites: *undisturbed, saintly, solemn* (versus trivial, for Milton), *victorious, devout, holy, undiscording.* The grammar ("That we . . . May rightly answer . . . O may we") underscores life's contingency with a new resonance. Indeed, the Fall gets recapitulated as a quasi-originary event: not quite a Manichaean opposite to the new creation in Christ, rather an ongoing "harsh din."

So "that Song" (25) has been posited as truly originary, the enactment of divine love, "consort" of disparities. A noble conception: harmonious song, even dance ("thir motion sway'd"), fulfillment in aesthetic action for all the committed, together. This heavenly perspective, construed from the fallen world, traditionally articulates itself in paradox: the Song both atemporal and temporal, and the "endles morn of light." Dark negatives and adversities which resist explanation or domestication — even by paradox — have been sighted but not grappled with.

III

The next seven poems circle closer to the issue and dally with false surmises: *An Epitaph on the Marchioness of Winchester, Song, on May morning, On Shakespear, On the University Carrier, Another on the same, L'Allegro,* and *Il Penseroso.* Four of these are occasioned by deaths, and the other three engage them antiphonally. The Marchioness has died of being what she is, a mother: "That to give the world encrease, / Short'n'd hast thy own lives lease" (51–52). Even the baby died. This speaker can assimilate some peripheral facts, but not that.

Assimilation of the peripheral means things like the poignant opening of the poem, epitaphically cataloguing her as almost (in Henry James's phrase) "heiress of all the ages": noble descent and alliance, art, virtue and breeding. But she's dead at twenty-three. So in a tactic elaborated in *Lycidas* we are reoriented to a metaphor of the world — or sample life-world, a shift from macrocosmic to microcosmic — as a mixed bouquet of entities and sequences: Hymen's garland with "a Cipress bud" (22). But this developing elegist cannot claim "you might have seen a cypress bud," only that "ye might discern" now, in retrospect.

And this uncertainty provokes a formula almost parody-Manichaean, at once so domestic and so classically distanced as to suggest a psychological avoidance in fantasy: "whether by mischance or blame / *Atropos* for *Lucina* came." (27–28).

Evidently, though, this formal-yet-troubled speaker resists the nightingale-song of fancy to return here where baby and mother are not "fruit and tree" but where the life-given may give death. He consults common experience: "So have I seen som tender slip, . . . Pluck't up by som unheedy swain" (35, 38). This approach might open toward the spirit of "As flies to wanton boys, are we to the gods." Instead we find ourselves reoriented out of the savaged garden into a comfortable convention: "Pearls of dew" on a flower as "presaging tears / Which the sad morn had let fall / On her hast'ning funerall" (43–45).

Still, the elegist does what he can: pray for rest, and certify the contributions of ritual and art to order the mourning. But what meaning does her life have in a world that would so interrupt it by death? The biblical analogue of Rachel, mother "after years of barrennes" to Joseph and then (fatally) to Benjamin, vexes the question. We seem to be told in those lines to honor that as the parallel; never mind other matters in the biblical context—broken bargains, stolen idols, slain Shechemites or the like. Yet if Rachel's death is not vindicated by her place in salvific history, why mention it at all? But the anxious assurance "much like thee, / Through pangs fled to felicity" (67–68) comes from the poet, not the Bible, and "no Marchioness, but now a Queen" is mere assertion. Is not a more appealing feature of this poem the growing sense of "House," of society organized, of maturation and lineage embedded in destiny which may on occasion mysteriously allow a fatal vicissitude?

Modern editions which break the 1645 order obscure the degree of antiphonal resemblance between *Epitaph* and *Song*. Shawcross helpfully reminds us that the meter of the "salute" (5–8) replicates that of *Epitaph* and of the later *L'Allegro* and *Il Penseroso*. There's more than that. "Garland . . . fruit and tree . . . flowr . . . vernall showr . . . blossom . . . som Flowers, and some Bays" on the "sad morn" of the death-stricken mother modulate to the "bright morning star" of "flowry *May*, who from HER green lap throws / The yellow Cowslip, and the pale Primrose" (my emphasis). The metrically accented *Now* beginning this song to a May *morning* and the phrase "wish thee long" which concludes it surely emphasize a poignant transience. And the floral names anticipate that more famous catalogue in *Lycidas*. But this is not so much dalliance with a "false surmise" as a kind of acknowledgment of limitation: to "welcom . . . and wish . . . long" what cannot be so is at least lively and generous, neither deathly nor mean-spirited.

On Shakespear balances liveliness not against death or meanness but rather against ineffectuality: "To th' shame of slow-endeavouring art, / Thy easie numbers flow." The orders of nature and of art or vocation cohered for the playwright, the culture-hero whose achievement transcends politics. But the poem invites a question about what order other doers and makers may stand in who can only wish for so noble a "Monument."

It is a world order of long and mixed lineage. "My *Shakespear*" seems to command the various generative forces. He embodies classical being: "son of memory" and author of "Delphick lines" more vigorous than (Latinate) monuments.[9] He is akin to some Hebrew prophet, the witness of his name in leaves of a sacred "Book." He is no mere fading theme of medieval Fame, rather her "great heir." And the stones of the mostly Anglo-Saxon words in his lines monumentalize him in our Anglo-Saxon astonishment. Such quick, shorthand marshaling of his society's resources — which becomes one of Milton's identifying moves — does not always proceed so univocally, as we shall see.

Milton's two poems *On the University Carrier* stand as finely buoyant, partly because placed as — so to speak — satyr-pieces to the solemn celebration of Shakespeare. However much humbler Hobson the campus character was, he resembled Shakespeare for Milton's young-poet speakers in doing the work that was his. If Hobson's work was not completed in some senses in which Shakespeare's work was, who would fault orders of nature, of culture or language which provided that "ease was his chief disease" — at age 87? Death domesticated to a long-due "Chamberlin" in the first poem, the dying man himself conceived in the second as chirping "for one Carrier put down to make six bearers" — everything coheres in the most jolly-serious elegiac performance in English between Jonson's *On S.P.* and Dryden's on Anne Killigrew. In *Shakespear*, we find suggested a kind of nation, a permanent society of English readers and writers, and in the Hobson poems a homelier community of students and letter-writers. Yet there's a leavening of historicity in the near-dialectic — perhaps not quite a dichotomy here — of inspiration with "slow-endeavoring art" in the one, of Hobson's perennial activity with his wittily pointed death in the others.

There is some cost in immediacy, in presence. Shakespeare's fluency reproaches "slow-endeavoring art," yet Shakespeare lived long and a young poet has long, does he not? Hobson is Other to collegians, almost an archetypal Old Man, "obedient to the Moon . . . to the mutual flowing of the Seas." What of more present options and consequent life-ways?

It is in this kind of ideational-psychological context that we find *L'Allegro* and *Il Penseroso*, as texts and as life-trials. This is not to unsay what has been observed about the twin poems. We can usefully bracket for the moment the lively arguments as to whether the two options are balanced, joined, tilted, or cyclical.[10]

IV

Whatever Milton himself may have felt at one youthful hour or another about personal ways of life available to him, the finished *L'Allegro* and *Il Penseroso* should be understood as ironic — poignantly, wryly, or humorously so at differing moments. The irony starts in the titles: deliberate, Miltonic joking mystifications, which betoken by their foreignness both the distance of what follows from the author and its familiarity to him. Milton could be polite and witty and poetic in Italian. Had he wanted to be impolite, blunt, and prosaic, he might have given English titles, not as editors do in notes ("Happy man" and "Thoughtful man"), but more like "Sport" and "Muser," almost "Ninny" and "Pedant." I risk exaggeration to clarify the subsiding — almost a night-sea voyage — into estrangement of these middle poems, thirteenth and fourteenth of twenty-seven.[11]

We have been presented with considerations of birth (and death coming with it) and lineages and fulfillment in a cosmic order, in the Winchester, Shakespeare, and Hobson poems, likely the productions with *L'Allegro* and *Il Penseroso* of little more than a year. If those last two have the general form of a "scholastic exercise," still, whence such verve, and why place them just here?

Everyone notices that they both begin with alternative generations: (1) the "horrid shapes, and shrieks" which unlike the "pangs" of Rachel (and Jane Paulet) herald no flight "to felicity"; (2) the contrasting easy triplets, the graces perhaps by Bacchus out of "lovely Venus at a birth" or else by a pagan *hagia pneuma* in a kind of creeping inflation; (3) the subhuman "*brood* of folly without *father bred*," in ghastly contravention of human or sacred nature; (4) even more startlingly the fantasized incestuous generation of Melancholy out of Vesta by her father, "solitary Saturn." Whether or not armed in the complete steel of Lévi-Strauss or more traditional anthropology, one recognizes Milton's own suggestion of the radical irregularity, inversion, and impoverishment of Melancholy's line. Milton's speaker gives us the otherwise pointless word *solitary*, and proposes the pedantic and alienating nonexplanation: "In

Saturns reign, / Such mixture was not held a stain." Surely if any explanation is needed, no explanation will help, and so much the more foolish for the pedantic Penseroso (call him) to think otherwise. He is caught like the Saturnine father in self-focus tending toward self-pity, with no possibility of exchange or reciprocity; or somewhat like the egregious Adam of *PL* VIII, 5–38, "fixt" as if asleep in "thoughts abstruse."

Allegro's way (call it) of being in the world seems similarly disabled. Set aside, for now, the rousing conclusion of the couplet at lines 31–32 ("Laughter holding both his sides") to look at the first half ("Sport that wrincled Care derides"). Sport, hypostatized as boisterous personification, can deride "Care," and chase it out of mind — one of the reasons that play is recreation. But sport, play, game, virtually by definition, presuppose a delimiting, contrastive context; cares may be temporarily ignored, but Care abides. Is something like that implicit in making "sweet Liberty" a "Mountain Nymph," distant and estranged from a speaker who strolls the plow-furrowed lowlands?

Allegro pledges (37) that if he gives Mirth "honour due" then he will be admitted to or will join her "crew." His efforts in that ritual vein are almost as compendious as the BCP Canticle of praise for the works of God, especially in the visual and the audible. We note that specially Miltonic alternation of near detail and framing structure, as in "nibling flocks . . . mountains . . . clouds . . . Daisies pide . . . Battlements . . . high in tufted trees . . . tann'd Haycock in the Mead . . . Nut'brown Ale . . . bed and whispering winds . . . Towred Cities."[12]

Yet there's something wrong. Giving Mirth due honor in parsing the horizon of her world — "mine eye . . . Whilst the Lantskip round it measures" — seems costly. Allegro walks "not unseen," but that has a detached, passive ring to it. He "hath caught new pleasures," with eye or ear (or other senses) only in a severely limited mode, a detached and noncommittal manner. What is really given or even received? Nor is it adequate to suppose that Allegro fantasizes an anatomy of Mirth's world as a set of possibilities (hence with dreamily abrupt shifts like that of Mirth and self from cottage to "Towred Cities"). Allegro evidently cannot both imagine Mirth's world and imagine himself in it, implicated, committed. Contrast a congregation jointly singing a canticle of praise.[13]

The poem develops the consequences of an opening choice which like the jealousy of Leontes or the disburdened exactions of Lear must entail some exorbitant price. Beautiful women, for example, subsist far from the "mirth and youth, and warm desire" of May songs, hover if anywhere in a scenically/existentially distant "perhaps," objects of anonymous gaze, "Cynosure of neighboring eyes" remote from the speaker's own. Propinquity yields hardly more intimacy: the cottagers "creep" to bed as if insectival; similarly, the "busie" speech of cities, not urbane, polite, civil, even political — a mere "humm of men" (118).

But service in Mirth's crew evidently becomes more hectic. The ceremony of cities involves "Ladies, whose bright eies / Rain influence" (121), not the mere presumed beauty of line 79. True, those eyes have the familiar office of stars, but they are existentially near enough to judge prizes "of Wit, or Arms," and poets are witty. Yet abruptly the nearness is distanced by the ambiguous status of dream and its dispersion among bemused "Poets" (127–28). If the stage be furnished with a play by one of the most celebrated playwrights of the speaker's national drama, Jonson is reduced to merely "learned" and Shakespeare reduced to "Fancies child" warbling. Ezra Pound could never have damned this as Milton's obtuseness had he considered the external context as including *On Shakespear,* and the internal context as the opening lines of *L'Allegro* and these, which follow immediately the reference to Shakespeare: "And ever against eating Cares, / Lap me in soft Lydian Aires" (135–36). It seems the wood-notes must *ever* be accompanied — not with madder music and stronger wine but — with the support and release of Lydian airs to "lap me in," with voice to unchain the "hidden *soul* of harmony" (144, my emphasis). The Melancholy kicked out the door to begin the poem has reappeared in the heart's core. The speaker may still dream of simple freedom from a Plutonic underworld, may only have learned enough caution to change the pledge of lines 37–38 to the tougher conditional of "if thou canst give" (151) — not "if I can take." But the poignancy of the irony is enforced by the behavior of Allegro's creator, who abruptly projects a trial of the antithetical option.

That very different partial or tentative or intermittent self — as Milton invites us in line 8 of *Il Penseroso* to consider — can see the mote in his neighbor's eye but not the beam in his own.

He is made to propose the pseudo company of Peace, Quiet, and "Spare Fast, that oft with gods doth diet." He does not say "spare time, oft with gods to diet" in Spenserian temperance or even a conventional austerity. He is made to personify skinny abstinence, as if a Miltonic joke on his speaker. What a later poet characterized as "eternal passion, eternal pain" in the song of Philomela is reduced by Penseroso and "Cherub Contemplation" to "sweetest, saddest plight, / Smoothing the rugged brow of night" (57). Not unlike Orsino on music, or Comus speaking of the Lady's song "smoothing the raven dawn / Of darkness till she smil'd" (*Mask,* 251–52).

In line 56, the instruction of quasi companions gives way to fancied circumstances, through line 97, when fancy shifts to stage scenes apparently inspired by texts (implying private study rather than playhouse), to lines 120–21 when dawn is supposed – all a night world. This darkness reiterates the ingrown estrangement of opening matters (including Melancholy's own "looks commercing [inconsequentially, it seems] with the skies," [38]). Does Penseroso attenuate the personal immediacy and consequentiality – the presence – of the Philomela legend in vaguely noting the nightingale's song as "most musicall, most melancholy!" as opposed to "noise of folly"? More than that, he separates entirely: "And missing thee, I walk unseen" (65). This walker's odd darkness has not the omnipresence of acoustical or dance space, yet it lacks also the differentiating qualities of visual/geographical or goal-oriented space: the protagonist is unseen, the moon is a confused or confusing marker even though near the zenith, the curfew-cry is apparently an identifier of separation ("far-off") more than connection, the macro-element of the ocean's (?) "roar" is indefinite ("som"), the micro-element of embers almost as decharacterized as the celebrated "darkness visible." The cricket on the hearth does not sing to this night fellow, though propinquitous like the bell-man (83), whose "drousie" (failing?) speech addresses "dores" rather than lone thinkers.

This contingent mode of being seems the most reclusive self Milton can imagine choosing to be. Not quite a recluse. Penseroso does speak as in his own voice. "Unseen," he proposes himself passively inferable from his tower lamp. As if shrinking from this faint hint of human contact, though, Penseroso thereupon supposes himself not reciprocally inferring the Other but instead aggrandizing himself in cosmic speculation. These removals immediately measure themselves by their effect: whereas Allegro's way with drama and life automatizes it, Penseroso's withdrawal of self into abstraction reduces the tragedy he hypothesizes to costumed spectacle; even "Pelops line" and the Trojan war become a passing parade. Similarly, the parade-like sequences in the ear, of a denatured Spenser or the cluttered tale of Chaucer's Squire. We may attribute more substantial qualities to this speaker or his occasions. But for him, in lethargic passivity, the very moon in "pale career" is a kind of parade figure. The sun – uncomfortably importunate – must be avoided, in favor of a dream parade projected on the screen of inner "eyelids." Heaven itself is the ultimate spectacle before the eye, not even in it, like beauty. Interhuman time and history have evaporated in this contingent as-if time.

We have slighted certain lines embarrassing to this chronicle of abstraction and detachment. Milton makes the embarrassment Allegro's or Penseroso's. The power of poetry evidently resists reduction to mirth, musing, or schema: it tugs back toward the society that constructed the language and its life, toward love that resists death, toward committed action, engaged sympathy, failure, whatever else we find in the potent figures of Orpheus and Eurydice, whose story defines by contrast both Allegro and Penseroso, as these familiar fragments can remind us: "would have *won* the ear"; "His *half*-regain'd Eurydice"; "Drew Iron *tears*"; "made Hell *grant* what Love did *seek*" (*L'Allegro* 148, 150; *Il Penseroso* 107, 108; my emphasis).

But Melancholy cannot raise Musaeus nor secure a song from murdered Orpheus, any more than Mirth can anesthetize with Lydian airs, at least not for Milton or his speakers. Evasions cannot prevail; they can only deny even a subsistence, as Milton has caused the Orphic references and other touches in both poems to suggest, and as he reiterates when he leaves Penseroso groping in subjunctives.[14]

Penseroso finally proposes a motion which would have the labor of journey but no *telos*, the repetition of dance but little expression and no joy: "Never fail / To walk the studious Cloysters pale." He proposes a quasi-liturgical "service high" but supposes himself uninvolved in that "people's work," instead rather estranged "into extasies" and spectacle-heaven.

For the remainder of *Poems* (1645), the poet seems resolved not to sidestep the trials of life and commitment but rather to embrace them and either appraise them through more wholeheartedly mutual and straightforward speaking selves than we saw before, or render them actively and interpersonally in the secular liturgy of entertainment or masque.

The speaker of *Sonnet I*, "O Nightingale," acknowledges radical adversity ("bird of Hate . . . hopeless doom") and puzzles, in phrases like "hast sung too late . . . no reason why." He stops short of asking "What am I doing wrong?" But in *Sonnet VII*, "How soon hath Time," it will by implication be the speaker's wrongdoing if he does not accept the grace to abide his time somehow fruitfully. Similarly, the Italian sonnet and "Canzone" present us a speaker involved with love. The acquaintance of Italy and the state of love provoke him to a good-naturedly ironic self-awareness of change, of "new flower of alien speech" ("il fior novo di strania favella"), "unknown and alien language" ("lingua ignota e strana"), and his confession to Diodati in *Sonnet IV* that he has earlier scoffed yet now entangled himself ("s'impiglia"). He knowingly joins the conventional and perennial society of young lovers — which by generic and historic definition is a high comic society.

The speaker in *Sonnets VII, VIII, IX* and *X* — to say speakers seems unnecessary — shows a growing confidence in the power of the imaginative word, as a mode of action and participation in the world. The imaginative word "can requite thee," "can spread thy name," can become a directive to the self (as in *Sonnet IX*), can define the virtue of a father and daughter so as to give that virtue a kind of presence for the hearers (in *Sonnet X*).[15] But a new split seems to be suggested by these successive sonnets, different from that between committed life and uninvolved mirthfulness or contemplativeness. The world has come to be seen as fallen, yet offering Christian redemption, a world in which it may make sense either to wait or to do, if waiting is not slack but oriented toward the hill of heavenly truth, and if to do is to do what one is — to wield with words insofar as one is a poet. If the immediate public realm is more fallen than the private, then it makes sense either (1) to seek privacy, or (2) to seek an alternative, already existing public realm, or (3) to reform the public realm, which might begin as (4) reforming the private self, as model and antecedent for reforming the great world.

Such an anatomy helps to identify the troubled moves of the last English portions of *Poems* (1645). These terms also help delineate the profundity of the crisis in *Lycidas*.

Solitary privacy seems never for Milton to have been a life-supporting answer to the questions posed by the fallen world. His Messiah in *Paradise Regain'd* finds Satan and all the world in solitude. The Bard there as in *Paradise Lost* is a public character. Messiah and Bard minister in their respective ways to society. Blind Samson defines himself as a public character even "at the mill with slaves." Compare with Allegro and Penseroso the followers of Comus, headed like various animals, and forgetful of their native homes.

The great world is reciprocally necessary to authenticate the self, Parliaments are exactly the place to certify an "old man eloquent," a medium necessary for certain "noble Vertues," as are "feastfull friends." These sonnets imply elements in classical, Hebraic, natural, and public English worlds which can sustain and be sustained by the poetic voice, in the cause of virtue, on behalf of what the *Book of Common Prayer* had always called "the company of all faithful people."

Arcades seems to have as its main claim to space in the volume its animated tableau of such a grace-given public reality: a noble matron and social hierarchy al fresco, night itself redeemed by "glad solemnity," the "daughters of Necessity" lulled, an order constituted where rightly

Alpheus "by secret sluse" steals "under seas to meet his Arethuse." More than the Mask, this may claim to be Milton's festive comedy.[16]

Lycidas claims its just celebration not least as the climactic struggle of *Poems* (1645). The universe is called in question because the prepublic self, the model or reflection of the unrealized speaker, can die absurdly aborted. Reforming a public world or even seeking out an already achieved, less-fallen public world may be alike vertiginous projects in a world which drowns a would-be poet-priest "ere his prime." Yet the long time of preparatory learning must be spent, for without it a priest will be at best an unread "blind mouth." The insufficiently learned priest-poet's songs will be insubstantial, in contrast both to the presencing words of "Honourd Margaret" and to the words of this poet who makes present "thy loss to Shepherds ear" (49).

So this speaker, the last variant in the series, comes to us as an engaged man who is simultaneously a man in profound crisis. In a world contiguous with the other scenes of *Poems* (1645) (even if the speaker does not at first know that), what can he do? He can act fraternally in loyal rituals of mourning. He can acknowledge the kinship of work and of death: the sable shroud will be the speaker's, might have been already; an *intimacy* of death is finally achieved. After a few more steps in this poem he will be able to confront (as in the Piedmont sonnet) the indignity of death: no sable shroud but "bones . . . hurl'd" in the "monstrous world" imaginatively visited and acknowledged.

That he and Lycidas were creatures of history — of the same culture, apprenticeship, and mentorship — renders the loss more poignantly as loss of self, analogous to an epidemic of small deaths in nature (45–49). So he begins what seems to me the major coping tactic of the poem, that tactic familiar from life of marshaling one source of reinforcement after another.

Except for the last, the reinforcements are destroyed, like troops committed piecemeal in a debacle. Nymphs of Druidic association, folklorish attribution, "the Muse her self that *Orpheus* bore" — all the aids from the deeps of the mind or Orphic life-seeking powers of poetic vocation — are savagely negated by "hideous roar" and "goary visage." Allegro's balletic youths dancing in the checkered shade are hailed into the immediacy of "tangles of *Neaera's* hair," a painful move because ambition for achievement has precluded that, the more painful because "the blind Fury" may preclude achievement and love alike.

That fame for earthly deeds is rightly tabulated in heaven is an Apollonian thought which establishes a line of resistance to engulfment by desperation, but only so long as the world permits such deeds. The spirits who represent Nature fail to engage such realities as "a perfidious bark" or "curses dark." Similarly, the (perhaps significantly male) representative of alma mater, Camus, can only lament. And the "Pilot of the Galilean lake" can neither explain nor assuage this sinking. He can identify abusers of the tradition for corporately dealing with mysteries he represents, but his harshness only shrinks the streams without recovering Lycidas. Condemnatory judgment lacks life-fostering power, even when just.

The struggling poet can gain brief respite by the familiar Herrickean strategy of fractionation into fine bits, like "bells, and flowrets of a thousand hues." This strategic withdrawal "to interpose a little ease" affords strength to address the otherness of the "monstrous world." The life-world of "som melodious tear" (14) balances the death-world of "watry bear" in an important sense. But that otherness of fable and hurled bones "to our moist vows denied" (159) must be confronted.

Remarkably, doing so permits the train of association which leads to the last emotional, intellectual, geographical reach, the crisis from which help comes. Surely William Madsen is right: St. Michael's voice answers.[17] He it is who can report — whether from within the speaker's entranced mind or outside — the mysterious ways of Heaven, and of transcendence. He does not provide a new name of God, not the Greek-ecclesiastical name *Christ*. Rather, he gives the particularly appropriate power and quasi-Hebraic definition-by-thing-done: "the dear might of him who walked the waves."

The dear might was both precious and costly alike to the Saviour and to those who would be saved. Such ambiguity signifies involvement. And the image enables the poet to accept it, and accept Lycidas as an image of fidelity. In fidelity to his vocation he persevered past the boundary between the known and unknown, and by that doing is "genius of the shore." He is that, too, because his fidelity and salvation attest to the boundedness of the sea; the monstrous world cannot utterly engulf being. Yet the coexistence of that monstrous world attests to the mysterious power of his God. All this in turn gives the poet strength to accept realistically the world and move "to fresh woods and pastures new" even if they lie beyond the boundary of the known. A "great redemption" from the desperately realized hopelessness of our deathly world has been brought, both "from above" and from below, to a poet who, in *Lycidas*, has come far from the poet who applauded redemption with such poignant innocence in the Nativity hymn. This poet is eligible for the company who would repair the ruins of our first parents (as he defines duty in "Of Education"). Now he qualifies to attempt the instruction of his country (as he proposes in his preface to Book II of *The Reason of Church Government*). He has come to a thing which a bard must know, that it is "the very essence of history to impute to us responsibilities which are never entirely ours."[18]

Louisiana State University

NOTES

1. See especially Louis L. Martz, "The Rising Poet," in *The Lyric and Dramatic Milton*, ed. Joseph Summers, English Institute Essays (New York, 1965), pp. 3–33, and Arthur Barker, "The Pattern of Milton's 'Nativity Ode'," (*UTQ*, X (1940–41), 167–81). See also Anna K. Nardo, *Milton's Sonnets and the Ideal Community* (Lincoln, Neb., 1979), for persuasive and roughly analogous argument about the sonnets. The 1645 edition is readily available in *Poems of Mr. John Milton: The 1645 Edition with Essays in Analysis*, ed. Cleanth Brooks and John Edward Hardy (New York, 1951).

2. "The Sacred Head: Milton's Solar Mysticism," *Milton Studies*, IX, ed. James D. Simmonds (Pittsburgh, Pa., 1976), p. 61.

3. "On the Morning of Christ's Nativity," (1–5), in *The Complete Poetry of John Milton*, rev. ed., ed. John T. Shawcross (Garden City, N.Y., 1971).

4. See Edward W. Said; "Notes on the Characterization of a Literary Text," in *Velocities of Change*, ed. Richard Macksey (Baltimore, 1974), pp. 32–57; and "Narrative: Quest for Origins and Discovery of the Mausoleum," *Salmagundi*, IX (1970), 63–72; rpt. in *Beginnings: Intention and Method* (New York, 1975). John Spencer Hill helpfully summarizes and persuasively argues from much previous scholarship in "Poet-Priest: Vocational Tension in Milton's Early Development," *Milton Studies*, VIII, ed. James D. Simmonds (Pittsburgh, Pa., 1975), pp. 41–69.

5. See Norford, "The Sacred Head."

6. For summary of the debate on this poem, see *Variorum Commentary on the Poems of John Milton*, ed. A. S. P. Woodhouse and Douglas Bush (New York, 1972) II, pts. 1, 2, and 3. See for "Nativity," II, i, 38–63.

7. William Riley Parker found Joshua Sylvester's "manner . . . simple riming with ornate language" (*Milton, A Biography* [Oxford, 1968], I, p. 20). ·

8. Commonplace here in the semitechnical sense. See Walter Ong, *Rhetoric, Romance, and Technology: Studies in the Interaction of Expression and Culture* (Ithaca, N.Y., 1971), esp. chs. 2, 4, and 11.

9. Shawcross notes Horace's "exegii monumentum aere perennius," p. 94.

10. Cf. especially the point tangent to this made by Leslie Brisman, "'All Before Them Where to Choose': 'L'Allegro' and 'Il Penseroso,'" *JEGP*, LXXI (1972), 226–40, esp. 228; and Leonora Leet Brodwin, "Milton and the Renaissance Circe," *Milton Studies*, VI, ed. James D. Simmonds (Pittsburgh, Pa., 1974), pp. 21–83, esp. 45–46.

11. Brodwin, "Milton and the Renaissance Circe," pp. 44–45, likewise notes estrangement, as do Woodhouse and Bush in *Variorum Commentary* (II, i, 25–26). The latter also adduce as sources Jonson's Mere-Foole and Sir Thomas Overbury's Melancholy Man, who "thinks business, but never does any . . . all contemplation no action" (II, i, 239).

12. Perhaps too problematical to belong in the main argument is: "barren mountain brest . . . on which labouring clouds do often rest." That sounds oddly abstractive and un-implicated, given the context of blessed and fatal fertility in *Poems* (1645). Cf. Jonson's Cokes.

13. Two centuries ago, Samuel Johnson observed in his "Life of Milton" that "both Mirth and Melancholy are solitary, silent inhabitants of the breast that neither receive nor transmit communication; no mention is therefore made of a philosophical friend, or a pleasant companion. . . . No mirth can indeed be found in his melancholy; but I am afraid that I always meet some melancholy in his mirth. They are two noble efforts of imagination." Brooks and Hardy, *Poems*, tried to resolve the seeming (but not actual) non sequitur of his last sentence above. See especially pp. 131 and 139.

14. Those subjunctives are too often glossed over; but see John Spencer Hill, "Poet-Priest," p. 56. Penseroso's final proposal may superficially look priestly-poetic enough to be Miltonic; but it is neither preacherly-active enough nor poetic-prophetic enough to repre-sent the Milton whose studying was always study for some kerygmatic purpose.

15. For this condensed assimilation to my thesis of the sonnets in *Poems, 1645*, I've found support in Nardo's extended and persuasive treatment of all Milton's sonnets as a coherent series in exploration of community. *Milton's Sonnets*, esp. chs. 2 and 3, and pp. 60–66.

16. I allude, of course, to C. L. Barber's *Shakespeare's Festive Comedy* (Princeton, 1959), and to his disinclination to treat *Comus* that way, in "The *Mask* as a Masque," in *The Lyric and Dramatic Milton*, ed. Joseph Summers (New York, 1965). I agree with Barber more emphatically now than I did in "Milton's Ludlow Mask: From Chaos to Community," *ELH*, XXXIII (1966), 23–42. But see also Thomas O. Calhoun, "On John Milton's *A Mask at Ludlow*," *Milton Studies*, VI, ed. James D. Simmonds (Pittsburgh, Pa., 1974), pp. 165–79; Rosemary Mundhenck, "Dark Scandal and the Sun-Clad Power of Chastity: The Historical Milieu of Milton's Comus," *SEL*, XV (1975), 141–52; and Barbara Breasted, "Comus and the Castlehaven Scandal," *Milton Studies*, III, ed. James D. Sim-monds (Pittsburgh, Pa., 1971). The *Mask* seems as distinct generically as it does biblio-graphically from the other English works of *Poems, 1645*. I suggest it is a counterritual. See Mara Selvini Palazzoli, *Self-Starvation: From Individual to Family Therapy in the Treat-ment of Anorexia Nervosa* (New York, 1978), esp. chs. 23–27; and, with Luigi Boscolo, Gianfranco Cecchin, Guiliana Prata, *Paradox and Counter-paradox: A New Model in the Therapy of the Family in Schizophrenic Transaction* (New York, 1978).

17. "The Voice of Michael in 'Lycidas,'" *SEL* III (1963), 1–9.

18. Maurice Merleau-Ponty, "The Yogi and The Proletarian," in *The Primacy of Perception*, trans. Nancy Metzel and John Flodstrom, ed. James M. Edie (Evanston, 1964), p. 223.

MILTON'S NATIVITY ODE:
THE FUNCTION OF POETRY AND
STRUCTURES OF RESPONSE IN 1629
(with a Bibliography of
Twentieth-Century Criticism)

I. S. MacLaren

T HOSE CONCERNED with the composition of *On the Morning of Christ's Nativity*, a poem which recently enjoyed the tercenquiquagenary of its own nativity, may avail themselves of nearly one hundred twentieth-century critical views citing approximately three dozen pertinent source references for the poem's imagery, theme and structure. Still, the saturation point of critical study remains on the horizon when we remind ourselves — by a cursory glance through the marginalia and Milton's own appended index in his copy of Pindar (purchased by him on 15 November 1629, and thoroughly studied, he tells us, between 17 June and 28 September 1630) — how prolific were Milton's powers of and penchant for collating allusions and synthesizing ideas in what he had read at the age of twenty-one.[1] One vital area of inquiry which seems to have been oddly neglected by this century's criticism is what the immediate poetical and political purposes of Milton's poem might have been. We too often have stopped short at agreeing that the poem marks Milton's coming of age, that it boldly demonstrates the poet's first success at combining Christian and classical elements, and that it is meant, plainly, to celebrate Christmas and to be Milton's present to his God and to his friend, Diodati, who had requested a poem.

Thus, in an effort to understand the political/social purpose of the poem, I will consider its poetical purpose — specifically, the question of how reader response is elicited by the generic and stanzaic forms employed in the work. These will be treated as mimetic functions of what Milton later would delineate as poetry's purpose — to challenge the reader to respond to the opportunity of God's grace, provided at the Nativity and provided continuously at each successive anniversary of it and other events in Christ's life. Implicit in this approach and worthy of preliminary attention is the developing continuity of poetic purpose discernible throughout Milton's *oeuvre:* all of his major and many of his minor poetic achievements are, in some sense, occasional poems, relating poetics and aesthetics to religion and politics in England. Discussion of the poetical and political purposes of this early ode in terms of the genres and forms it employs therefore requires a prefatory review of the development of Milton's concept of the function of poetry.[2]

Professors Barker and Leishman, among others, agree that Milton was referring to the experience of composing the Nativity ode when he wrote in 1642, "And long it was not after, when I was confirmed in this opinion that he who would not be frustrate of his hope to write well hereafter in.laudable things, ought himself to be a true poem."[3] The experiences of 1629–1630 gave Milton not only his first great poetical success, but also what recently has been termed the "shipwrecked effort" of *The Passion*.[4] This pattern of success followed by failure, discernible at many stages in Milton's life, was not (perhaps surprisingly) something he chose to conceal. When preparing his poems for publication in 1645, still a time when he could ill afford a public self-portrait which he was not wholly prepared to defend, Milton chose to include both success and failure in the volume, a fact which suggests that both represented to him parts of a struggle to achieve an ideal.[5] A veteran by 1645 of the pamphlet wars, Milton had often succeeded and failed, and had been repeatedly forced to recollect and reconsider what he had thought were his firm religious and political convictions and allegiances. This exfoliation of his own ideas made him acutely aware that the ideal of the true poem, on paper and in his life as a man, could not mean writing one great poem after another any more than his ideal of Christian liberty could be achieved with facility by England. The 1645–1646 poems attest to the former, while *Areopagitica*, published thirteen months earlier, deals with the latter. As investigations of similar ideals, both works are founded on the rhythms of human experience, of success and failure, which are audible in them. This passage from *Areopagitica* is apposite:

For this is not the liberty which we can hope, that no grievance ever should arise in the Commonwealth — that let no man in this world expect; but when complaints are freely heard, deeply considered, and speedily reformed, then is the utmost bound of civil liberty attained that wise men look for.[6]

The diazeugma of the verb phrases, "freely heard, deeply considered, and speedily reformed," both defines and mimetically represents the rhythm of human experience. Such a rhythm is clearly audible, as we shall see, in the structure and stanzaic form of the Nativity ode. More-over, given its prominent place in the volume, this poem might have been considered by Milton as a most successful mimesis of the rhythms of human experience, which poetry can achieve when it fulfills all its functions. Four years before publishing the Nativity ode Milton had de-lineated them.

These [poetic] abilities, wheresoever they be found, are the inspired gift of God rarely bestowed, but yet to some (though most abuse) in every nation; and are of power beside the office of a pulpit, to inbreed and cherish in a great people the seeds of virtue and public civility, to allay the perturbations of the mind and set the affections in right tune, to celebrate in glorious and lofty hymns the throne and equipage of God's almightiness, and what he works and what he suffers to be wrought with high providence in his church, to sing the victorious agonies of martyrs and saints, the deeds and triumphs of just and pious nations doing val-iantly through faith against the enemies of Christ, to deplore the general relapses of kingdoms and states from justice and God's true worship. Lastly, whatsoever in religion is holy and sublime, in virtue amiable or grave, whatsoever hath pas-sion or admiration in all the changes of that which is called fortune from with-out, or the wily subtleties and refluxes of man's thoughts from within, all these things with a solid and treatable smoothness to paint out and describe. Teaching over the whole book of sanctity and virtue through all the instances of example, with such delight . . . that whereas the paths of honesty and good life appear now rugged and difficult, though they be indeed easy and pleasant, they would then appear to all men both easy and pleasant, though they were rugged and dif-ficult indeed.[7]

To purge and to inbreed, to allay and to restore, to deplore and to cor-rect, to lament and to celebrate, to teach and to delight — these are the offices of the poet whose experience of the rhythms of life and whose natural abilities entitle and oblige him to convey God's ways to men mimetically, to the end that they may know how to hear, what to con-sider, and when and how to reform their own lives.

Its embodiment of these functions of poetry and its integrity of form are, it seems to me, the features that distinguish *On the Morning of Christ's Nativity* from any of Milton's earlier poems, and are what provoked Milton's optimism in his letter to Diodati. Examination of the poem's stanzaic structures and its two-part form will clarify how the ode fulfills all the functions of poetry in Milton's terms, and not merely those of celebration and entertainment.[8]

Starting at the start of this poem has repeatedly caused difficulties because of the sense one has that Milton does not really start until "The Hymn." But one must confront the problem of the opening stanzas' relation to the hymn. Frank Kastor, who reads the poem as a response to the Renaissance humanistic poetic tradition of the "mythological and narrative formalization of the Christian version of history which Milton would make, later and vastly more expanded, the subject of *Paradise Lost*," divides the proem into two sections, each comprising two stanzas.[9] The first two stanzas establish both the occasion and "the large framing story with its time scheme of pre-fall heaven to post-judgment heaven. Also . . . they establish Milton's point of view as omniscient author." By using the past tense almost exclusively in this section, the poet has served notice that he is recalling a well-known tradition. As he moves from the omniscient view of the Christian world to his own participation in the occasion at hand in stanzas three and four, the narrator brings the first celebration of the Nativity into the focus of 1629. The verb tense accommodates this turn by switching to the present in stanza three, thereby stylistically effecting the distinction between the historical/omniscient/heavenly and the current/personal/earthly. Thus, there are two distinct parts in the proem, both of which are conventional, but neither one, I submit, necessarily representing Milton's view. The proem might suggest an autobiographical reading but the unique form of the hymn, its breadth of vision and its much more complex view of the Nativity, all suggest that Milton employs the hymn as a learning experience for his narrator. By harmonizing the proem's confusedly dualistic view, the hymn figures forth the process by which the narrator learns to respond to the Nativity, and, in terms of the poem's narrative, works his way to the stable by poem's end. And, it hardly need be pointed out, the harmonization of the omniscient and the personal, the heavenly and the earthly, mimetically celebrates the Nativity of the being who first managed such harmony for man's sake.

Generically, the poem is composed of two sections and employs two terms, ode and hymn. Sorting out this confusion has attracted much attention. David B. Morris calls the poem a Pindaric ode, while Philip Rollinson views it solely as a liturgical hymn. They were corrected by Hugh MacCallum to the extent that he perceived how the subject matter of the poem could be regarded as proper for ode *and* hymn, given Milton's prescriptions for those genres in *The Reason of Church Government*. There, as we have seen, Milton orders the ode after Pindar, as the mode of celebrating "the victorious agonies of martyrs and saints," and the hymn, after Callimachus, as the mode of celebrating "the throne and equipage of God's almightiness." MacCallum's correction was a simple but needful one: it demonstrated that Milton treats the Son as both a member of the Trinity and a man, both Pan and

Hercules, both Son of God in heaven and son of man in the manger and on the cross.[10]

In the light of Kastor's salutary study, however, it appears that Milton is collating not only the subject matter of the two genres, but also their structures. Rather than offer another possible breakdown of the hymn's structure, I would suggest that the hymn be regarded alone as one discrete part of a tripartite poem which also includes the two-part proem already delineated. This provides the general pattern of a Pindaric ode: the strophe and antistrophe (the two parts of the proem) are structurally identical and together are distinct from the structure of the epode. Moreover, the hymn of Milton's poem fulfills the thematic function of the Pindaric epode (etymologically, the part which is "sung after") by responding to the dialectic built between the strophe and antistrophe. This pattern — one not dissimilar to, though "more simple, sensuous, and passionate" than, the structure of rhetorical debate upon which Milton's *Academic Exercises* of this period are modeled — may help to resolve Milton's use of the two terms "Hymn" and "humble ode" in the poem: the hymn is a discrete entity, has its own stanza form, its own beginning and end, but also it participates in a larger poem — an ode — as its epode, harmonizing the apparently disparate points of view that introduce it. Thus, the poem proceeds in a manner analogous to both Christ's effort to harmonize apparent misfortunes and refluxes of thought with God's ways, and a similar response required of the poem's reader, the Nativity's celebrant.

The hymn also weaves together the past and present tenses used in the two sections of the proem. The result is not the "biplanar" perspective found by Lowry Nelson, Jr.;[11] nor is it a view of the Nativity "as an isolated and static event occurring at a particular moment in time and as an essential episode in the comprehensive drama of history," as Morris argues.[12] Both these approaches ultimately distinguish, as do the strophe and antistrophe, between the poem's eternal and temporal perspectives, suggesting that the poem fluctuates between them. Rather, the hymn's variations of tense permit a continuous rhythmic infusion of the eternal with the temporal, the temporal with the eternal, and thereby adumbrate the role of Christ. The hymn is not a linear string of conceits as Warton suggested, or a Mystery Cycle of static tableaux, but a continuous struggle to represent simultaneously several views of and reactions to Christ's arrival, to balance the mystical awe of the "glorious and lofty hymn" and the sober respect one pays the mortal, odic hero who "on the bitter cross" (152) must suffer the "agonies" of mortal life. Readers are thus encouraged to moderate their ecstasy at Christmas and their anguish at Good Friday by striving to understand God's purpose for two such apparently disparate occasions, as Christ must have striven when, "on the bitter cross," he could say, "today shalt thou be with me in Paradise."

This process of understanding begins for the narrator at the lost harmony of the "winter wild" of life in the hymn's first stanza. It proceeds, gradually, to a regeneration of lost harmony by allaying the perturbations of the mind and setting the affections in the hymn's right tune. But that process is not straightforward or formulaic: it is punctuated by the rhythms of human experience, of success and failure, which are mimetically presented in the hymn's stanza form, a form unique in English poetry.

Balachandra Rajan remarks that the effect of the form is "reminiscent of a carillon of church-bells," partly for the rhythms built by the "to and fro movement" caused by lines of different length, and partly for the way those lines are rhymed. But if the poem serves more poetic functions than "celebrating a happy event with a kind of crystalline joy,"[13] and is a song to be sung by human voices, then perhaps the madrigal is the musical form behind this unique stanza.[14] That Milton was home from Cambridge for the Christmas of 1629 is not definitely known.[15] That he would have turned to his father's favorite art form for his first inspired work requires even dizzier speculation. It is important, however, that the madrigal, heard on an organ (the instrument Milton played best), or sung, provides the kind of contrapuntal variety capable of accommodating the rhythms of advance and retreat being worked out in the epode. And it was the madrigal's contrapuntal variety, its ability to synthesize a number of different human voices, that caused it to flourish in English music before 1629. This quality suited Milton's purpose in the epode: the rhyme scheme ($a\ a\ b\ c\ c\ b\ d\ d$) suggests a lyrical form, but the variety in line-length distinguishes the stanza from anything recognizably lyrical. The first, second, fourth and fifth lines in each eight-line stanza are trimeters; the third and sixth are pentameters; the seventh is a tetrameter and the eighth an alexandrine. A dynamic rhythm, not to say a struggle, culminating in the gradually achieved integrity of the alexandrine, is played out dramatically, rather than lyrically, at the structural level of the verse. A pair of trimeters advances to a pentameter, and retreats again; another pair advances to the pentameter and, though unsuccessful, is repulsed only to the tetrameter before the final assault achieves the alexandrine. This infrastructure does not correspond strictly to any explicit thematic dialectic in each verse, but it does imitate the rhythm of struggle in the ode's epode. The trimeters are amplified and then moderated, gradually gathering the pentameters and the tetrameter with them, struggling to a harmony (*d* is composed of *a*, *b*, and *c* in the rhyme scheme) that none of them alone can produce. "The modulation that is orchestrated by the epodic contraction and expansion of the metrical line," is, as Don Cameron Allen notes, the poem's structural mimesis of its theme. And, as Isabel MacCaffrey observes, the stanzaic form is analogous to the poetic form employed: "The long and short lines of the stanzaic pattern, alluding to the alternation of strophe, antistrophe and epode in the Pindaric ode, expand and contract in a movement answering to the rhythmical widening and narrowing of the speaker's vision."[16]

Clearly, the rhythm of the stanza is linked to the hymn's function as epode, and is representative of Milton's later conception of poetry's need to "paint out and describe" "*all* the changes of that which is called fortune from without, or the wily subtleties and refluxes of man's thoughts from within" (emphasis added). The effect is not that of "remoteness and the tranced deliberation of movement appropriate to the dream vision," as Brooks and Hardy argue.[17] Instead, those disparate fluxes and refluxes are interfused dynamically in a progressive dialectic, and their eventual synthesis, like the cohesion of previous line-lengths in the alexandrine, exceeds its constituents. Nevertheless, whatever achievement appears to have been made in the alexandrine's (all of which but one are end-stopped) is modified ironically by the trimeter in the next stanza's first line. The temporary union or harmony is dispersed, as in a madrigal, into its original, distinct parts. This pattern might well suggest a parody of progression, as in the myth of Sisyphus, and the close of the hymn on the image with which it set out might confirm such an interpretation. But the alexandrine, as has so often been remarked, clearly displays an impressive energy, and that energy accumulates with each successive regeneration of the rhythm and the rhyme. Combined with the reader's expectation that a poem on this subject will conclude positively, that energy urges the struggle at least in the direction of resolution.

When one approaches the hymn in this way, regarding it as the fulfillment of its function as epode, this sense of progression is crucial. Many critics have complained, Malcolm Ross, John Broadbent, and John Carey perhaps most vociferously, that the poem is not enough about the humanity of the manger, attributing that deficiency to Milton's Puritan, dehumanizing self-indulgence.[18] Rather, we see that Milton is gradually working out the process by which to get his narrator and his reader to the manger as participants, not merely as spectators.

This process involves harmonizing the omniscient view of the event —
God's purpose and the Son's acceptance of that purpose — with the conventional, misguided, human reaction of blind adoration and mere
astonishment at the arrival of the Redeemer. That baroque reaction,
depicted in the poem by the shepherds, is being modified by Milton.
The "present" (16) which one should be preventing the "Star-led Wiz-
ards" with should not be blind faith in a life saver, but the willingness to
follow the model Christ offers. That alone offers an "order serviceable";
that is some use to men in their own lives on earth. And as the narrator's
understanding of this dawns on him gradually — Barker's study of the
pattern of light imagery is invaluable here — we remember his stark,
dormant view of the Nativity in the hymn's first stanza. It is lifeless because the narrator is not participating in the event. But by stanza xxvii,
much has been accomplished; the writing of the hymn, and the setting
of one's affections in right tune in order to fully respond to the event,
have produced that sense of alacrity one feels. We are, as it were, "attending" (242) the scene as well, and if our perception is unperturbed,
then, coincidentally and consequently, the Sun/Son sheds the light we
require to "But see!" it (237).

The "rest" in the hymn's last stanza implies a deserved respite before the resumption of the struggle: the "Bright-harness'd Angels" have
polished their uniforms; the "car" is "polisht" and all are "attending"
the example of their venerated and respected leader. It is as if the hymn
merely has prepared the characters and set the scene for a drama that is
about to unfold (which is, of course, the ongoing drama already re-
hearsed in the poem). When we look back to stanza i, the scene seems
barren and dehumanized by contrast, composed of nothing but the
forms and Nature's apparently equivocal response to them. By poem's
end the narrator's perception has improved to the extent that he now invites us to see what previously he could not. We are invited, Diodati is
invited (if not commanded by the imperative), not just to look, "But
see!" — see the part we have to sing in "*our* tedious song" (emphasis
added), so that a Nativity tableau will be generated with life and the
historical event will be rejuvenated and celebrated in the present. We
should celebrate, not by overindulgence in food and drink at "festivals
which honour the heaven-forsaking god,"[19] as Diodati had done, but by
responding to Christ's gift of the opportunity to order our lives in a harmonious, "serviceable" way (244).

Just as the narrator's perception must be modified, other responses
occur and are tempered by turns in the hymn. George Smith labels this
aspect of the poem "the pattern of mistake then correction."[20] His terms

are slightly too rigorous, for they imply a "biplanar" dualism of right and wrong again, a concept too restrictive for Milton's sense of how God challenges men by providing them with new, continuously exfoliating opportunities for response. Nevertheless, Smith's analysis bears much fruit. He sees that Nature, the stars, the shepherds, the sun, and "our fancy," one after the other, mistake the vehicle of the Nativity for the tenor, and that "by repeating with variations the pattern of mistake then correction, Milton achieves structural continuity." One enactment of that pattern is the initial response by Nature: "naively beseeching winter snow to be her redemption, she has seized on the vehicle without the tenor, on the sign with no comprehension of the inward and spiritual grace." Similarly, "our fancy" wanders to an apocalyptic view of the event at the center of the hymn, and would "abridge Christian indirection and have the millennium occur immediately upon Christ's birth." This response occurs as a series of associations unguided by reason.

Each step in the misjoining of associations is very short: from the angels' music to the last time it was heard, from the music of the spheres at Creation to the prelapsarian participation of the earth, then to the vision [of the Golden Age restored at the millennium]. This sequence is unimpeded and . . . Milton is demonstrating how easily made, how plausible is fancy's mistake. . . . But it is on the pre-Christian vehicle rather than the Christian tenor that "our fancy" seizes; and the three parts are misjoined through the vehicles rather than through the association with Christ's birth. The vision not only attributes redemptive power to the angelic chorus, but also ignores entirely the person and role of Christ.[21]

What Smith seems to overlook in his otherwise perceptive analysis is that the narrator also participates in each of those responses and moderations, and thereby learns to modify his own perturbations of baroque joy and his unreasonable expectations of the Nativity as a universe-transforming spectacle. Milton is aware, moreover, that many of his readers (as much subsequent criticism bears out) will share the narrator's expectations. Thus, he manipulates those expectations by offering the transcendental vision as one potential response to the event, and, as an alternative, potential resolution of the heavenly/earthly dialectic established in the proem's strophe and antistrophe. Stanzas xiv–xvi, with their extended "if/But" grammatical relation (133, 149), tease us with the song which has the power to "touch our senses" (127), "enwrap our fancy" (134), and guide us to the "Gates of [heaven's] high Palace Hall" (148). But this potential response is meant to remind us of the self-annihilating tendency in Nature's earlier response to the music. She "was almost won / To think her part was done, / And that her reign had here its last fulfilling" (104–06). The shepherds respond similarly: the music of the spheres "*all* their souls in blissful rapture took" (98, emphasis added).

These incidents, and, similarly, the stature accorded many of the pagan gods in the hymn's catalogue, testify to the human potential for perverting God's purposes by submitting to enchanting tones instead of responding actively to the models of harmonious human endeavor provided by God. For the poet who "cannot praise a fugitive and cloistered virtue, unexercised and unbreathed," the potential for not acting, for listening but not singing, is anathema. "But wisest fate says no"—the monosyllabic blows shatter the visionary dream as the if/but structure is completed at the start of the hymn's middle stanza. This marks Milton's most dramatic use of a stanza's opening trimeter to modify the temporary achievement won by the preceding alexandrine. "We are," as Nelson remarks, "brought 'down to earth' again in being reminded that the Christ child is still a child, and will grow up and suffer death on the cross."[22] Having been teased out of ourselves, we are ruthlessly made to turn and see the person in whom our fancy's transcendental aspirations originated, now apparelled in the corporeal form (which we so lately were willing to abandon) and suffering pain and humiliation for our sake.

Yet, our perturbed hopes are not entirely dispelled in the way that Smith argues; they are allayed, tempered, and redirected by the presence of "yet" in the next line: "This must not yet be so" (150). Combined again with the "gift of reason," as Milton calls it in *Areopagitica*, "our fancy" can celebrate and sponsor an active response to the Nativity in our lifetime. Like the angelic song which "*Could* hold all Heav'n and Earth in happier union" (108), Christ "*Can* in his swaddling bands control the damned crew" (228, emphasis added), and the "order" (244) his presence offers us as a model for our lives can be of service. But these too are potentialities: only if men play a part in this "symphony" (132), only if our different voices are heard will the "hideous hum" (174) be restored to harmony. The dragon has been subdued, not vanquished; the prospect of regeneration has been presented but in no wise has Paradise been made sure, as Rosemond Tuve would have it.[23]

We have seen how the dramatic pattern of the hymn deals with the dialectic of the proem's strophe and antistrophe by describing, moderating, and reforming a variety of responses to the Nativity, and we have seen how the stanzaic form of the hymn mimetically represents the struggle of that dramatic pattern. Similar relations of structure and theme are, of course, discernible throughout the Miltonic *oeuvre*. From the "Nativity Ode," Rajan tells us, "it is a far cry . . . to the bleak prophecies of Michael."[24] Yet, as the remark implies, that cry is audible in *Paradise Lost*, however far it may have traveled. One hears it, though in another key, in Michael's postlapsarian advice to Adam for his reformation and regeneration:

> know I am sent
> To show thee what shall come in future days
> To thee and to thy Offspring; good with bad
> Expect to hear, supernal Grace contending
> With sinfulness of Men; thereby to learn
> True patience, and to temper joy with fear
> And pious sorrow, equally inur'd
> By moderation either state to bear,
> Prosperous or adverse: so shalt thou lead
> Safest thy life, and best prepar'd endure
> Thy mortal passage when it comes.   (XI, 356–66)[25]

The dramatic rhythms of Books XI and XII are based on Adam's oscillations between extremes of joy and fear as he reacts to events in history. His elation is qualified by Michael; his despair is mitigated. His exuberant response to the story of Christ's Nativity is not too dissimilar to our fancy's: he praises Michael as the "finisher / Of utmost hope" (XII, 375–76). His conclusion that man will be rescued from Satan and that Satan will suffer a "capital bruise" (XII, 383) echoes the Nativity ode and requires similar modification. Michael warns Adam to "Dream not of thir fight, / As of a Duel" (XII, 386–87) — not to dichotomize in a world of wish fulfillment, but to remember joy in fear and fear in moments of joy; to remember that Satan is only "in straiter limits bound" (Nativity ode, 169), and that the pagan gods are not routed, but can only be controlled (228).[26]

Gradually, the oscillating responses of Adam and the Nativity ode narrator diminish, but the process never stops and is far from complete as Adam and Eve leave Paradise or as the narrator reaches the "Courtly Stable" (243). Faith alone is not enough: it must be exercised and breathed by men into an order useful to them in their lifetimes. Clearly, poetry's purpose of conveying these understandings was understood similarly by the twenty-one-year-old student and the sixty-year-old epic poet. As previously noted, its placement at the beginning of *Poems* (1645) suggests that "On the Morning of Christ's Nativity" enjoyed Milton's approval at a time when parts of *Paradise Lost* and *Paradise Regained* may already have been embarked upon.

In Milton's theory, poetry also had a public function — its social, religious and political utility, beside the office of the pulpit, to men. It is difficult to imagine that Milton, who becomes so publicly engaged, not to say embroiled, in the affairs of his country a mere decade later, and who dates his relation of a true poem to a virtuous life from the composition of the Nativity ode, would have held no strong views of public affairs in 1629. Yet this is the impression given by much criticism of the poem, especially that which views it as a dream vision or meditation. But 1629 had been anything but a dream vision in England. In May, the Queen had prematurely delivered a baby which died in a matter of hours, an event which sadly disappointed a nation awaiting its first native birth of a sovereign in almost a century.[27] Henrietta Maria was pregnant again by October, but fears for her welfare and successful accouchement were widespread and intensified by a growing plague in London. Prayers for her success were popularly offered in England and Scotland from November on, and Laud, newly made the Bishop of London, spent the Christmas season "concocting a special prayer," as Elizabeth Hamilton puts it, and arranging a special fertility Thanksgiving service to be held in the New Year.[28]

But this was not the only factor which might have prompted Milton's concern about the celebration of a more significant Nativity. In the spring of 1629, Charles had repeatedly prorogued Parliament to avoid having the Commons pass legislation outlawing the levying of his tonnage and poundage taxes without a parliamentary grant. Charles finally countered by dissolving Parliament and beginning an eleven-year reign, effectively without the voice of the English people. Further, he instructed Laud to muzzle all controversial preachers later in the year.[29]

The events are cited not to suggest specific sources for Milton's poem, but to demonstrate how "momentous," as one critic calls it, the year 1629 was for England as well as for a young poet coming of age.[30] And because we are dealing here with an occasional poem whose chosen subtitle is a specific date, the public events of 1629 should not be ignored. The very pointed reference in the poem's opening line — "This is the month, and this the happy morn" — juxtaposes the pattern of history with 1629, when the voice of the people was dissolved, the voices of God's word and the celebrants of His Son's Nativity muzzled, and the attention of the nation, as well as the Bishop of London, focused on the imminent birth of a secular prince. The nation was perhaps not sufficiently responsive to the opportunity afforded by Christ's Nativity, and Milton's own response realizes that possibility. The morning of Christ's Nativity, 1629, represents the dawning of new hope for men, but it easily might be ignored, as the pun on "Morning" in the poem's title and the remembrance of the Passion at the hymn's centre suggest. Milton recognizes that Christ is not often accorded attention and response until He is "on the bitter cross" on Good Friday. This recognition is dramatized through Milton's combination of two separate traditions telling of the cessation of the oracles, at Christ's birth and at Christ's death.[31] The date in the title also calls attention to the irony that 1,628 celebrations of Christ's Nativity had not, especially given the events of 1629, produced the millennium or restored the Golden Age. Thus the date serves to temper the baroque idealism and the "crystalline joy" of the ode. But if it tempers one extreme response, it guards against the other extreme—indifference. "This is the Month, and this the happy morn" when those who can and will "But see!" will find the Son/Sun arise in a stable far more courtly and a court far more stable than any secular prince could provide.

We have no facts to substantiate this political reading as we have for some of Milton's later poems — only the sense that Milton had his nation's current response in mind when writing any of his poems, including many written before the Nativity ode, such as the Gunpowder Plot poems and "Elegia Quarta." Here, in 1629, was an opportunity being squandered, if not perverted, by the bishop's concern for another nativity, and if the pulpit was not fulfilling its functions, then poetry must, and one of its functions, described immediately after the remarks on the hymn and ode in the passage from *The Reason of Church Government* mentioned earlier, is "to deplore the general relapses of kingdoms and states from justice and God's true worship." In a kingdom whose sects, religious and political, were beginning to polarize, it must have struck Milton as profoundly ironic that, while on this day was born into the world one who could balance the greatest of polarities (heaven and earth, the spirit and the body), the attention of his fellow men may have been diverted from the very model of "our peace" being sought. Just as Virgil, in his anticipation of the Nativity in the *Messianic Eclogue*, had recognized that the opportunity to restore the Golden Age could have been either realized or squandered, so Milton, in 1629, could see that the pattern of reform offered at the Nativity in the person of Christ could be either imitated or desecrated by the English people. As we have seen, the poem allows for both possibilities, while sharply insisting that England must respond with alacrity and assiduity if, as he suggested in a different but not unrelated context in 1641, it was to serve Christ's purpose and "be the first Restorer of Buried Truth."[32]

We can be sure that Milton's concern in 1629 was shared by at least one other Englishman, John Donne. His sermon for Christmas Day, which Milton may or may not have heard,[33] challenges his congregation to respond actively to the Nativity. He presents this challenge by bringing Christ immediately before them, as Milton's first line does, and as such other treatments as *Christ's Victorie and Triumph* could not:[34]

> But I bring it closer then so; now, and here, within these wals, and at this houre, comes Christ unto you, in the offer of this abundance; and with what penurious-nesse, penuriousnesse of devotion, penuriousnesse of reverence do you meet him here? . . . *God standeth in the Congregation;* does God stand there, and wilt thou sit?

The argument of prose does not, of course, employ the rhythms of poetry, but the idea resembles Milton's theme. So too does Donne's encouragement to put to use the "order serviceable" offered by Christ:

> That grace which God offers us in the Church, does not onely fill that capacity, which we have, but gives us a greater capability then we had: And it is an abuse of God's grace, not to emprove it, or not to procure such farther grace, as that present grace makes us capable of.[35]

Donne and Milton are not exceptions in their focus on response to grace rather than merely the celebration of its offer. Milton could have found a similar approach, though not so emphatic, in the sermons of Lancelot Andrewes (to whom Milton's *Elegia Tertia* is dedicated), which had been published earlier in 1629; and, doubtless, his formal education served to initiate the concern. What is unique in Milton's poem, besides the stanzaic form and the manipulation of hymn and ode which structure it, is the process by which the narrator gradually perceives the significance of both God's offer of grace through the Son and man's responsibility for response entailed in that offer. Neither the "repentant, world-stained sinner, nor a transported meditator"[36] (common roles for Nativity poem personae, both of which involve a privacy that tends to exclude immediate reader participation), Milton's narrator is humble, and, therefore, able to invite the reader's participation in his education, in what he calls "*our* tedious song." The harmony to be sung cannot be sung alone: it is "ninefold," includes all men on earth—the "Bass of Heav'n's deep Organ" (130)—and the rhythms of their human experience. Milton's poetic effort, searching for the best response, considers others and modifies them. The result, thematically and structurally, is a controlled complexity, a precarious harmony capable of purging and inbreeding, allaying and restoring, deploring and correcting, lamenting and also celebrating the Christmas of 1629, its attendant and attentive celebrants, and their responsive descendants three hundred and fifty years later.

University of Western Ontario

A CHRONOLOGICAL BIBLIOGRAPHY OF TWENTIETH-CENTURY CRITICISM

A chronological ordering has been chosen to indicate more readily the kind of critical attention which the Nativity ode has attracted at different periods in this century. As well, this method of listing facilitates the referral of one study to its immediate contemporaries, and to all studies prior to it. This format thus demonstrates both the "state of the art" of the poem's criticism at any one point in the century and the gradual composition of the body of criticism through eight decades. Publications in the same year are arranged alphabetically.

Grierson, Sir Herbert. *The First Half of the Seventeenth Century.* New York, 1906. P. 182.

Cook, Albert S. "The 'Ode on the Nativity' and the Poems of Mantuan." *MLR*, II (1906–07), 121–24.

Leach, A. F. "Milton as Schoolboy and Schoolmaster." *Proceedings of the British Academy*, III (1907–08), 15–16.

Cook, Albert S. "Notes on Milton's Ode on the Morning of Christ's Nativity." *Transactions of the Connecticut Academy of Arts and Sciences*, XV (1909), 307–68.

Saintsbury, George. "Milton." *Cambridge History of English Literature*, (1911), VII, pp. 110, 111, 132, 133.

Spaeth, Sigmund Gottfried. *Milton's Knowledge of Music: Its Sources and Its Significance in his Works.* Princeton, 1913. Pp. 90–92, 100–03.

Shafer, Robert. *The English Ode to 1660: An Essay in Literary History.* New York, 1918. Pp. 93–95.

Grierson, Sir Herbert. *Metaphysical Lyrics and Poems of the Seventeenth Century.* Oxford, 1921. P. xlviii.

Rand, E. K. "Milton in Rustication." *SP*, XIX (1922), 109–35.

Hanford, James Holly. "The Youth of Milton." In *Studies in Shakespeare, Milton and Donne.* University of Michigan Publications: Language and Literature, I. New York, 1925. Pp. 122–24. Rpt. 1964, and in *John Milton, Poet and Humanist, Essays by James Holly Hanford.* Cleveland, 1966. Pp. 35–36, 38.

Tillyard, E. M. W. *Milton.* London and New York, 1930. Pp. 35–42.

Knight, George Wilson. "The Frozen Labyrinth: An Essay on Milton." In *The Burning Oracle: Studies in The Poetry of Action.* London and New York, 1939. Pp. 59–113.

Whiting, George. *Milton's Literary Milieu.* New York, 1939. Rpt. 1964. Pp. 85–86, 177, 180, 184, 199, 211.

Shuster, George N. *The English Ode from Milton to Keats.* New York, 1940. Pp. 67–70.

Barker, Arthur E. "The Pattern of Milton's 'Nativity Ode.'" *UTQ*, X (1941), 167–81. Rpt. in *Milton: Modern Judgments.* Ed. A. Rudrum. London, 1968. Pp. 44–57.

_____. *Milton and the Puritan Dilemma 1641–1660.* Toronto, 1942. Rpt., 1955, 1964, 1971. Pp. 6–10.

Woodhouse, A. S. P. "Notes on Milton's Early Development." *UTQ*, XIII (1943), 66–101. "Nativity Ode," 73–77.

Myhr, Ivar L. [Duncan, Mrs. E. H.]. "Milton's HYMN ON THE MORNING OF CHRIST'S NATIVITY, Stanza 8." *Explicator*, IV (1945), item 16.

Ross, Malcolm M. "Milton and the Protestant Aesthetic: the Early Poems." *UTQ*, XVII (1948), 346–60. Rpt. in *Poetry and Dogma.* New Brunswick, N.J., 1954. Pp. 183–204.

Highet, Gilbert. *The Classical Tradition: Greek and Roman Influence on Western Literature.* London, 1949. Pp. 237–38.

Warner, Rex. *John Milton.* London and New York, 1949. Pp. 50–51.

Mack, Maynard. Ed. and intro. *Milton.* Vol. IV. *English Masterpieces.* Gen. ed. Maynard Mack. Englewood Cliffs, N.J., 1950. Pp. 5–7.

Mahood, M. M. *Poetry and Humanism*. London, 1950. Pp. 171–75.

Brooks, Cleanth, and John E. Hardy. *Poems of Mr. John Milton: The 1645 Edition With Essays in Analysis*. New York, 1951. Pp. 95–104.

Hutton, James. "Some English Poems in Praise of Music." *English Miscellany*, II (1951), 43–45.

Stapleton, Laurence. "Milton and the New Music." *UTQ*, XXIII (1953–54), 217–26. Rpt. in *Milton: Modern Essays in Criticism*. Ed. Arthur E. Barker. New York, 1965. Pp. 31–42.

Allen, Don Cameron. *The Harmonious Vision: Studies in Milton's Poetry*. Baltimore and London, 1954. Pp. 24–29.

Martz, Louis L. *The Poetry of Meditation: A Study in English Religious Literature of the Seventeenth Century*. New Haven and London, 1954. Pp. 164–67.

Nelson, Lowry, Jr. "Góngora and Milton: Toward a Definition of the Baroque." *CL*, VI (1954), 53–64. Rpt. in *Baroque Lyric Poetry*. New Haven and London, 1961. Pp. 41–52.

Prince, F. T. *The Italian Element in Milton's Verse*. Oxford, 1954. Pp. 58–62.

Muir, Kenneth. *John Milton*. London, 1955. Pp. 24–27.

Sypher, Wylie. *Four Stages of Renaissance Style: Transformations in Art and Literature 1400–1700*. Garden City, N.Y., 1955. P. 106.

Daiches, David. *Milton*. London, 1957. Pp. 38–48.

Tuve, Rosemond. *Images and Themes in Five Poems by Milton*. Cambridge, Mass., 1957. Pp. 37–72.

Broadbent, J. B. "The Nativity Ode." In *The Living Milton: Essays by Various Hands*. Ed. Frank Kermode. London, 1960. Pp. 12–31.

Maddison, Carol. *Apollo and the Nine: A History of the Ode*. London, 1960. Pp. 107–08, 151–52, 321–27.

Fletcher, Harris Francis. *The Intellectual Development of John Milton*. Urbana, Ill., 1961. II, pp. 494–98.

Sirluck, Ernest. "Milton's Idle Right Hand." *JEGP*, LX (1961), 756–57.

Finney, Gretchen. *Musical Backgrounds for English Literature 1580–1650*. New Brunswick, N.J., 1962. Pp. 163–64.

Cohen, J. M. *The Baroque Lyric*. London, 1963. Pp. 151–53.

Nicolson, Marjorie Hope. *John Milton: A Reader's Guide to his Poetry*. New York, 1963. Pp. 31–42.

Røstvig, Maren-Sofie. "The Hidden Sense: Milton and the Neoplatonic Method of Numerical Composition." In *The Hidden Sense and Other Essays. Norwegian Studies in English*, IX. Oslo, New York, 1963. Pp. 1–112, esp. pp. 44–58.

Bush, Douglas. *John Milton: A Sketch of His Life and Writings*. New York and London, 1964. Pp. 36–38.

Frazier, Harriet. "Time as Structure in Milton's 'Nativity Ode.'" *Universitas: A Journal of Religion and the University*, III i (1965), 8–14.

Martz, Louis L. "The Rising Poet, 1645." In *The Lyric and Dramatic Milton: Selected Papers from the English Institute*. Ed. Joseph H. Summers. New York and London, 1965. Pp. 22–33.

Patrides, C. A. "The Cessation of the Oracles: The History of a Legend." *MLR*, IX (1965), 500–07.

MacCaffrey, Isabel G. *John Milton: "Samson Agonistes" and the Shorter Poems*. New York, 1966. Pp. xii–xviii.

Patrides, C. A. *Milton and the Christian Tradition*. Oxford, 1966, P. 258.

Feinstein, Blossom. "On the Hymns of John Milton and Gian Francesco Pico." *CL*, XX (1968), 245–53.

Kastor, Frank Sullivan. "Miltonic Narration: 'Christ's Nativity.'" *Anglia*, LXXXVI (1968), 339–52.

Lawry, Jon S. *The Shadow of Heaven: Matter and Stance in Milton's Poetry*. Ithaca, N.Y., 1968. Pp. 27–41.

McQueen, William. "Prevent the Sun: Milton, Donne, and the Book of Wisdom." *Milton Newsletter*, II (1968), 63–64.

Parker, William Riley. *Milton: A Biography*. Oxford, 1968. I, pp. 61–69.

Rajan, Balachandra. "In Order Serviceable." *MLR*, LXIII (1968), 13–22. Rpt. in *The Lofty Rhyme: A Study of Milton's Major Poetry*. Coral Gables, Fla., 1970. Pp. 11–22.

Carey, John. *Milton*. London, 1969. Pp. 26–35.

Cullen, Patrick. "Imitation and Metamorphosis: The Golden-Age Eclogue in Spenser, Milton, and Marvell." *PMLA*, LXXXIV (1969), 1559–70.

Friedman, Donald. "Harmony and the Poet's Voice in Some of Milton's Early Poems." *MLQ*, XXX (1969), 523–34.

Grundy, Joan. *The Spenserian Poets*. London, 1969. Pp. 207, 213.

Leishman, J. B. *Milton's Minor Poems*. Ed. Geoffrey Tillotson. London, 1969. Pp. 51–67.

Butler, Christopher. *Number Symbolism*. London, 1970. Pp. 140–43.

Hyman, Lawrence W. "Christ's Nativity and the Pagan Deities." *Milton Studies*, II. Ed. James D. Simmonds. Pittsburgh, Pa., 1970. Pp. 103–12. Rpt. in *The Quarrel Within: Art and Morality in Milton's Poetry*. Port Washington, N.Y., and London, 1972. Pp. 10–20.

Meier, T. K. "Milton's 'Nativity Ode': Sectarian Discord." *MLR*, LXV (1970), 7–10.

Webber, Joan. "The Son of God and Power of Life in Three Poems by Milton." *ELH*, XXXVII (1970), 177–78.

Morris, David B. "Drama and Stasis in Milton's 'Ode on the Morning of Christ's Nativity.'" *SP*, LXVIII (1971), 207–22.

Potter, Lois. *A Preface to Milton*. London, 1971. Pp. 113–17.

Swaim, Kathleen M. "'Mighty Pan': Tradition and an Image in Milton's Nativity Hymn." *SP*, LXVIII (1971), 484–95.

Kingsley, Lawrence W. "Mythic Dialectic in the Nativity Ode." *Milton Studies*, IV. Ed. James D. Simmonds. Pittsburgh, Pa., 1972. Pp. 163–76.

Woodhouse, A. S. P. *The Heavenly Muse: A Preface to Milton*. Ed. Hugh MacCallum. Toronto, 1972. Pp. 36–38.

Woodhouse, A. S. P., and Douglas Bush. *A Variorum Commentary on the Poems of John Milton*. New York, 1972. I, pt. 1, pp. 34–110.

Grose, Christopher. *Milton's Epic Process: "Paradise Lost" and Its Miltonic Background*. New Haven and London, 1973. Pp. 17, 20–21, 72–73, 95.

Jordan, Richard Douglas. "The Movement of the 'Nativity Ode.'" *South Atlantic Bulletin*, XXXVIII:4 (1973), 34–39.

Sage, Lorna. "Milton's Early Poems: A General Introduction." In *John Milton: Introductions*. Ed. J. Broadbent. Cambridge, 1973. Pp. 265–67.

Jacobs, Lawrence H. "'Unexpressive Notes': The Decorum of Milton's Nativity Ode." *Essays in Literature*, I (1974), 166–77.

Barthel, Carol Ann. "Milton's Use of Spenser: The Early Poems and Paradise Lost." *DAI*, 36 (1975), 297A (Yale).

Davies, H. Neville. "Laid artfully together: stanzaic design in Milton's 'On the Morning of Christ's Nativity.'" In *Fair Forms: Essays in English Literature from Spenser to Jane Austen*. Ed. Maren-Sofie Røstvig. Cambridge, 1975. Pp. 85–117.

Erlich, Victor. "Milton's Early Poetry: Its Christian Humanism." *American Imago*, XXXII (1975), 77–112.

Pecheux, Mother M. Christopher. "The Image of the Sun in Milton's 'Nativity Ode.'" *Huntington Library Quarterly*, XXXVIII (1975), 315–33.

Rollinson, Philip. "Milton's Nativity Poem and the Decorum of Genre." *Milton Studies*, VII. Eds. Albert C. Labriola, Michael Lieb. Pittsburgh, Pa., 1975. Pp. 165–88.

Røstvig, Maren-Sofie. "Elaborate song: conceptual structure in Milton's 'On the Morning of Christ's Nativity.'" In *Fair Forms: Essays in English Literature from Spenser to Jane Austen*. Ed. Maren-Sofie Røstvig. Cambridge, 1975. Pp. 54–84.

Behrendt, Stephen C. "Blake's Illustrations to Milton's 'Nativity Ode.'" *PQ*, LV (1976), 65–95.

Sadler, Lynn Veach. "Magic and the Temporal Scheme in 'On the Morning of Christ's Nativity.'" *Ball State University Forum*, XVII: ii (1976), 3–9.

Nitchie, George W. "Milton and his Muses." *ELH*, XLIV (1977), 75–84.

Clanton, Jann Aldredge. "Love Descending: A Study of Spenser's *Fowre Hymnes* and Milton's 'Nativity Ode.'" *DAI*, 39 (1978), 3593A (Texas Christian).

Falle, George. "'a solemne measure . . . a just proportion.'" In *Familiar Colloquy: Essays Presented to Arthur Edward Barker*. Ed. Patricia Bruckmann. Toronto, 1978. Pp. 209–26.

MacCallum, Hugh. "The Narrator of Milton's 'On the Morning of Christ's Nativity.'" In *Familiar Colloquy: Essays Presented to Arthur Edward Barker*. Ed. Patricia Bruckmann. Toronto, 1978. Pp. 179–95.

Neuse, Richard. "Milton and Spenser: The Virgilian Triad Revisited." *ELH*, XLV (1978), 606–39, esp. 623–25.

Smith, George William. "Milton's Method of Mistakes in the Nativity Ode." *SEL*, XVIII (1978), 107–23.

Mercer, Lemoyne Brooks. "Trinal Unity: The Sources, Traditions and Craftsmanship of Milton's 'On the Morning of Christ's Nativity.'" *DAI*, 39 (1979), 4280A (Bowling Green State).

NOTES

1. See David M. Robinson, *Pindar: A Poet of Eternal Ideas* (Baltimore, 1936), pp. 26–27.

2. I am indebted to Professor Arthur Barker's perceptive suggestions and extremely generous encouragement of this and other ideas presented here.

3. "Apology for Smectymnuus," in Merritt Y. Hughes, ed., *John Milton: Complete Poems and Major Prose* (Indianapolis, 1957), p. 694. This edition is used throughout, except for references to *Of Reformation*.

4. George W. Nitchie, "Milton and His Muses," *ELH*, XLIV (1977), 77.

5. Indeed, with the Nativity ode at the outset, *L'Allegro* and *Il Penseroso* virtually at the centre, *Lycidas* as the culmination of the English poems, and numerous translations and such poems of less stature as *The Passion* interspersed among them, it is possible that Milton intended some sort of rhythm of success-followed-by-failure (or at least qualified success) followed-by-success by his unchronological ordering of the poems. Although *A Maske Presented at Ludlow Castle* completes the section of English works, it was likely intended to be considered separately, as its generical distinction deserves and its own title page suggests. See Nitchie, "Milton and His Muses," p. 84.

6. *Areopagitica*, in Hughes, p. 718.

7. *The Reason of Church Government*, in Hughes, pp. 669–70.

8. My reading is not intended to supplant all others. Certainly, the idea that Milton is manipulating Virgil's *Messianic Eclogue* for a Christian purpose requires close attention. See E. K. Rand, "Milton in Rustication," *SP*, XIX (1922), 127–129; and Patrick Cullen, "Imitation and Metamorphosis: The Golden Age Eclogue in Spenser, Milton and Marvell," *PMLA*, LXXXIV (1969), 1565–68.

9. "Miltonic Narration: 'Christ's Nativity,'" *Anglia*, LXXXVI (1968), 341.

10. "The Narrator of Milton's 'On the Morning of Christ's Nativity,'" in Patricia Bruckmann, ed., *Familiar Colloquy: Essays Presented to Arthur Edward Barker* (Toronto, 1978), pp. 179–95.

11. *Baroque Lyric Poetry* (New Haven and London, 1961), p. 45.

12. David B. Morris, "Drama and Stasis in Milton's 'Ode on the Morning of Christ's Nativity,'" *SP*, LVIII (1971), 215.

13. Balachandra Rajan, *The Lofty Rhyme: A Study of Milton's Major Poetry* (Coral Gables, Fla., 1970), pp. 12, 11.

14. One problem is the apparent unsuitability of the madrigal to a religious subject. Most madrigals in Italy and in England dealt with secular subjects even though a great many English madrigals were composed by church organists, like Thomas Weelkes (1575?–1623), organist at Chichester, and Thomas Morley (1557–1603), organist at St. Paul's and the Royal Chapel, who edited the volume of madrigals *(Madrigals, the Triumphs of Oriana)* in which the works of John Milton Sr. appeared. That Milton would have used the madrigal for a different purpose seems as likely as his using the hymn and ode genres for his Nativity poem. Indeed, if madrigals are what Louis L. Martz means by "Elizabethan songs," the possibility has already been raised; see his "The Rising Poet, 1645," in Joseph H. Summers, ed., *The Lyric and Dramatic Milton: Selected Papers from the English Institute* (New York, 1965), pp. 25–27. Carol Maddison, in *Apollo and the Nine: A History of the Ode* (London, 1963), p. 321, remarks that "there is also much of the traditional English poetry-making alliteration and assonance. We do not yet hear the mighty-mouthed organ voice of England, but still the almost Elizabethan singer."

15. For a note on where Milton likely spent Christmas 1629, see Mother M. Christopher Pecheux, "The Image of the Sun in Milton's 'Nativity Ode,'" *Huntington Library Quarterly*, XXXVIII (1975), 319 and 322, n. 11.

16. Don Cameron Allen, *The Harmonious Vision: Studies in Milton's Poetry* (Baltimore and London, 1954), p. 29; and Isabel G. MacCaffrey, *John Milton: "Samson Agonistes" and the Shorter Poems* (New York, 1966), p. x.

17. Cleanth Brooks and John E. Hardy, *Poems of Mr. John Milton* (New York, 1951), p. 104.

18. Malcolm M. Ross, "Milton and the Protestant Aesthetic: the Early Poems," *UTQ*, XVII (1948), 346–60, rpt. in *Poetry and Dogma* (New Brunswick, N.J., 1954), pp. 183–204; John B. Broadbent, "The Nativity Ode," in Frank Kermode, ed., *The Living Milton: Essays by Various Hands* (London, 1960), pp. 12–31; and John Carey, *Milton* (London, 1969), pp. 23–35.

19. William Riley Parker, *Milton: A Biography* (Oxford, 1968), p. 68.

20. "Milton's Method of Mistakes in the Nativity Ode," *SEL*, XVIII (1978), 107.

21. Ibid., 117.

22. Nelson, *Baroque Lyric Poetry*, p. 45.

23. *Images and Themes in Five Poems by Milton* (Cambridge, Mass., 1957), p. 68.

24. *The Lofty Rhyme*, p. 21.

25. Michael's "Prosperous or adverse" represents the balance of temperance which

Adam's education is meant to achieve. The phrase ironically echoes and moderates Mammon's perverse plan to forsake God and create "prosperous *of* adverse" (II, 259, emphasis added), believing in Satan's baroquely bold but actually nonsensical contention, "Surer to prosper than prosperity / Could have assur'd us" (II, 39).

26. Tuve, *Images and Themes*, comments instructively on Milton's treatment of the pagan gods (pp. 63–64). Lynn Veach Sadler, "Magic and the Temporal Scheme in 'On the Morning of Christ's Nativity'," *Ball State University Forum*, XVII:ii (1976), p. 9, perceptively modifies Tuve's view to incorporate the idea of reader response.

27. At least one historical account of the infant's death suggests it was the consequence of the king's decision to "rather save the mold than the cast," since Henrietta Maria's life apparently was in danger as well. See Quentin Bone, *Henrietta Maria, Queen of the Cavaliers* (Urbana, Ill., 1972), p. 70. It is feasible that the pagan gods represent historical figures of the day. Moloch, the prototype of kings who sacrificed children, may obliquely portray Charles I and his decision to sacrifice the first Charles II.

28. See Elizabeth Hamilton, *Henrietta Maria* (London, 1976), pp. 96–101.

29. See E. M. Simpson and G. R. Potter, eds., *The Sermons of John Donne* (Berkeley and Los Angeles, 1958), IX, pp. 8–9.

30. Ibid., p. 8.

31. See Lemoyne Brooks Mercer, "Trinal Unity: The Sources, Traditions, and Craftsmanship of Milton's 'On the Morning of Christ's Nativity,'" *DAI*, 39 (1979), 4280A, 47–48 (Bowling Green State). Mercer shows that Eusebius, Lavater, and E.K. of *The Shepheardes Calendar* (Maye) set the cessation at the Crucifixion, while Prudentius and Giles Fletcher would have offered Milton precedents for dating it from the Nativity. Mercer, however, does not suggest that Milton uses both traditions.

32. "Of Reformation in England, and the Causes That Hitherto Have Hindered It," in Don M. Wolfe, ed., *Complete Prose Works of John Milton* (New Haven, 1953), I, p. 526.

33. Pecheux, "Image of the Sun," suggests that because Milton had no quarrel with the Anglican church at this point, and was still considering the Anglican ministry as a vocation, he might have attended St. Paul's on this date.

34. Milton may have been trying to work the whole panoply of Christ's life into his poem, with the Passion as its epicenter, rather than write separate, companion poems as Fletcher had done. This may suggest why there was nothing left when Milton attempted a separate poem on the Passion four months later. Certainly, the Nativity ode attests to Milton's unique sense of both the simultaneity of Christ's acts and the universality of their significance. That concept called for a more sophisticated handling of the subject than Fletcher's linear structure could accommodate. Likewise, the concept of simultaneity takes the metaphysical conceit's use of paradox from simple juxtaposition to contrapuntal harmony — a blending together without violence.

35. *The Sermons of John Donne*, IX, pp. 152, 150. See also p. 13 of this volume for Simpson's and Potter's argument for according the date of 1629 to this sermon.

36. MacCallum, "The Narrator," p. 186.

THE POWER OF THE COPULA
IN MILTON'S *SONNET VII*

William A. Shullenberger

I N H I S description of Milton's grammatical practice, R. D. Emma notes that although Milton uses the copula less frequently than Shakespeare or Eliot, Emma's Elizabethan and modern controls, Milton's use of the copula is semantically loaded, so that the verb functions as more than a predicative linkage.[1] The use of the copula by Milton is theologically in-structed. The biblical God identified himself to Moses as Yahweh, a sublime tautology which has been translated as "I am who I am," or "I will be who I will be."[2] The term achieves God's intimate association with the idea of "being," so that it is virtually impossible to conceive of "being," in any context informed by biblical discourse, apart from God. The bearing of God's biblical self-disclosure will probably always be a vital topic for theologians and philosophers. But its bearing upon language, and in this case upon the language of poetry, is more likely to be overlooked.[3] This is in part because of our habit of looking *through* language as a virtually transparent medium for the ideas it carries. If we tend to listen only for the "message" in ordinary discourse, the tendency becomes exaggerated as language strains to indicate the transcendental: one of the conventions of religious discourse is to confess that words fail when the subject of the discourse is God. Yet the biblical conception of a name involved a different semiotic structure, a different understanding of how words stood for the things to which they referred: the name was a true bearer of a person's self; the disclosure of a name was a manifestation of a person's real power, presence, and identity.[4] The Christian idea of Incarnation reinforced this interpenetration of sign and referent, for the figure of the Word becoming flesh,[5] as in John i, 14, suggested not only the Deity's claiming of the fallen world but also his claiming of the language through which he could be mediated to the world, and by which he could effect the world's renovation. "Yahweh," then, has linguistic implications. God's association with "being" provides the fundamental linguistic structure in which a biblically educated poet can compose his existence, and the copula, the conjugations of the verb "to be," is the clearest signifier of divine involvement in human existence.[5]

Milton's *Sonnet VII*, "How Soon Hath Time," develops into a play on the conjugation of the copula as the foundation for authentic speech and true action. Woodhouse has argued that this poem marks the threshold of Milton's poetic maturity, sealing the commitment to religious and ethical themes of which the Nativity ode had been the inaugurating gesture: "Here, in *How soon hath Time*, one encounters at last, though in a simple and rudimentary form, the full Miltonic pattern and function (the resolution of conflicts by the imposition of aesthetic pattern)."[6] It is an indication of the kind of pressure to which Milton subjects a received form, that this early Petrarchan exercise carries the same instruction about faithful waiting upon the timeliness of divine grace which Michael delivers to Adam in the closing books of *Paradise Lost*. The density achieved by verbal compression and by the syntactic enactment of its transcendental theme marks this poem as an instance of Milton's monumentality, and indicates how Milton in his maturity transforms the occasional poem into an occasion for the saving history which wrote itself out not only in Scripture, but in the poetry written in light of Scripture. *Sonnet VII* traces a pilgrim's progress, from the dead end of life considered in the shadow of mortal passage, to a comprehensive because divinely structured understanding of time and temporal existence as an unfolding of conditions and possibilities, overseen by the unconditional presence of God himself.[7] God's structuring presence is marked by the appearance and the varied reiteration of the copula which organizes the poem's sestet, its final and confirmatory utterance.

The linguistic pilgrimage is enacted in three stages, which correspond to the two quatrains and sestet of the sonnet. The most notable features of these stages are the progressive complication of the clause structures, and the change in the kind of verbs which activate the sentences. The first quatrain indicates a speaker trapped in the foregone conclusions of his declarative statements. There are three simple indicative statements, uncomplicated by any subordination or shift in mood, each reiterating the same lament over time irrecoverably lost. The final word of the quatrain, however, provides the first hint of complication in the speaker's attitude toward time, for the outward orientation of "show'th" contains at least the potential of its opposite, the hidden. The second quatrain enters this breach, countering the assertive "showiness" of the first quatrain by an extended complex sentence with two levels of subordination, which traces a tentative movement inward. This movement is both encouraged and continually cast in doubt by the buildup of verbs of seeming, deceiving, appearing: the clearcut evidence of the initial declarations thus dissolves into the uncertainty of the second quatrain. The final movement of the verbal drama is the steady crescendo of the sestet, which stations the ambiguities of the previous quatrain in parallel sets of temporal possibilities within a large and complex structure governed by the verb "to be." The copula climaxes its flexible power in the sublime assurance of the final syntactic couplet,[8] which locates the conditionality of human existence in the imperturbable existence of the Deity who is the condition of all being.

A closer look at each stage of the poem's progress will clarify Woodhouse's remark about the poem's "resolution of conflict by the imposition of aesthetic pattern," for the pattern is discovered to be a display of syntactic force. The initial quatrain registers its nostalgic frustration in the imagistic efflorescence and the transitive velocity of its statements. The three clauses are set in motion by indicative verbs of action: "hath stol'n," "fly on," "show'th"; their cumulative effect is to strike a note of sudden and too late retrospection in the middle of time's headlong course. The declarative haste of these statements is impeded only once, by the appositive, "the subtle thief of youth," in the first line, an uncomplicated personification which serves, like every other phrase in the quatrain, to underscore a single point: the speaker's youth has been stolen, wasted, lost. Instead of slowing the tempo, the appositive interruption in fact accelerates it by splitting the initial verb phrase, so that "Stol'n" jumps out at the head of the second line: the statement indicates a crime just committed, and just realized. The quatrain is elaborately overwritten, as every phrase and every qualifier sounds the note of temporal flight. The whole quatrain is implicit in the initial adverbial sigh, "How soon," and this deliberate redundancy reaches its climax in the third line, "My hasting days fly on with full career," where the participial modifier of the noun phrase, "hasting," the verb phrase "fly on," and the prepositional modifier of the verb, "with full career," virtually reduplicate each other in every place in the sentence. There is little room for reflection in this kind of rhetoric. From the first two words, the speaker represents himself as the victim not only of time but of his own assessment of it. The one-dimensionality of his statements indicates a conception of time as linear, measurable, and irrecoverable. Time is represented as an alien force which has rendered him a terminal case.

Brooks and Hardy note an abrupt shift in the mode of discourse as the sonnet's second quatrain unfolds: "With the second quatrain, the play of imagery is apparently abandoned for a rather sober, even prosaic statement, although the 'spring' metaphor is carried on in the phrase 'inward ripenes.'"[9] This shift can be accounted for, not by the disappearance of imagery, but by a shift of the speaker's attention to the problematic nature of the imagery by which he has represented himself; it is not so much that imagery is abandoned as that it is opened to question by the quatrain's concentration on the potential ambiguity of phenomena. As the flourish of imagery fades, what emerges is a more difficult kind of poetry which foregrounds its syntactical relationships as the field in which understanding is to be questioned and ultimately disclosed. This movement, in which the poem's language clarifies itself by an apparent shift from the sensuous to the abstract, from concrete particulars to a "vital symbolic geometry,"[10] is so characteristic of Milton that it is virtually a poetic signature. The movement is as significant thematically in *Sonnet VII* as in *Comus* or in *Paradise Regained*, for in each case what is accomplished by the radical shift in poetic diction is not a repudiation of the material existence toward which a more sensuous, "imagistic" poetry is oriented, but the placing of such existence in a large and coherent ontological structure, even as the poetry disciplines itself in more comprehensive and self-understanding linguistic patterns.[11]

The initial effect of such a shift in *Sonnet VII*, however, is severely disruptive. As I indicated earlier, the verb "show," which closes the first quatrain, has the potential for a double semantic valence which no other word in the first quatrain carries. The potential ambiguity erupts in the difficult fifth line, which demands yet eludes paraphrase by means of the multiple interpretative options it presents. The subject noun phrase, "my semblance," sustains the potential uncertainty invoked by the verb "show," in fact intensifying that uncertainty by the stronger connotations of appearance, of deliberate illusion, which the noun sets in play.[12] "My semblance" seems to refer to the condition of wasted youth established in the first four lines of the poem; it may look forward to the near-manhood indicated in line 6; however, it creates at least the possibility for an inward condition which may or may not correspond to outward appearance, and which the poem has not yet described. In the verb "deceive" all the ambiguity surfaces, although it has already been strenuously qualified by the double conditionality of "Perhaps" and "might." The verb anticipates an indentifiable object, in whom the reader might expect the ambiguities to be at least temporarily settled: if the sentence discloses *whom* the speaker's "semblance" might perhaps be deceiving, it would close out on a stabilizing note. Instead, the final word of the line is the abstract "truth." Ordinary discourse does not prepare us for the coupling of this verb with this object; we expect that the speaker's "semblance" might *conceal* the truth, or that it might deceive *someone*. If both these semantic expectations crowd the edges of our attention to this clause, nevertheless the literal reading of it prevents an interpretative rewriting of the clause into something more intelligible.[13] The sentence, that is, resists paraphrase, and its extension through subordinate clauses into the rest of the quatrain forces us to hold our desire to interpret in suspension, in the hope that something may appear later to resolve the uncertainties as the larger structure of the sentence unfolds.

The lines which complete the second quatrain are syntactically less perplexing and semantically more transparent than the fifth line. We seem to return to the point of the first quatrain: the speaker's youth is behind him, he is approaching manhood, and he has little to show for it. In fact, the speaker's sense of temporal passage has deepened and complicated, in the very transit of his discourse, as his consideration develops from the abrupt assertions of the first quatrain into the subordinate structures of the second and fourth lines of the second, which mark out a potential introversion:

> Perhaps my semblance might deceive the truth,
> That I to manhood am arriv'd so near,
> And inward ripeness doth much less appear,
> That some more timely-happy spirits endu'th.

The appearance or nonappearance of "inward ripeness" does create a disturbance in understanding, because of its resonance with the distinction between outward seeming and inward potential established in the fifth line. Has the speaker achieved an "inward ripeness" which is simply not visible, or has "inward ripeness" failed to appear even to him? That inward ripeness doth much less *appear* does not necessarily prohibit its presence: the showy external evidence of growth, indicated by bud and blossom in the fourth line, are here replaced by an image which correlates maturation to internal development, not to clock or calendar time, nor to physical growth. If the manifest evidence of this quatrain seems to reinforce and develop the point of the first quatrain— that is, if the speaker is declaring his lack of the "inward ripeness" which has graced more "timely-happy spirits"—the internal evidence, the speaker's handling of complicated syntax, which allows for the extended comparisons not only between outward and inward signs of growth but between himself and others, suggests a measure of poetic maturation at odds with such a self-assessment.

Nevertheless, the emerging potentiality of an attitude toward time which is not confined to the indicative mood and the linearity of clock time is framed by the initial "Perhaps" which presides over the entire sentence. Furthermore, the three lines which unfold this more complex attitude stand in an uncertain relation to the initial uncertainty of the main clause. It is impossible to locate the place in the main clause on which the hinge of subordination, the joining "That" of line 5, turns. The subordinate clauses of 6–8 could stand in relation to one of the nouns in the main clause, either "semblance" or "truth"; it is also possible for the subordinate clauses to explicate the verb, the act of deception. As the extended subordinate structure of the sentence floats between these three possible linkages, it activates a number of distinct ideas, which oscillate like the emerging and dissolving foreground of an optical illusion, with no single idea capable of attaining an interpretative priority. Consider, for a moment, several possible paraphrases: "my appearance, that I am approaching manhood with no visible evidence of true maturity, might perhaps deceive the truth"; "my appearance, that I am approaching manhood with a sense of inward ripeness that is not yet manifest, might be deceptive"; "my appearance of near manhood proves false to the truth of my lack of inward ripeness"; "my appearance of wasted youth is deceptive, in that I possess an inward ripeness which isn't manifest." The number of ideas generated by the sentence is incalculable, because each of the points of syntactic or semantic ambiguity increases logarithmically the potential ways to read the sentence. Some of the distinctions between possible implications are slight, and some are antithetical; they are sufficient to finish the octave in a sense of profound uneasiness. The more one grapples with the task of explicating these lines, the more one is left with a sense of fleeting implication, which simply cannot be fixed in paraphrase. All the possibilities must be held in a simultaneous awareness of the intimacy by which appearance and truth, inwardness and outward evidence, are related; the multiple possibilities place the reader in the difficult position of trying to discover a calculus which is adequate to correlate the contrary measurements of time which the poem has thus far suggested. And this is precisely the point: Milton throughout his work demands that his readers suspend interpretative judgment as they work through an increasingly complicated syntactic structure, any juncture of which may open several new interpretative possibilities which must also be held in mind, until the poem itself stands forward to resolve the reader's perplexity by presenting a redeeming word or figure which will interpret the dilemma.

The redeeming word in the poem's final movement is, as I have indicated, the copula, whose forms are the manifestation in human speech of what Coleridge called "the infinite I AM."[14] The sestet does not so much resolve the multiple difficulties of the second quatrain as it absorbs the semantic overload into a larger and more balanced syntactic structure indicative of an imagination instructed by the power of the copula. The way in which the sestet comprehends what has led up to it may be explored by attending to what appears to be yet another referential difficulty, the antecedent of the pronoun "it," which has not yet appeared in the poem, but which assumes a prominence now as the heavily used "I" and "my" pronouns disappear from the discourse until its consummative lines. What seems to take place in this pronominal displacement is a shift of the speaker's attention, from a self-centered perspective to a virtual objectivity derived from a divinely structured grasp of experience as a totality. The speaker no longer conceives of his life and time on earth as a possession of which time has unfairly deprived him; he accounts for his life as an element of an existence ordered by God, beyond his power to circumscribe or claim. The ambiguous "it" of lines 9, 10, and 13 is included in this enlarged sense of temporal structure, so that its ambiguities are not so troubling as the ones which shook us in the second quatrain. Whether "it" represents time, or maturity, or "inward ripeness," or the entire condition marked out in the octave, "it" is firmly placed by the stately syntactical parallelism of the poem's close. There is a great deal of semantic potential compressed into the pronoun; yet the ease of its accommodation to the unfolding of the sentence where it occurs indicates a quantum leap in perspective, the kind of shift achieved at the close of Chaucer's *Troilus and Criseide*, where Troilus looks upon "this litel spot of earthe" as a part of a comprehensive design, and laughs.[15]

The turning point of a Miltonic poem, or of a soliloquy uttered in the context of a larger poem, is marked by an expressive act of will, as the speaker accedes to the potential influx of grace and reverses the psychological momentum of a thought train which has lost its bearings.[16] The firm brief syllables which compose the sestet indicate such a turning in *Sonnet VII:* "Yet be it less or more, or soon or slow, / It shall be still." In lines 9, 10, and 13, a form of the copula inhabits the second place in the verse, receiving a primary stress and setting the line in motion. The sestet consists of two complex conditional sentences; the controlling verb of each sentence is the copula. What emerges here is the authorizing power of the verb "to be," whose multiple operations organize and contain the existential perplexities and variabilities of the poem's octave. The first fruits of the verb's power are displayed in the change of the speaker's relation to his discourse, which indicates a change in his attitude toward what time accomplishes, or toward what can be accomplished in time. The protasis of the first conditional sentence contains the first subjunctive verb form to appear in the poem: "Yet be it." The switch from the indicative into another verbal mode intensifies what John Searle calls the "illocutionary force" of the speaker's language.[17] Whereas the indicative mode emphasizes the propositional quality of a statement as a reference to existing condition, a subjunctive or imperative involves the speaker's active commitment to question or to change existing conditions by the very effect of his statement. Milton notes the difference in modes in his Latin grammar:

The Indicative Mood *sheweth* or *declareth*, as *Laudo* I praise.
The Imperative *biddeth* or *exhorteth*, as *Lauda* Praise thou.
The Potential or Subjunctive is Englished with these signs: *may, can, might, would, could, should.*[18]

The absence of an auxiliary word not only intensifies the stress of the verb "be," but permits its act of predication to operate through two circuits which reinforce rather than interfere with each other. The overall structure of the sentence as a conditional statement encourages us to supply the auxiliary "whether," thus making the protasis a statement which acknowledges and accepts the temporal and maturational options: "Whether it be less or more, or soon or slow." Yet the word order, "yet be it," suggests a more forceful engagement of the speaker with his discourse in the form of a jussive subjunctive,[19] by which the speaker actually wills the alternative conditions which will be taken up and accounted for by the inclusive apodosis. If "yet be it" carries such an imperative force, then we might render the phrase, "Yet *let* it be less or more, or soon or slow." Such bidding carries an echo of the divine fiat which originally brought into being the conditions of world and time: "And God said, Let there be light: and there was light." The speaker, then, is not only accepting the uncertain conditions which had so perplexed and defeated him in the octave; by the adjustment of his speech to the perspective afforded by a language which transcends his own, it becomes possible for him to participate in the determination of temporal conditions through the "illocutionary force" of that language.

  The expectation of the subjunctive is fulfilled in the future-oriented assurance of the verb in the apodosis: "It shall be." This is the first note of a prospective rather than retrospective attitude in the sonnet. It counts on a stability provided by a strict measure of life, not according to the natural cycle of bud, blossom, fruit, nor to the progressive stages of human development toward "manhood," but according to divine appointment, the will of heaven which coordinates the action of time. The duration of this penultimate sentence in the sonnet, suspending the alternative possibilities of time in a set of poised options which no longer demand resolution, represents the supercession of an eternal moment upon the haste of temporal passage, the generation and containment of the conditionality of existence by the unconditional "being" of the Deity. The verb, "shall be," generates a third pair of terms of measurement, "mean or high," which relocates the scale on a vertical axis of spiritual accomplishment, rather than on the horizontal axes of material accumulation or of temporal movement, "less or more, or soon or slow." Yet the verb securely places in a comprehensive syntactic structure all these pairs, without repudiating any of them, even as "Time" is placed in a new situation as the divine guide rather than the enemy of man. The final pairing of the sentence, Time and the will of Heaven, is the first ramification of a subject structure in the sentence; it reveals thereby the agents by whom the acts of predication which constitute temporal existence are accomplished. The *and* joining the subjects answers the coordinating *or* of the earlier predicate pairings, which had threatened an indeterminacy or pure relativity of measure; the *and* places Time under the disposition of Heaven. Throughout the sentence, prepositions have been the occasion for the ramification of sentence structure as the sentence tries to render the complicated intercourse between the conditional and the unconditional.[20] The final prepositional phrase, to which the others have led, brings the sentence to an inclusive closure in a totality which admits of no further ramification: "the will of Heav'n."

The final sentence closes the poem quietly by means of a simplified clause structure; it is a coda which sums the movement of the entire sonnet. This is also a conditional sentence, yet one in which the protasis is contained in, surrounded by, the apodosis. This embedding implies a resistance to the apparent meaning of the sentence. A reordering of the sentence according to ordinary discourse would render, "If I have grace to use it so, all is / As ever in my great task-Master's eye." This more familiar structure establishes a cause-effect pattern, in which the result, contained in the apodosis, depends upon the fulfillment of the conditions stated in the protasis. This implies the religious impossibility that the divine being, or the divine realization of the world, depends upon human accomplishment. Most interpretations of the poem resort to some kind of paraphrase which elides the difficulty;[21] Woodhouse, who meets the problem head on, proposes a punctuation change and subsequent paraphrase which in my estimation only make the sentence more difficult.[22] Rather than asking what the sentence means, and providing an answer through a paraphrase which inevitably alters the literal statement at some point, we might consider again how the syntactic arrangement of the sentence establishes a relationship between its divine and human subjects. Milton's sentence establishes fulfillment or accomplishment before the conditions under which it can be accomplished are even stated: "All is" is a final, absolute and unconditional statement of the authority of the divine perspective. Milton's subsequent embedding of the protasis in this large and unconditional affirmation establishes the human and the divine activities, not in a cause-effect structure, which would imply the priority of a temporal perspective, but in a hierarchy of causes. This hierarchy is not temporally determinate, because it has to do with man's immediate and time-shattering presence before the Deity, and with a human gracefulness in action which is possible only because of a "prevenient grace" conditional only upon the human willingness to admit it.[23] The speaker's "I" now reappears, chastened of anxiety and of its sense of loss, restored to its seat as agent of its life's progress and subject of its discourse, because it is now underwritten, overseen, contained, and echoed in the unconditional eye/I/aye which is the name of God.

This sonnet of Milton's youth, then, is a brief syntactical drama which enacts the same story as Milton's later and grander works. Like those later works, it closes and comments upon itself in a way that requires us to read its beginning in light of its ending. Given the radical restructuring of time, action, and identity accomplished in the course of the poem, it is not altogether surprising to discover that the poem's initial figure derives less from seventeenth-century convention than from Scripture:

But know this, that if the goodman of the house had known in what watch the thief would come, he would have watched, and would not have suffered his house to be broken up. . . . Therefore, be ye also ready; for in such an hour as ye think not the Son of man cometh.[24]

Like *Sonnet XIX*, to which it is often compared, *Sonnet VII* transforms the speech of personal complaint into the scripturally in-structed language of parable.

University of Massachusetts, Amherst

NOTES

1. Ronald David Emma, "Grammar and Milton's English Style," *Language and Style in Milton: A Symposium*, ed. John T. Shawcross and Ronald David Emma (New York, 1967), pp. 242, 250.

2. Exodus iii, 14. For a brief discussion of the name Yahweh, see "Names of God," *The Interpreter's Dictionary of the Bible*, (New York, 1962), II, pp. 407–17. In *The Christian Doctrine*, Milton interprets the divine name Jehovah as "*he who is, or which is, and which was, and which is to come.*" Of the contraction of the divine name into Jave, Milton writes "the name Jave appears to signify not only the existence of his nature, but also of his promises, or rather the completion of his promises." *The Christian Doctrine*, I.II, in *John Milton: Complete Poems and Major Prose*, ed. Merritt Y. Hughes (New York, 1957), p. 907. Unless otherwise noted, subsequent references to Milton are taken from this text, and will be indicated parenthetically.

3. In classical language theory, Michel Foucault states, the verb "to be" is the "essence of language, which sustains the possibility of all discourse." Although his points of reference are different from mine, his notes on the semiotic charge of the copula show how the verb "to be" underwrites whatever ontological functions the philosophers may assign to "being." Michel Foucault, *The Order of Things* (New York, 1971), pp. 94–96.

4. *The Interpreter's Dictionary of the Bible*, II, p. 422.

5. *The Interpreter's Dictionary of the Bible* notes that, whereas the simple Hebrew stem of the name Yahweh produces the meaning "I am," the causative stem, "which is precisely the grammatical form of the word 'Yahweh,'" yields the meaning "I cause to be"; "When the whole enigmatic formula is changed into the causative, it means 'I cause to be what comes into existence'" (II, p. 410). That Milton understood the double implication of the name is suggested in the quotation above, n. 2.

6. *The Heavenly Muse: A Preface to Milton*, ed. Hugh MacCallum (Toronto, 1972), p. 52; revision of "Notes on Milton's Early Development," *UTQ*, XIII (1942–43), 66–101.

7. On the divine restructuring of time in the Nativity *Hymn*, see Kathleen M. Swaim, "Mighty Pan: Tradition and an Image in Milton's Nativity *Hymn*," *SP*, LXVIII (1971), 484–95.

8. The "syntactic couplet" is noted by Taylor Stoehr in "Syntax and Poetic Form in Milton's Sonnets," *English Studies*, XLV (1964), 289–301.

9. *Poems of Mr. John Milton: The 1645 Edition with Essays in Analysis* (1952; rpt. New York, 1968), p. 153.

10. Isabel Gamble MacCaffrey, Introd. "*Samson Agonistes*" *and the Shorter Poems of Milton* (New York, 1966), p. xvii.

11. Stanley Fish is perhaps our most cogent expositor of this process in Milton; Fish's paradigm is presented concisely in "Inaction and Silence: The Reader in *Paradise Regained*," *Calm of Mind: Tercentenary Essays on "Paradise Regained" and "Samson Agonistes" in Honor of John S. Diekhoff*, ed. J. A. Wittreich, Jr. (Cleveland, 1971), pp. 25–47. Fish's arguments, however, often seem to construct a spiritual one-way street, by which the reader passes "above the smoke and stir of this dim spot / Which men call Earth" (*Comus*, 5–6; Hughes, p. 90). I would argue that Milton upholds human language as the place in which we live and move and have our being; he does not consume it in a movement toward a silent transcendence.

12. Cf. *OED*, n. 3: "A person's appearance or demeanor, expressive of his thoughts, feelings, etc., or feigned in order to hide them."

13. I find the *Variorum* commentary on this very difficult line quite unenlightening: deceive means "prove false to the truth (*OED*: deceive 3). The construction seems to be modelled on deceive, i.e. betray, one's trust." *A Variorum Commentary on the Poems of John Milton*, (New York, 1957), II, pt. 2, p. 371.

14. *Biographia Literaria*, ch. XIII, in *Samuel Taylor Coleridge: Selected Poetry and Prose*, ed. Elisabeth Schneider (New York, 1951), p. 268.

15. *Troilus and Criseide*, V, 1815, in *Chaucer's Poetry: An Anthology for the Modern Reader*, ed. E. T. Donaldson (New York, 1958), p. 836.

16. Examples of this peripeteia in speech include the Lady's soliloquy in *Comus* (210–11; Hughes, p. 95); the turnings of Adam's soliloquy in *Paradise Lost* X, 720–844 (Hughes, pp. 424–26); and the resolve of the disciples and Mary to wait upon the reappearance of Jesus in *Paradise Regained* II, 49, 102 (Hughes, pp. 495–96). A variation on this turning indicates its origins more clearly by the incursion of a voice of "higher mood": the Nativity *Hymn*, 149–50 (Hughes, p. 47); *Lycidas*, 76–84, 113–31 (Hughes, pp. 122–24). The "strong motion" which leads Jesus into the wilderness (*Paradise Regained*, I, 290–91; Hughes, p. 489) and the "rousing motions" which lead Samson to the Temple of Dagon (*Samson Agonistes*, 1381–83; Hughes, p. 584) are inward equivalents to this disposition of speech toward God.

17. *Speech Acts: An Essay in the Philosophy of Language* (Cambridge, Eng., 1970).

18. *Accedence Commenc'd Grammar*, in *The Works of John Milton* (New York, 1932), VI, p. 305.

19. I borrow this term from Latin grammar because I am unaware of an equivalent in contemporary English grammatical description. The jussive subjunctive (from *iubere: to command or order*) has the force of an imperative yet is addressed to a first or third person.

20. Organizing the sentence according to its prepositional phrases will clarify this point:

> Yet be it less or more, or soon or slow,
> It shall be still
>   in strictest measure ev'n
>   to that same lot, however mean or high,
>   Toward which time leads me, and the will
>   of Heav'n.

21. For instance, "All that matters is whether I have grace to use my ripeness in accordance with the will of God as one ever in his sight," K. Svendsen, *Explicator* (1949), VII, item 53; "All time is, if I have grace to use it so, as eternity in God's sight," D. Dorian, *Explicator* (1949), VIII, item 10; "'All is . . . As ever in my great task Masters eye,' but only 'if I have grace to use it so': that is, only if I have the grace to use everything as if it were being observed by Him," Brooks and Hardy, p. 154.

22. "The meaning is then clear, with no redundance: All [that matters] is: whether I have grace to use it so, as ever [conscious of being] in my great taskmaster's [enjoining] eye." Woodhouse, *The Heavenly Muse*, p. 353, n. 47.

23. *Paradise Lost*, XI, 3 (Hughes, p. 433).

24. Matthew xxiv, 43–44. Milton is thinking of his life in terms of parable in the "Letter to a Friend" in which the sonnet is enclosed; the parable of the Talents is in the same textual vicinity (Matthew xxv, 14–30) as the parable of the thief. In all the parables, the motif of immediate accountability before the Lord (the great task Master) is dominant, as it is in the letter and in the poem. The letter appears in *The Complete Prose Works of John Milton*, ed. Don M. Wolfe et al. (New Haven, 1953–), I, pp. 318–21.

"UNEXPRESSIVE SONG": FORM AND ENIGMA VARIATIONS IN *LYCIDAS*, A NEW READING

Michael Fixler

A T T H E climax of *Lycidas* Milton draws on the visionary terms of the Apocalypse to describe the apotheosis of his dead friend, who "hears the unexpressive nuptial Song, / In the blest Kingdoms meek of joy and love" (176–77). The song is for the Marriage Supper of the Lamb, that ultimate union of Christ and his saints, and "unexpressive" here means ineffable, beyond words. But where words die music begins, and this most lyrical of all of Milton's poems can itself be read as meant, somehow, to sound in consort with that "unexpressive" music of beatitude. For, insofar as it evokes heavenly song, *Lycidas* exists in much the same imaginative relationship to such song as do the choral harmonies of *At a Solemn Music*, where sound would, Milton wrote, "answer" heaven's "undisturbed Song of pure concent." To "answer" means both to respond to heaven's music and to correspond with it, approaching that ideal concord "all creatures made" once "In perfect Diapason" before the Fall (21, 23), and to renew which is the point of Apocalyptic consummation, as in the beatitude evoked at the climax of *Lycidas*. Like the "answerable style" of *Paradise Lost*, there is a decorum of technique in the style of Milton's elegy.

"Unexpressive" takes on the sense, then, not only of a song beyond mortal words, or as ineffable as beatific music and as inaudible as the music of the spheres — all of which figure, for example, in the Nativity Ode — but becomes a latent attribute of that kind of *musica humana* which reaches out to approximate the transcendent music with which it participates harmonically and which in a curious way serves as its inimitable model. In *Ad Patrem* Milton has the "poet's work" or "divine song" (17) cognate with those Apocalyptic harmonies awaiting both his father and himself when "we too shall move with golden crowns . . . blending sweet songs with the soft notes of the lyre" (33–35). Nor was it mere extravagance that led the young Milton to write three tributes to the singing of Leonora Baroni in Rome, whose voice "declares God's

213

presence" (I, 4), evokes angelic harmonies, and effects spiritually reno-
vating and "soul animating" (II, 11) responses in her listeners. The reality of the effect went beyond the gifts of the singer, while comparably
Milton's terms for poetic worship, devotional verse, or doctrinal poetry
involve with these kinds of expression resonances that intimate analogous powers, always to suggest, if not directly to express, the unutter-
able. In *At a Solemn Music* the "mixt power" (3) or wedding of voice
and verse first quickens the rapture that later climaxes in the ultimate
Apocalyptic harmony. In *Il Penseroso* another mixed power, of organ
and choir, evokes ecstasies that bring, as the cloistered recluse has it,
"all Heav'n before mine eyes" (166). But we know well that these answerable correspondences between heard and unheard music were for
Milton recurring motifs of high significance. I would suggest that there
is a further significance in the correspondences of heard and unheard
music, namely the derivation from them of unheard latencies in Milton's
audible music — meanings whose unexpressed qualities in some sense
imitate the unheard harmonies he thought of as the ideal of heavenly
music, grasped perhaps, if not by the ear, then by the spirit in its "high-
rais'd fantasy."[1]

In practical terms this means that *Lycidas* may be conceived as
working at distinct levels of consciously and subliminally apprehended
effects, which is to claim for the poem no more than we might expect
from most poetry. With *Lycidas*, however, the distinguishable effects of
audible and "unexpressive song" were, I think, deliberately wrought in
accordance with a theory and practice Milton had been perfecting almost from the time he wrote *At A Vacation Exercise* and certainly had
mastered with *L'Allegro* and *Il Penseroso*.[2] This is not the place to consider Milton's poetics at any length, nor its illustrations in the varieties
of his practice. For the moment, it should be enough to take as our cue
the term "unexpressive song" and trace how related ideas lead to an
apparent differentiation of effect in Milton's conceptions of the consciously and subliminally apprehended elements of lyric poetry. By a
certain modulation in *Lycidas* these distinctions turn into differences of
theme and structure, of meaning and form — but only analytically, for
the effect of the poem is truly harmonic. And in a musical sense also its
processes remain obscure, eluding verbal definition, while even the full
range of its harmonies is never altogether consciously heard. In the light
of the poem's purpose its effects are apparently deliberate. Partly we
are to grasp its intelligible effects, the complex but overt sense it communicates. Partly we are to apprehend subliminally a species of effects
audibly produced yet silent in nature.

The silent powers of Renaissance poetry were in fact recognizable attributes of poetic song, powers that Milton both took note of and involved allusively with his verse. I will address myself to some elements of the theory in a moment, but it is worth remarking that in *Lycidas* itself the Orphic voice sounds unheard, a symbol of unavailing song, though it was a song whose powers were well-nigh superhuman. Orpheus could quicken inanimate things into life, move nature beyond itself, and nearly charm death to recover Euridyce. In myth Orpheus sings even as his severed head, resting on his silent lyre, races down the swift Hebrus. But in *Lycidas* that song is "unexpressive" in yet a further sense, being implicit, a part of the allusion. It cannot be heard, nor does its power help to ease the distress voiced by the poet as he evokes Orpheus. Yet, for all that, his song still sounds silently, a symbol of the range of Orphic effects inherent in poetry, an art that for Milton was always a fusion of sense, or argument, and *melos*, or musical sound.

The symbol serves to isolate a certain literalness in Milton's use of the word "song" for poetry, especially since in *Ad Patrem* he emphasized that all the powers of Orpheus were those of "his song, not his lyre" ("Carmine, non cithara," 54) — that is, of words musically modulated. Even the extent of musical modulation could be minimized as simply the acoustic properties of poetic form, which is clearly the case when Milton quotes in his *Commonplace Book* the opinion of Basil of Caesarea that God endowed the poetic gift to enable those possessing it to teach well, mixing with doctrines "the delights of melody so that we might unconsciously receive the benefit of the discourse through the charm and sweetness of sounds." The key term here is "unconsciously," signifying that poetic meaning, expressed as a verbal music, has access to levels of response within us that prosaic or rational arguments of the same order do not. Specifically, poetic meaning, as verbal music, has power over our emotions. This is the point of Milton's saying that some verse is able "to allay the perturbations of the mind and set the affections in right tune."[3] We may note how even here there is a division of powers corresponding to the component elements of poetry as song; that is, a semantic effect, the doctrine or argument addressed to the rational mind, and a musical effect which worked upon the emotions in less obvious ways. This programmatic summary of one kind of poetry could have been written with *Lycidas* in mind. Akin to its effects is a kind of catharsis, as the chorus of *Samson Agonistes* suggests when it observes how ineffectual mere prosaic argument tends to be where a mind is truly and deeply perturbed. Such argument too may have its music, but seems "a tune / Harsh, and of a dissonant mood," unless somehow it

carries with it a mysteriously infused grace, "consolation from above; /
Secret refreshings" (653–66). In *Samson Agonistes* such grace does come
to the hero, not musically, but through a climactic series of dialectical
encounters. The counterpart in lyric poetry is the dialectic of complementary and interacting elements, most immediately those of voice and
verse, one being the vehicle of the musical form so wedded to the other,
the verbal sense, that as song it carried a grace and power beyond the
sense of its words. Nowhere is the idea more dramatically phrased than
in the words of the Attendant Spirit in *Comus*, who hears the lost Lady,
inspired by her "new enliv'n'd spirit," sing "strains that might create a
soul / Under the ribs of Death" (228, 561–62). The phrase is singularly
apt to suggest an imaginative context for the kind of poetry on which
Milton meditated when he had been asked to commemorate the death
of Edward King.

Such a poem must move, as *Lycidas* does, from the turbulence of
grief to consolation, and beyond that to visionary triumph. But in so
moving it harmonizes, as a rising climactic progression, with the most
powerful physical rhythms of human life, those "great revelatory moments," as Paula Johnson calls them, "of ecstasy and childbirth." She is
describing the effects of certain seventeenth-century musical and poetic
forms, in their kind similar to the formally rising progression of *Lycidas*. And the movement of *Lycidas* is indeed both musical and verbal,
or sensuous and intellectual. It is a rising from grief and ignorance to
consolation and illuminative insight, a movement of both form and
theme. Necessarily, for both form and theme to climax at their appropriate moment, the nature of their end must be, at the outset, inhibited
or obscured. The poem's method is unfolded — retrospectively, as it
were — as what gradually emerges quickens into a triumphant revelation. For example, the Arcadian pastoral guise serves to obscure the evident meaning of death until it can be triumphantly revealed. But the
revelation comes only after a succession of artificial delays has forced
the poem through a climactic progression toward an overwhelming answer. Similarly the movement of the poem seems in its beginnings hesi-
tant and formally ambiguous, reflecting that "perturbation of the
mind" which it was the function of *Lycidas* "to allay," but in the end it
harmonizes the reader's responses by setting his "affections in right
tune." The clarification of theme and movement in the poem parallels
what Milton would have conceived as a clarification of spirit from its
physical nature, where it may be held "clotted" by excessive sorrow, or,
worse, by immorality. But with gracious help and pure intention spirit
etherializes, and in its most volatile condition becomes more apt for in-

tuitive or unconsciously spontaneous, rather than merely intellectual, understanding. Such would be the visionary insight into death's function and God's purpose in the scheme of things that the climax of *Lycidas* seems meant to impart.[4]

But the climax does not necessarily illumine every level by which it was reached. Some of the processes remain obscure. My object in what follows is specifically to identify two principal "unheard" progressions in the formal and thematic movements of the poem, upon which the sounding harmonies largely depend. These are, I suggest, the sustaining bases of the poem, much as, in the scheme of things that caught Milton's own fancy, the unheard harmonies of the heavens, and corresponding harmonies at every level of the universal "concordia discors," set the musical frame for any harmonic vindication of the divine order in human affairs. The formal progression of the poem evolves as a hierarchical structure Milton uses elsewhere and which is based on a Platonically derived theory of inspirational composition. The virtues of this extraordinarily flexible poetic structure are many, but from Milton's point of view I think its most appealing quality was its intrinsic participation in the form by which grace seemed to descend and, completing a spiritual circuit, the aroused religious sensibilities of those affected by it returned heavenward as devotional impulses. It was a way of infusing a transitive grace through the poetic effect. I have already shown how in *Paradise Lost* Milton used a traditional progression keyed to the *furor poeticus*, in a four-phased climactic sequence, beginning with things of the lower and lowest worlds and moving toward a unitive vision of the divine love that holds the cosmos together.[5] This sequence fundamentally structures the progression of *Lycidas*, but it is so unobtrusive that it is easy not to recognize its autonomous and paradigmatic nature. In discussing the sequence later we will see that it serves the poem best by not calling attention to its formal character.

The "unheard" thematic progression is keyed to the poem's need, as a pastoral elegy, to conceal the mystery of death's meaning, namely death's ultimate cause in original sin, and the mystery of that regenerative power in Christian election which redeems from death the fallen saints of God. These themes develop throughout the poem, mediated between the upward sequence of the poem's formal structure and the outward movement from doubt to resolution by which *Lycidas* reflects the cathartic release experienced by the poetic speaker. But the thematic movement is particularly obscure. It figures in the poem as a series of apparently discontinuous enigmas, to which our attention is specifically directed in such a way as to suggest that we grasp their sense even though their particular references seem to elude clear identification.[6] Unheard then, in this progression, are the ulterior contexts and precise meanings of these allusive references, and also the unsounded continuity that in a very particular way threads through all of them — or flows through them, if we accommodate our metaphor to the poem's motif of the alternately open and hidden flow of destructive and regenerative waters. I shall briefly illustrate what I mean, although the full discussion of these sequential enigmas must come later.

Death, of course, is the poem's primary enigma, a mystery expressed by insistent questions, the answers to which are obscurely framed in images that relate the flowing stream of the poet's inspiration to the waters that signal death, regeneration, and resurrection. Then at a more recessed level we find an intermittent but evocative sequence of apparently unrelated allusions, literal enigmas, so used as somehow to resolve periodically the tensions generated by overt thematic progressions, as in the lines ostensibly addressed to the drowned friend but absolving the sea of complicity in his death, for

> It was that fatal and perfidious Bark
> Built in th'eclipse and rigg'd with curses dark,
> That sunk so low that sacred head of thine.   (100–02)

Here, without directly explaining anything (what "fatal and perfidious Bark"?), these lines check and seem to resolve the sequence of questions meant to elicit purpose and sense from Lycidas' drowning.

Then next the passage on the corruption of the Church is climaxed enigmatically by "that two-handed engine at the door" that "stands ready to smite once and smite no more" (130–31). Again the demonstrative pronoun "that" forcefully suggests that we are meant to grasp what in fact we do not grasp, namely, *what* "two-handed engine"?[7] This two-handed mystification is immediately compounded by some implied but unclear relationship between itself and the transition to the poem's next section. There Alpheus, the mythologically personified river, is invoked to return because (with a varied use of the misleading word "that") he is assured "the dread voice is past / That shrunk thy streams" (132–33). Now clearly some dread voice elsewhere sounded something ominously terrible in some other context, one we are apparently supposed to recognize but which, judging from the scholarly record, nobody does. Yet the poetic voice seems to assume our assent to the dread voice's passing, and builds upon it a phenomenally subtle transition to a passage so marked (to vary the artistic metaphor) by *chiaroscuro* that it rivals in its mysteriousness Coleridge's *Kubla Khan* or any hermetically conceived symbolist poem. For clearly the unclear symbolism of the ensuing flower passage relates particularly to some aspect of the mythological history of Alpheus, and to the river's relation with the unknown (and unheard) dread voice.

Further, all these allusions are linked by suppressed associations to the final enigma, the figure of "the great vision of the guarded Mount" (161) who, whichever way he looks, mediates a revelation to the poet the grounds of which are never expressed, though the Christian reader presumably grasps the essence of the transition from doubt to open and triumphantly consoling faith. Here at the end, at last, Milton's relative term in all these enigma variations now has a clearly identifiable antecedent, the saving knowledge of "the dear might of him that walk'd the waves" and who leads Lycidas into the beatific "sweet Societies / That sing, and singing in their glory move" (179–80). In the final resolution the reader himself is included, as Lycidas becomes symbolically, through the poem, a public blessing, "the Genius of the shore, / . . . good / To all that wander in that perilous flood" (183–85) of the world's journey.

The poem leaves us then with a clear sense of an overt thematic progression from doubt to knowledge, from grief to consolation; correspondingly, we must accept implicitly that connections exist between the sequence of enigmatic allusions and their climactic resolution in the final vision. In the course of this discussion I hope to make plain the nature of that progression, identifying in turn the "unheard" sense of each enigma by reference to the context from which each seems drawn, showing how they develop as a sort of sustaining musical ground bass within the poem's structural movements, an accompaniment to its more overtly sounded effects and meaning. But to do so I must show how the covert and overt voices of the poem are functions of its genre and form. About these there has been a good deal written recently, notably by the late Clay Hunt and by Joseph A. Wittreich, Jr., who, however they differ, concur in finding *Lycidas* generically complex, blending different models, so that the poem lends itself to a musical expressiveness which determines both its own thematic development and our grasp of its overall or formal progression.[8] My own view accords with theirs, but more specifically attributes to the poem's underlying structural form its climactic movement through the Platonic hierarchy of ascending poetic raptures, the assured basis of *all* its movements.

II

Clay Hunt's concern is to explain the precise significance of Milton's choices in shaping his poem as both a pastoral lyric and a monody. His

conclusion is that *Lycidas* must be read and *heard* as a tragically conceived musical composition, a new art form Milton derived from lyric
pastoral, and then modified in the light of the monodic theory that had
evolved with the musical humanism of the later Italian Renaissance.
Wittreich finds Milton mingling pastoral and elegiac modes in *Lycidas*,
to which mingled genres he adapted the verse forms of the *canzone*
(which is very likely) and of the madrigal (which is less likely), using both
to transform the poem into a vehicle of prophetic vision. Wittreich's interpretation is relevant here insofar as his emphasis on the poem's prophetic function has some bearing on one of my concerns — distinguishing
its levels of clear and obscure meanings. But it is Clay Hunt's work
which, by virtue of its scope and approach, enables me to take as relatively proven some of the poem's formal musical characteristics.

Both Hunt and Wittreich distinguish the genres of *Lycidas* from its
structures, since it is evident that the poem develops through a mingling
of structural forms and that it mingles genres and formal or expressive
modalities. The preeminent genre, as Hunt rightly insists, is monody —
Milton's own word for it in his only direct reference to the kind of poem
Lycidas was — monody being understood to be a chiefly musical term. I
would emphasize the poem's monodic character for two reasons Hunt
does not develop: the structural sequence of the four Platonic raptures
is, in Renaissance musical speculation, specifically involved with monodic theory; and monodic music is characterized by just such an expressive interplay of clear and obscure effects as I find in Milton's poem.

In the sixteenth century Scaliger defined monody, in both musical
and literary terms, as a type of Greek composition, a lament or "mourn-
ful song" in "memory of the dead" played on a flute by a single performer who stepped out of a chorus of mourners. It is (and the term fits
Lycidas in its conception and publication) a solitary voice sounding in
modulating tones in the context of a more general grief. Puttenham, for
example, described funereal songs sung by many voices as *epicedia*,
whereas monody was the proper term for the lament "uttered by one
alone." As such it would be a specialized form of funereal elegy, within
which all the more complex effects of poetry as song could somehow be
expressed. This is important because monody became identified more
broadly with the particular union of poetry and music as song. But as a
wedding of voice and verse, of melodious sound and words, it was as-
similable by Milton to that quickening of both poetic rapture and visionary insight he recorded in *At a Solemn Music*, *Comus*, and elsewhere. This fusion was, therefore, a precondition to and attribute of
poetic inspiration, thereby linking monody to a wide range of lyric ef-

fects that involve the transitive power of grace infused into works which may in turn animate or religiously arouse a reader or auditor.[9]

While Hunt connects monody and lyric, he is careful to distinguish the poem's monodic form from its primary character as a pastoral lyric. For although *Lycidas* "adheres in large part to the form of pastoral elegy, [it] would be a subspecies of the genus lyric." As in a pastoral lyric, "the poetic voice is that of the poet himself, metaphorically disguised as a shepherd but speaking in *propria persona*, in a mode of discourse alternatively narrative and reflective." The lyrical mode of pastoral is distinguished also from the eclogue, where shepherds and their kind "engage in contention or discussion" in dramatic exchanges. Thus the lyric-pastoral genre of *Lycidas* is primary.[10]

But its lyric qualities underscore the nature of *Lycidas* as song, the point with which we began. Hunt emphasizes that the poem's lyrical or song-like properties are a function of its *lyric* pastoral genre, and goes to great lengths to develop the more-than-metaphorical sense in which such poetry is song or music. He traces the transposition of effects from music to lyric poetry back through a line of Italian practitioners and theorists, at the head of which stands Dante's justification of the musically unaccompanied poetic *canzone* as veritable song itself. An ambiguity remains inherent, however, for Hunt writes that at the end of the Renaissance lyric is "a mode of poetic discourse in which words worked *in various kinds of combination with music* in order to produce a special kind of artistic effect" (emphasis added). But the actual "music" is often hypothetical, being an effect transposed into the poem and therefore formally part of it. Though it is not easy to isolate, Hunt sees that effect as a kind of vitality; and, falling back on a generative metaphor, he describes the lyric pastoral as a procreative fusion, akin to the "dynamic interaction between . . . two principles [which] is the cause of the distinctive life of every created thing." Form is somehow the musically active generative element, while the lyric's theme, sense, or meaning is the passive material upon which the male power, if we may call it so, works.[11]

To the extent that Hunt's metaphor really gets to the point of how Milton conceived his work, Hunt is assuredly right, so much so that one wonders at his evident caution in amassing so much documentation in order to approach *Lycidas* as a lyric or as poetic song. To be sure, he does clear away whatever doubts we might have about a convention by which a composition (the *canzone*), originally conceived for the voice, retained the name of song when, preserving essentially only a formal resemblance and acoustic euphoniousness, it was later conceived entirely for the page and eye, and not with an audible voice for the ear. However, about song's dual elements, mixed voice and verse, or the procreative duality of the mixture, Milton himself leaves little room for doubt. In *At a Solemn Music*, the metaphor (if it is only that) is loaded, voice (music) and verse (meaning) wedding their sounds, "Dead things with inbreath'd sense able to pierce" (4), just as the procreative fusion becomes magnificently regenerative in *Comus'* "strains that might create a soul / Under the ribs of Death." I have discussed elsewhere Milton's use of the latent power of such procreative fusions, on a larger scale, as the dynamic process at work in *L'Allegro* and *Il Penseroso*, and we know that he saw the transitive grace of poetry as a breeding power like that of the word of God preached from the pulpit, procreating souls in listeners.[12] The commonplace that poetry's music works on us unconsciously, which he quoted from Basil, is introduced with the key word, "mixed," to describe the procreative mingling of doctrine and melody, the word being also used in his reference to the "mixt power" of voice and verse in *At A Solemn Music*. Variations on this theme of the energizing, generative power inherent in poetry as song or lyric are scattered, therefore, throughout Milton's work, partaking of that larger generalization about the genders, the male and female properties of sunlight and moonlight in *Paradise Lost*, "Which two great Sexes animate the world" (VIII, 151). The point is that the significance of poetry as song can be stated boldly, that for Milton the melic and semantic components of lyric necessarily work together, procreatively as energized power, by means of which alone poetry transcends rhetoric, and becomes, most characteristically, a power to communicate both audibly and inaudibly, consciously and unconsciously. For me, this is the primary purpose of establishing the monodic character of *Lycidas* as poetic song, so that, within the framework of Milton's technical presuppositions and at the heart of his poetic theory, we are enabled to consider its extraordinary deployment of covert or allusive effects.

Yet the lyric aspects of *Lycidas* as pastoral is segregated by Clay Hunt as peculiar to its generic nature, rather than assimilated directly to its *form* as monody. Presumably he wanted to establish the autonomy of the poem's musicality first as lyric, since it is the lyric character, as *canzone*, which derives from Italian tradition back through Dante, and is rooted in Aristotelian rather than in Platonic or Neoplatonic aesthetics.[13] But monody, which for Hunt is "formal" rather than "generic," is involved (though he does not say so) with Renaissance Neoplatonism, not Aristotelianism. Hunt sees monody as "formal" in that it derives from Greek tragic expression and hence provides a specifically monodic musical structure, as distinct from the tradition of the *canzone*, a structure within which the words or sense take precedence over their lyrical or musical qualities and possible accompaniments. Here I think Hunt's shrewd but too tentative guess as to the procreative nature of poetry's power as lyrical song should be transposed to monody, for Renaissance Neoplatonists characterized the life-giving vitality of song as monodic precisely by reference to the *furor poeticus* or Platonic rapture, and to the climactic progression that structurally it triggered.

According to Ficino the generative moment in the fusion of poetry and music as song was the rapture, and he even practiced monodic songs to elicit it. Pontus de Tyard, the theoretician of the Pléiade, wrote that a rapturous union of power in song is the necessary basis for the cultivation of those higher religious mysteries that had been signified in antiquity by the Dionysian rapture. Poetic rapture was the condition of musical rapture in song. In Tyard himself, these ideas led "to a demand for the reformation of French poetry and music on the model of antiquity. Poet and musician are to be identical or close collaborators. The music is to be monodic, and the poetry either vers mesuré à l'antique [quantitative] or rhymed verse written especially for music." Then, at a later stage, monodic theory, as directed to the reformation of song, encouraged the subordination of music to the clearly audible lead of the poetic words, the dominance of sense over musical effect. It became the argument for overturning the prevailing subordination of poetry to music in polyphony and the madrigal. The effect of monodic theory, therefore, was to divide the power of words and the power of music, with the sense or meaning of the words dominating their sound and those instrumental sounds which supported it. And so, analogously, the *melos* or music technically inherent in all poetic composition must have been conceived as supporting the meaning or sense of the poet's words, as the music of song. To the tradition of the *canzone*, which encouraged Milton to fashion a musically unaccompanied poem as song, we may then add the tradition of the monody, which, as we now see, tended in the same direction.[14]

The relevance of monodic theory to *Lycidas* is even more particular. In its musical revival it led ultimately from an interesting form of nearly incantatory song to the art of the recitative or musically accompanied verbal declamation. Already in the early seventeenth century monody had emerged as "a solo voice declaiming phrases of paramount emotional interest and supported by instruments that play such chords as will heighten the poignancy of the voice." Only intermittently sounded, the chords themselves were often varieties of discord intended to heighten the vocal surface. To this end they were made "parts of an intelligible scheme and not merely . . . uncontrollable expressions of emotions," a development which in turn gave "formal symmetry and balance to the vocal surface." Characteristically then, the recitative function of the voice was dominant, being the overtly intelligible part, though it was sustained by a succession of chords, generally on a harpsichord or played on a lyre, as a thoroughbass accompaniment (the *basso continuo*), in a form that was seldom explicitly scored but had to be understood by the performer from minimal indications in the key system.[15]

Given Milton's designation of *Lycidas* as a monody, and a minimal familiarity with the sounds of early seventeenth-century monody, these characteristics of the form suggest we attend most closely, as Hunt would have us do, to the overt musicality of the poem.[16] Not only is it in itself the most "musical" of all Milton's poetic compositions (if we except the songs of *Comus* and *Arcades*), but no other poem by Milton shows such a density of musical terms, figures and images. The Muses, like Phoebus Apollo, are evoked in a lyric strain, that is, to the sound of the lyre, with specific indications as to dynamic register and range: "Begin, and somewhat loudly sweep the string" (17) and, "That strain I heard was of a higher mood" (87). There are evocations of "rural ditties . . . / Temper'd to th'Oaten Flute" (32–33), while the poet's flute is related also to the vocal reed of Mincius and to Bacchic or Dionysian pipes. In the poem the argument is a song, happiness is a dance, while futility is the failure of song and the extinction of the singer. Discords are figured in the barbarous dissonance of "the rout that made the hideous roar" (61), or evoked at second hand in "the lean and flashy songs" of the "blind mouths" that "grate on their scrannel Pipes of wretched straw" (119, 123–24). An intermezzo, as Hunt notes, is figured in the scoring of the flower passage ("for so to interpose a little ease" 153), while the "shores and sounding Seas" become a sustaining continuo that bears at its climax the "unexpressive nuptial Song" (154, 176), where meaning and sound triumphantly rise to a musically expressive poetic crescendo. This is then modulated into a quietly closing statement in song, the poet "with eager thought warbling his *Doric* lay" (189), a fusion of effects itself sustained from below by a wind instrument, as he touched "the tender stops of various Quills" (188), a phrase that evokes a run of diminishing notes toward the end of the poem.

All this music suggests a relationship between a "recitative" component in *Lycidas* as a monody, represented on the one hand by the plangent directness of the grief expressed and the very quest for meaning undertaken in the most explicit vein of the poem's development, and a "musical" component of chords and discords on the other hand, linked throughout by a minimally scored bass figuration. The musical component is allusive, resonant, intermittently sounded, though it is really an extended pattern, and it interacts with the overt level of the poem's development as a species of discontinuous allegory.[17] These apparently dissociated elements of allegory bring together on the one hand the surface Arcadian fiction, expressing a certain naiveté about death, and on the other hand the underlying allusiveness which expresses in mythological and veiled Christian terms the poem's theological realism. The muffled associations of the two contexts (pastoral or mythological, and Christian) bear upon the poetic character of *Lycidas* as a cathartic vehicle for grief, since to achieve catharsis there must be an initial resistance to a Christian consolation, and the pastoralism provides this resistance.

By such means as this discontinuous allegory, working through the sustaining bass figuration of the poem, *Lycidas* — below its audible range, so to speak — resounds with the silent meaning of "unexpressive song." That is, the poem's music is related to the ineffable and unworldly music of beatitude, inaudible like the music of the spheres, and akin to the "harmony divine" which in *Paradise Lost* only God can hear truly but to which he "listens delighted."[18] There is an analogue for such audible/inaudible figuration in both sixteenth- and seventeenth-century "speculative" music, wherein either a kind of chromatic art or a symbolic structure might be visually and intellectually decipherable only from the score into which either would be incorporated, unrecognized and not to be heard, but assimilated unconsciously through the audible sounds of the score. The hidden effects of such music supposedly had a mysterious spiritual power relating to the ideal soul of the work (in a Platonic sense), whence it worked occultly upon the listener, while what was sounded took its overt significance from the total pattern of audible effects.[19] Notably too, the silent music of *Lycidas* sustains the poem's nature as a consolation that begins in grief's uncontrollable emotions, but ends explicitly in grief's catharsis. For the poem, as I have said, seems meant to work at two levels, intellectually and harmonically, on the understanding and the passions, on the perturbed mind and untuned affections. Given this cathartic function, Clay Hunt is right to identify its dominant tragic tonality as a major constituent of the monodic expressiveness of *Lycidas*.

Finally we return to the involvement of monodic theory with the animating effect of the poetic raptures, the sequence by which the inspirational power, as an *ad extra* grace,[20] is infused procreatively into the vehicle of poetic song. There is a sense in which the figuration for this sequence within the poem itself becomes part of the ground bass, the continuity of those enigma variations we identified at the outset, for its key image of the fountain of the Muses, from which inspirational grace wells, flows into the enigmatic imagery of sounding waters throughout the poem, just as Spenser, in his *Tears of the Muses*, imagines the stream of Parnassus as "taught to bear / A Bases part" to the Muses's "consort" (27–28).

III

What now follows briefly repeats, with the reader's indulgence, material I have presented elsewhere,[21] but without which some of the subsequent discussion of the intrinsic structure and development of *Lycidas* cannot be understood. The *furor poeticus* was the key term in a theory of poetry rooted in the premise that the reader is a direct participant in the poem's workings. Milton makes sure that the reader participates in *Lycidas* by virtue of his own personal involvement in the poem. Within the theory of the raptures, poetry at its best is presumed to be a channel of grace, moving in a sort of divine cycle. It begins outside the poet in the force that inspires him, and ends beyond the reader, in the final object toward which the poem has moved his mind and heart. It is a transitive process within which poetry's very essence appears as a species of energy, which is of course how Plato conceived poetry in the *Ion* (534): as a kinetic power possessing in turn poet, rhapsode, and listener. The Christian adaptation of the Platonic model simply completes the cycle implicit in this movement, so that poetry becomes one with all the descending and ascending cycles in the hierarchical yet circuitous scheme of things by which the One descends into the many and in the upswing recovers something of the spiritual power originally imparted to them.

Indeed, hierarchy ontologically means a divine cycle, defined by the Pseudo-Dionysius, for example, as "a sacred order and science and operation" in all the channels of being. In the poetic cycle, however, the sacred order, science, and operation of hierarchy were at times formally identified with the Platonic model for the movement of poetic energy, the scale of inspirational raptures known from antiquity onward as Plato's four poetic furors, the so-called frenzies out of which the momentum of poetic composition was initiated and sustained. I have already demonstrated elsewhere that this model structures the sequence of invocations to the Muse beginning Books I, III, VII, and IX of *Paradise Lost*, and hence fundamentally orders the poem's design.

I say the four "poetic" furors, although only the first of the Platonic raptures was, properly speaking, the *furor poeticus*, the other three being successively identified with the inspirational raptures of Dionysus, Apollo, and Eros (or Love). To the extent that the scale had long been assimilated to the Christian mystical scale of ascent—from the soul's awakening, to its purification, thence to its illumination, and finally to its apotheosis in unitive vision with the divine—it was identifiable chiefly by its highest level and end, divine love. But to the extent that it served as a structural basis for conceiving the role of inspirational rapture in composition as a graduated progression, the whole sequence tended to be identified by its initiating impulse, as the four "poetic" furors. In this sense the sequence translated a differentiated inspirational momentum into a thematic hierarchy and a structural form, but a form with the inherent ability to accommodate itself, apparently inexhaustibly, to any poetic matter embodying a hierarchical principle of order.

As a sequence, the furors or manias originated, we know, in Plato's *Phaedrus*, where Socrates describes Love's power to raise the fallen soul as a divine inspiration like that of the Muses, Dionysus, and Apollo, but of a higher order. In the *Phaedrus* the four raptures are not explicitly linked as a series, but to the Neoplatonists their sequential nature seems to have been taken as self-evident, confirmed for them by Plato's tendencies elsewhere to order such things as cosmogonic, epistemological, and dialectical processes in hierarchical, fourfold series. Given the interchangeability that the belief in correspondences built into all analogical series—cosmogonic, epistemological, dialectical, and poetic— the hierarchy of raptures became, in effect, a vehicle for ordering as one essentially two kinds of knowledge, the extraordinary revelations of inspiration or intuition (including the knowledge conveyed by myth or any strong passion) and the more rational processes of dialectic, or of logic and rhetoric.

The most suggestive English references to the Platonic raptures and their relation to poetic excellence are in Henry Reynoldes' *Mythomystes*, a work largely showing the influence of Pico. Unlike Ficino or Pico, Reynoldes does not outline anything like a compositional paradigm, but from his discussion of the "extaticke elevations" of poetry's raptures, which signify its divine character, he moves to consider its revelatory power, as in the Orphic Hymns, for poetry unfolds "the series or concatenations of the universall Natures"; indeed, the function of poetry, he suggests, is really to elucidate "the right scale of Nature," as "by the links of that golden chaine of Homer, that reaches from the foote of Jupiter's throne to the Earthe." Milton uses the same image in

Prolusion II as a symbol interchangeable with the Pythagorean harmonies, the essence of which, of course, is itself the interchangeability of all tetradic systems in the occult harmonies of the cosmic scheme.[22]

In discussing Milton's use of the sequence of raptures as a structural form underlying *Paradise Lost*, I cited as the most relevant precedents *Lycidas* and Dante's *Divine Comedy*. To be sure, the *Comedy* is in three parts, not four, and many readers would say this is also the case with *Lycidas*. But in the *Comedy*, as in *Lycidas*, there are four passages evoking inspirational raptures or passions. In Dante's work the first and last more or less bracket the poem, and the middle two, like the first, introduce the main divisions within the poem's narrative order. The *Inferno*'s invocation is to the Muses, the *Purgatorio* invokes Calliope specifically (for Milton "the Muse herself that Orpheus bore" (58), both Calliope and Orpheus being conventional Dionysian surrogates), and the *Paradiso* directly invokes Apollo. Finally, the last lines of the poem evoke the ultimate stage of the poet's inspiration in that unitive vision where the power of divine love is instantaneously grasped as the force moving everything, from the sun and all the stars down.

Were Dante the present concern, the intervening matter of his poem could be shown to correlate quite regularly in every detail to this inspirational succession. But here let us merely suggest the possibilities for some help in getting to know the general thematic topography of the various levels. The inspiration of the Muses, corresponding to the *Inferno*, has thematic associations with things either terrestrial or chthonic. The Dionysian inspiration is associatively purgatorial or cathartic and is often identified with the sphere of the moon, and, as in the *Purgatorio*, with the mutability and alternation of light and darkness in the movements of the sun and moon. It is often also associated with the human nature of love, and so with sexual or generative themes. The Apollonian inspiration is associated with prophecy, with the symbolic illumination of the sun, and with the immutability of the harmony of the spheres, elements sustaining much of the *Paradiso*. And the inspiration of divine love, evoked by Dante at the end of the *Paradiso*, is associated with transcendent intuitive or angelic knowledge and with the spiritual or visionary illumination emanating from the Good, the Beautiful, and the One.

Milton, I submit, follows a similar progression in a number of his early poems, but nowhere more overtly or to better effect than in *Lycidas*. Beyond its induction, *Lycidas* begins by invoking the Muses, proceeds to a turbulent and downward-thrusting Dionysian transition evoking the dismemberment of Orpheus, picks up again with the higher strain initiated by the words of Phoebus Apollo, and proceeds to a climax in its rapturous apocalyptic vision of resurrecting love. As in *Paradise Lost*, this fourfold progression is part, not the whole, of the work's structural form, so that the poem lends itself to alternative structural analyses. Like the ambiguities of its genre and its answerable style, the ambiguities of form in *Lycidas* are part of the poem's strategies, but once we are cued to attend to them the formal meanings of the inspirational evocations are hard to ignore.

At every transitional point of the scale in Milton's elegy there is a quickening movement, a special animation or excitation of spirit in the monodic voice we hear. The induction is a troubled descent, but with the sounding Muses of the sacred well there is, as it were, a plangent impetus to ascend from inspiration's hidden conduits to Olympian heights, to begin the first stage in allaying the perturbations of the mind and setting the affections in right tune. Then the evocation of "the Muse herself that *Orpheus* bore"—the Orpheus who was dismembered by the Dionysian maenads—comes as an intrusive and again a sensibly felt intensification of mood; underlying it this time we sense primitive terrors, and following it we have the characteristically Dionysian opposition of downward-tending sexual desire and upward-tending creative virtue. At the close of this section the terror returns, to be purged by the higher Apollonian voice, which for the first time in the poem refers the whole knot of its tensions to heavenly justice and the divine scheme. In the prophetic mode the Apollonian section, the longest in the poem, looks back (with the "perfidious Bark," as we shall see) to original sin and forward to Apocalyptic justice. Near its close the movement perceptibly intensifies with the evocation of the "two-handed engine," which is followed by a bridging passage wherein the theme of love, as the compassionate sympathy of the mourning flowers, is first sounded. But the real nature of the last stage is not fully revealed until the poem moves, in a climax of faith and love, from the homeward-looking angel to the flaming sun of the morning sky and the sweet societies of everlasting bliss. The fourth stage then, like the three preceding ones, begins in a descent in order to mount higher, achieving in its latter part a sustained rapture at the full and final revelation of divine love. In a comparable but reversed pattern the same progression is found in *Paradise Lost*.

In both poems the fourfold progression is linked successively to a multiple conception of death as the primal feature of the fallen world. Milton distinguished this fairly conventionally in the *Christian Doctrine* as death's four degrees.[23] Since death and transfiguration are the essential themes of the poem, the four degrees of death must be pass-

ingly reviewed if we are to follow the related unfolding of both structure and theme. The first degree is general death as the mortal condition all nature shares inherently through original sin, the Fall itself.
The second and third degrees are the death of the spirit and the death of
the body in humankind. Finally there is eternal death, the absence of
souls from God's presence or the punishment of the damned in hell.
Since the movement of *Lycidas* is from ignorance to knowledge, from
doubt to faith, and from death to resurrection, the implication of
death's four degrees becomes part of the pattern by which death brings
into focus life itself and life's fulfillment. Hence death as the mortal
condition is enigmatic in the poem until its place in the scheme of things
is both clear and felt. In the first stage, however, death's first degree,
original sin, though never stated, is dominant in the opening section.
Such sin, or the Fall, involves the alienation of nature, its sympathetic
disordering by the disordered human condition, which then becomes
the impossibility for nature fully to reflect human moods and needs.
More will be said about this later.

The second or spiritual degree of death involves the death we experience before death, what Milton referred to as the carnal imbruting of
the spirit in man, the gradual extinction of the light of reason by his re-
sponsiveness to lust, considered as a perversion of love and the human
instinct for immortality through offspring. Carnality even reaches toward the righteous man's vulnerability in what Plato described as the
sublimation of the procreative instinct, the desire for an immortality of
fame through our influence upon others, say as a poet or a teacher.
Fame then "is the spur that the clear spirit doth raise / (That last infir-
mity of Noble mind)" (70–71), and so forth.[24] Purgation from these
effects must reverse the spiritual movement between body and soul —
clarify the spirit and enlighten the mind. Such for now are the relevant
implications of the second or Dionysian stage in *Lycidas;* where once it
is admitted that nature is powerless in the face of death, the sympathy
between man and nature, both assumed and denied within the poem, is
then seen to be a pathetic fallacy.

The third degree of death is that of the body alone. In *Lycidas* the
corresponding stage is now Apollonian and involves at first the continued question as to why Lycidas died, a question that remains enigmatic
while it moves perceptibly toward a mysterious clarification, climaxing
directly after the imagined scene where the corpse is poetically strewn
with funereal flowers. Finally, in the apocalyptic transfiguration of Lycidas among the beatified in heaven, there is the inversion to triumph of
that fear of the fourth death, the eternal separation from God.

As the unfolding sequence of death's degrees suggests, Milton's governing strategy inhibits us at the outset from too quickly reaching the triumphant conclusion that death is redeemed by beatific transfiguration. The poem's pastoralism restrains the meaning from emerging too quickly. It imposes a kind of obscurantist naiveté. Clearly the pastoral convention of the elegy is used not so much to disguise reality — for example, the life King and Milton shared at Cambridge — but to veil the evident meaning of death until that meaning might be triumphantly made plain after a succession of partial, interim revelations. Constraint and delay then are the very terms in which the poet's grief is first expressed, and from the outset they make even the writing of the poet seem a problematic venture.

If we refer to reality, the nonpoetic world, no sooner does death occur than a surviving Christian friend or relative (in Milton's world) would be immediately offered, perhaps more soberly, the consolation that in *Lycidas* seems a final revelation. But in this same world of reality the young Milton was beset by real constraints and delays. At the age of twenty-nine he had as yet no socially apparent vocation; as far back as six years earlier, he had written that no condition was more spiritually disquieting and burdensome. Nor had he yet found the fulfillment in love and marriage a man of his passionate nature must have long looked for. Delay and constraint were therefore the very conditions of his life, justified to himself as a scrupulously comprehensive preparation for his calling to some anomalous vocation, that of a Puritan poet-priest, a calling difficult to project even imaginatively onto the contemporary scene of Stuart England. But the constraints must have engendered a need for some climactic release or revelation that would, in retrospect, explain or clarify the providence that delayed his fulfillment.[25]

Hence, the pastoral form of *Lycidas* as a climactic progression answered, I think, several understood or perhaps felt needs. The news of King's death, with the request to Milton that he contribute to a book of memorial verses, becomes in the poem's induction a "bitter constraint, and sad occasion dear" (6), interrupting some preparatory seclusion, into which, as into an idyllic setting, death intrudes. He may have been profoundly immersed in thinking about poetry in all its possibilities, but as something to be done *tomorrow*, not today. "I come," he wrote of the poetic coronals, to "shatter your leaves before the mellowing year" (5). But the constraint to write was also a distancing event that could set in perspective and yet absorb the contradictions of his immediate situation, all the more so because the very form with which art might most readily come to terms with King's death, the pastoral elegy, was singu-

larly apt to absorb his outward and inward conditions. His country retirement, transposed, became the Arcadian ambiance of an unready
shepherd, while his guilt about the lack of apparent commitment or accomplishment here had its correlative in death itself, as an intrusion
into Arcadia of insistently personal and historical reality.

For in Arcadia death was admitted, but only as an anomalous mystery. On the surface the Arcadian landscape is, or should be, golden and
happy. Yet poetically the condition of such happiness is a fiction that
drastically reduces the scale of experience and simplifies the images of
life, for to the extent that the pastoral admits death, it does so quizzi-
cally. In one of Poussin's pastoral paintings Arcadian shepherds group
around a stone cenotaph as if at once it was and was not there, or as if it
was, in all its rectangular and polished artificiality, a natural rather
than human feature of the golden landscape. Only from the whole formal composition does a sense of disquietude about the contrast emerge.
Inscribed on the marble is the legend of death's inexplicable presence
amid idyllic happiness. *Et In Arcadia Ego.* In *Lycidas* just that disquieting Arcadian contrast between near primal innocence and death
keys a deeper level of development than that to which the poem's apparent movement overtly testifies.

Perhaps this can be illustrated by what the poem does *not* say. It
does not say anything about the most obvious Christian elements in the
understanding of death. On the contrary, it withholds that understanding as an insight only to be realized climactically at the end, as if it were
a revelation vouchsafed — after both imaginative and spiritual obstacles
have been overcome — in ecstatic, visionary terms all the more powerful
for having been held back, and holding back, even at the end, complete
explicitness. In general the poem progresses along an upward curve
from grief to an evident Christian consolation, with internal complica-
tions of local movement, in swirls and eddies of renewing grief that mo-
mentarily check the rising swell of assuaging comfort. The restraining
element in that grief is always a nominal ignorance, and its form is conventional. With the pastoral stance, Milton adopted the studied naiveté
earlier used in his Latin poems on death and in the *Fair Infant Dying of
a Cough,* namely that he did not know why death should have so wide
and arbitrary a dominion. But this is the voice of a poetic fiction, of a
character who, unlike John Milton, has to discover death's meaning by
stages. In *Paradise Lost* the conclusion is put firmly before us at the outset: disobedience, the Fall, brought death into the world, where it must
have universal rule, "till one greater Man / Restore us."

The evasion of a straightforward answer to the questions as to what death is, what it means, why it happens, is of course scarcely noticed because of the Arcadian integument governing what Puttenham would have called the "depth of devise" in the "invention" of Milton's poem. The Arcadian allegory of *Lycidas* populates its landscape with pagan myths and the symbolic flora and fauna of a green pastoral world. But the fictive surface scarcely conceals the identity of "the Pilot of the *Galilean* Lake" and the even more forceful climactic presence of he who in his "dear might . . . walk'd the waves" (173). The water-associated aspects in which St. Peter and Christ appear — but are not and cannot be named — do not, however, mean that we forget altogether why they can be almost, but never directly, evoked in an Arcadian poem. They remain, for all the power of their allusive presence, pastoral figures in a mythologized context, and it is therefore in myth-sustained, pastoral terms that death must be reconciled to Arcadia. Hence the poem's very inspiration, namely its Christian intent, *must go underground and mingle as a thematic stream* with the poem's mimesis of the course of an ostensibly naive mind, a mind which, in the apparently inadequate terms of pastoral fictions, must account for death in an Arcadia that knows nothing directly of the Fall of Man but nevertheless is called upon to witness its consequences.

I suggest that into this convention Milton projected the complex private state of mind in which were balanced his apparently unproductive leisure and an active guilt such as appears in the "Letter to a Friend." Going further, one may speculate that the poem's formal development reflects the ability of art to resolve such contradictions and to transpose into a symbolic action — writing the poem — the needs posed by the larger complexities of the situation which produced it. For the contrast in Arcadia between death and naive innocence is also a contrast between reality, or one form of nature, and art, or another form of nature. The contrast is between death as the blunt reality of the fallen world of human knowledge, and a nature represented in the stylization of an art that seems to pretend to restorative powers, as if art itself could redeem nature — a point that the poet later ambivalently questions as he sees into the "false surmise" (which is, in one sense of that phrase, the pathetic fallacy) of the flower passage, where nature is imagined bringing flowers to "strew the Laureat Hearse where *Lycid* lies" (151). But the truth is that in the Christian scheme art redeems nature only insofar as art itself is an instrument of grace. Yet, in an Arcadia where even grace must be disguised, art itself, both in its ultimate inspiration and in what it represents, would offer, if not grace itself, then a sure earnest of grace's redemptive power. Even the very image of Arcadia's pastoral

world is really a vision touched by grace, a vision (shaped by convention, but revitalized in the inspired poet's mind) of a pagan golden age
that has taken on much of the coloration of the Eden that was and shall
again be, its green world become a haunted mirror of a lost perfection
to be regained.

Finding that lost world is part of the poem's business, while another part is to pose the mystery of the quest itself. Herein seems to be
the poet's justification for withholding what we know until the need for
it can be shaped into an insistent expectation that must be satisfied, or
even a longing to tell us something about our religious instincts. The restorative art of the poem, therefore, in some indeterminable or graduated sense related to its questing movement, first shapes our yearning
for a stable happiness into those Arcadian images set in tension with
morbid reality, and then uses the dialectical play between death here
and now, and the imaginative world where desires are fulfilled, as a
way of propelling the mind to that ultimate Christian point of insight,
where death and life become one. This apparent progression is both the
literal movement by which the poem's meaning comes to its climax, and
the psychological (or aesthetic) movement by which the reader participates in the poem's development to that climax, a progression rooted in
our physical natures.

IV

The rhythms of the poem are its movements, and what interests us
here are not the rhythms of sound, but those of meaning and structure.
Those of meaning more directly reflect the poet's divided consciousness
behind the contrasts of Arcadian innocence and morbid knowledge,
and they suffuse the surface of the poem with a gradually dissipated, in-
determinate, or obscured sense of direction. The structural and formal
rhythm is also indeterminable in appearance, in a way very nearly announced by the poet at the outset, when he mingles the coronal leaves of
heroic laurel, pastoral myrtle, and elegiac or Bacchic ivy.[26] The mixing
of modes is reinforced by the mingling of lyric inspiration, contrastively
expressed by the loudly swept strings of the Muses, with the elegiac
human voice with its symbolic oaten flute. All such mingling partly follows from what Hunt showed to be traditional characteristics of the
lyric pastoral and monodic techniques. But there is an even more fundamental structural and formal indeterminacy in what seems to be the
very absence of a self-evident and rigidly formal design. What seems to
appear is the concurrent presence of several schemes.

The largest is simply the undulating but mounting progression of the poem's eleven verse paragraphs, bracketed at either end by an induction and conclusion. More intriguing is the concurrence of the separable patterns of the poem seen as either three or four main movements. The movement in three phases is essentially the structure long since identified and analyzed by Arthur Barker,[27] where the movement is broad, overt, and thematically continuous, consisting, as we shall see, more or less of a sequence of modal statements and responses interacting upon one another. The fourfold pattern is, of course, the upward progress structured by the four Platonic raptures sketched earlier. At the turning point of each of the four stages the movement seems quickened by an antiphonal conjunction of voices, either speaking or represented by instrumental equivalents. The points of juncture suggest specific blendings of voice and verse, music and meaning, as the dual quickening power impelling the inspirational momentum forward.

In the three-part thematic development the voice heard first and most directly throughout is the poet's own, in its Arcadian guise. It is also a representative human voice asking questions for which, however, more than human answers are needed. This is the function of the other set of voices, which cannot be so easily identified by a dominant aspect, but which reflect an underlying theological realism aware of all the degrees and dimensions of death. The emerging Christian reality can find an outlet didactically only by responding to questions and doubts. It cannot spontaneously offer unsolicited solutions. And as the poet's voice expresses a natural condition, the responses, which refer to more than natural conditions, become obliquely revelatory, continually shifting the focus of concern from the questions about death to the real nature of life's fulfillment. While these alternations are rhythmically regular, they do not appear successively in the same form, since each set is a higher order of experience than the preceding one, and in each the answer varies from overtly clear meaning to the puzzling enigmas identified earlier.

The first and longest movement of the three-part rhythmic structure (15–84) has an extended opening in two sections (if we leave aside the inspirational invocation), juxtaposing the happy former days in Arcadia and the realization of the death of Lycidas. It brings together the fate of Lycidas, in his identity as a poet, and Milton's own more personal concern, the questions posed by the tensions within himself of equally unfulfilled sexuality and poetic accomplishment.

In the second part (85–131) the rhythm picks up pace, its two main sections again juxtaposing the physical fate of Lycidas (this time in Edward King's identity as minister and priest) to the meaning of unfulfill-

ment in the ministerial calling. The note of unfulfillment here is again
obliquely personal, insofar as Milton conceived his own poetic vocation
in ministerial terms and was to claim that he had been thwarted of fulfillment, "church-outed by the Prelats," who along with lesser clergy
are represented as the "blind mouths," the corrupting taint on the
larger pastoral body of Christ, thwarting there too the fulfillment of a
larger spiritual life. Death and unfulfillment are answered here more
mysteriously than in the first section, with the promise of that "two-
handed engine" that "stands ready to smite once and smite no more."

The third and last part (132–85) returns again to the fate of Lycidas, this time as everyman, whose death is the symptom of the universal
human condition. Hence even more enigmatically now his death involves the sympathy of nature. And if such sympathy is only artistically
imaginable as the "false surmise" of the pathetic fallacy, now the poet's
own voice sustains and answers that lamentation for the mortal body of
Lycidas, the voice exalted as if by a visionary fantasy, but responding to
the image of the body's death with the imagery of a triumphant beatific
fulfillment.

Now this progression is, in fact, loosely identical with the poem's
fourfold development, each phase of which is marked by an inspirational quickening. The very long section that Barker sees as one section I
take really to consist of two stages. The first stage is an inspirational invocation to the Muses, followed by the contrast of the happier days in
Arcadia, with the first realization of death as the human condition. The
second stage climactically leads toward and not away from its inspira-
tionally marked center. In the first stage the initial rapture of poetry,
the poetic furor, has two attributes that are repeated by variation in
every one of the three succeeding inspirational junctures, where the
momentum of the poem is renewed by a more intense or higher stage of
rapture. Both attributes are conventional but are exploited so as to
make of them elements of a sustaining network of symbolic associations
throughout the poem.

The first identifies the *natural* part of inspiration—the poetic
voice itself welling from within the poet—with flowing streams, while
the second identifies the *supernatural* part with a symbolic musical
accompaniment:

> Begin then, Sisters of the sacred well
> That from beneath the seat of *Jove* doth spring,
> Begin, and somewhat loudly sweep the string.   (15–17)

Simply put, these motifs of physical waters and imaginative airs respond both to the circumstances of Edward King's death by drowning

and to Milton's need to memorialize the occasion poetically—hence, among other reasons, the induction's mixed coronal leaves, signifying the mingled modalities in the garland of song offered to Lycidas' "wat'ry bier." But it is also a procreatively quickened mingling of human expression with transcendental music, subdued to a lower level again at the conclusion of the poem by the poet's touches on "the tender stops of various Quills," accompanying his "eager thought warbling his *Doric* lay."

In the second of the inspirational stages (50–84, beginning, "Where were ye Nymphs"), the two elements of flowing water and mingled music, associated with the renewal of inspirational rapture, are dramatically inverted to represent a powerful downward check upon the upward-tending course of poetic consolation. This is the point of the Dionysian rapture, which appears as a turbulent reversal of direction, for the Orphic inspiration seems fruitless in the face of a Dionysian fury that is at once natural or sexual and supernatural.[28] The intrusive dissonance is paralleled by the turbulence of the inspirational stream involved with the dismemberment of Orpheus,

> Whom Universal nature did lament,
> When by the rout that made the hideous roar
> His gory visage down the stream was sent,
> Down the swift *Hebrus* to the *Lesbian* shore.

The meaning here of the dissonance drowning out the procreative rapture, and thus checking the upward ascent, is spelled out more explicitly in the evocation of the Orphic tragedy in *Paradise Lost:*

> where Woods and Rocks had Ears
> To rapture, till the savage clamor drown'd
> Both Harp and Voice, nor could the Muse defend
> Her Son.   (VII, 35–38)

In both cases the poet's invocation of the Muse encounters the fact that poetry deals with unavailing fictions unless its secret powers draw their strength from a higher source. But in *Lycidas* the quickening of imagination aroused by the Dionysian rapture seems energized by a formal terror with deep roots in Milton's personal life.

The symbol of Orpheus dismembered by the orgiastic women leads immediately, in a natural though implicit transition, to thoughts of dalliance, of sexual fulfillment, as something better to pursue in the face of death than the fruitless efforts to write great poetry.

> Were it not better done as others use
> To sport with *Amaryllis* in the shade
> Or with the tangles of *Neaera's* hair?   (67–69)

As we noted earlier, at the Dionysian level there is a conventional link-age, derived from Plato's *Symposium*, of the drive to beget children with a sublimation of that drive in the quest for an immortality of fame. In *Lycidas* this movement from the sexual need to the sublimation of it becomes the last purely natural impulse in purifying the spirit:

> *Fame* is the spur that the clear spirit doth raise
> (That last infirmity of Noble mind)
> To scorn delights, and live laborious days.   (70–73)

But earthly fame as an end is also threatened by Fate, who comes as the "blind *Fury* with th'abhorred shears / And slits the thin spun life." The terror of the image goes beyond death simply understood, being rooted in an implicit sexualized relationship between life's fulfillments and po-etry's fulfillments. Nor is our reading only a modern, post-Freudian as-sociation. It is classically Greek. Aeschylus in the *Eumenides* describes the Furies in terms that assimilate them to the Dionysian Maenads who dismembered Orpheus. They are man-renders, castrators whose pun-ishments are "heads / . . . severed, eyes torn out, throats cut, man-hoods unmanned."[29]

Then the strains of the third or Apollonian rapture are first sounded within the second stage as the intervening voice of Phoebus Apollo, mu-sically figured — a voice that dramatically arrests the imaginative tur-moil, the sensual music, of the downward-tending Dionysian mood, converting its movement upward again. Apollo's reply sets the nature of fame in its rightful perspective, not as rooted in the sublimation of sex but in its heavenly aspect. That voice is also symbolically identified with Apollo's music, and immediately induces the poetic voice, figured as the oaten flute, to complete the invocation to the renewed Apollo-nian strain by calling on its natural counterparts, the streams of Arca-dian inspiration:

> O Fountain *Arethuse*, and thou honor'd flood
> Smooth-sliding *Mincius;* crown'd with vocal reeds,
> That strain I heard was of a higher mood.   (85–87)

This stage (85–131) is illuminative, as it must be by virtue of its formal Apollonian nature.[30] Altogether the section begins to get closer to the es-sential truth in which the relationship of mortality to fulfillment, *the* question of the poem, will be clear. But the clarity is partial, the bright-ness that of *chiaroscuro*, for the Apollonian strain is in itself an incom-plete revelation, as is symbolized at the outset by the pairing of the fountain Arethuse with the Theocritean river Mincius, whereas the powerful and far more mysterious complement of Arethuse is really the river Alpheus, into which it will flow in the fourth and last inspirational stage of the poem. Here, however, the conventional prophetic aspect of the third stage of poetic rapture is sounded firmly enough in the closing lines of the section, with the apocalyptic prophecy of the two-handed engine foretelling divine vengeance upon the abusers of the church.

The important thing is that the transitions from one section to another have become more and more mysterious, because inspiration, as the sustaining energy of the poem, becomes increasingly a mystery of intermittent revelatory grace, and a Christian grace, moreover, necessarily disguised by the constraining pagan fictions of Arcadia. I know of no more enigmatic lines in all of Milton's poetry than those which open the poem's fourth stage (132–85):

> Return *Alpheus*, the dread voice is past
> That shrunk thy streams.

As we noted earlier, on the face of it, nothing connects "the two-handed engine at the door" with some dread voice and a shrunken stream. Our full understanding of these lines must abide the next stage of analysis, as we follow the allusive workings of monodic composition in the poem's techniques. But clearly they evoke one last, essentially natural inspirational power, figured as a self-transforming underground stream. Changing his nature as a god into a stream to pursue the nymph Arethusa underground, where she changed herself into a fountain, Alpheus finally mingled with her waters in Sicily. The music to which Alpheus responds is inaudible in two ways: first, because some dread voice is *past*, and second, because another strain begins to be sounded above the renewed pastoral music ("Return *Sicilian* Muse"), the strain of the intermezzo, as Hunt calls it (p. 140), of flowery natural grief. This higher music — whatever it is — must be angelic since it is inexplicably linked to the foregoing "two-handed engine" and begins the mounting movement toward the angel in the "great vision of the guarded Mount." More evident as a transition is the strangely masterful movement from the angel of the mount to the theme of apotheosis in divine love, a theme that is the center of almost every Christian expression of the climactic stage of inspirational rapture.

Retrospectively, we see then that the relationship to one another of the four levels in *Lycidas* is not simply progressive. Specifically, they connect in a way that expresses symbolically the modulation in the sense of death itself and the stages of ascending insight and spiritual happiness or consolation. Thus the beginning of the first level, that of the

Muses, with its reference to the sisters of the sacred well, is linked to the end of that level and the beginning of the next, or the second, level by the fact that in the Dionysian stage Orpheus is introduced as the Muse's son, one higher than they, but as the surrogate and priest of Apollo, lower than the god. Then when Apollo himself appears it is "as emissary from All-Judging Jove."[31] And when St. Peter appears as the most explicit development of the Apollonian prophetic character, his last words are not only prophetic but apocalyptic, and his whole speech reverberates with anticipation of the two great apocalyptic moods he signals, divine wrath and divine love. But divine love is God himself, knowledge of whom will set the very height of the poem's reach. Then, between Peter's words and the evocation of the great angel, the intervening "intermezzo" passage significantly begins with the return of Alpheus, the flowing again of the underground stream connecting the apparently disconnected elements.

V

At the climax of *Lycidas* all the poem's movements come together. Along with the broad three-part ascent from death to life there is the progressive unfolding of the inspirational movement through its four raptures, while binding both movements together is the tacitly developing consciousness of those differences between death and life signified by death's four degrees. The first, death as the mortal condition, involves coming to terms with its cause in the Fall of Man by original sin. At the poem's first stage we are far from that realization; rather the mortal condition is then translated into the general sense of the alienation of a natural world sympathetically accessible to us but unable either to prevent death or account for it. The second degree, or spiritual death, is threatened at the second stage by the intrusive awareness that inspiration alone ("the Muse herself") will not exempt the poet from either spiritual death or the fear of its consequences, the fear being paradoxically what might tempt him into mistaking sexual or poetic fulfillment here below for our need to survive ourselves. The parenthetical reference to fame indirectly states that such a mistake would threaten the clear or rising spirit of the poet, the very essence of the aspiring spiritual life threatened by spiritual death. All the effects of death's first degree, as Milton recorded them in the *Christian Doctrine*, are now intensified in the second degree, which thematically cues the motifs of this section, as alienation, guilt, terror, degradation of mind, and "a lessening of the majesty of the human countenance" are evoked.[32] The second movement notes, as its point of departure and culminating awareness, that both nature and inspiration (as a measure of grace) are powerless in the face of death, that nature's sympathy is futile.

The third degree of death, that of the body alone, is the most familiar and pressing awareness we have of our mortal condition, for which the Apollonian reassurance must break through as a premonitory revelation that, to triumph over that death, we must look well above nature. In this stage the poem's allusive strains become significantly deepened. Hitherto death was a fact without any theological underpinnings. Now the question about death elicits that strange answer which seems meant to suffice but which tells us little that is specific. There was, we are told, no immediate or apparently natural reason for this death.

> The Air was calm, and on the level brine
> Sleek *Panope* with all her sisters play'd.
> It was that fatal and perfidious Bark
> Built in th'eclipse, and rigg'd with curses dark,
> That sunk so low that sacred head of thine.   (98–102)

Like the Orpheus passage, with the sacred head of the poet-priest sent "down the swift *Hebrus*" (64), the reference to that fatal and perfidious bark is clearly to something discordant outside the pastoral context of the poem, yet, as representing sudden death by water, puzzlingly identifiable with the death of Lycidas. But apparently both the Orphic evocation and this passage derive from one source, one which, moreover, also helps illumine the other most enigmatic passages in *Lycidas*. Here we begin to bring to the surface the deliberately recessed senses of the apparent meaning, and they point toward that answer about the meaning of death which in the Arcadian setting can never be made explicit.

In Seneca's *Medea*, the symbol of the primal evil that destroyed the innocence of the golden age is the voyage of the Argonauts, in which Medea herself became a prize before, rejected by Jason, she murdered their children. The Argo, in which both sailed, is thus an accursed ship, destroying all who sailed. Prominent among the Argonauts was Orpheus.

> he, the tuneful Muse's son,
> At whose sweet strains the streams stood still,
>
> .   .   .   .
>
> Over the Thracian fields was he hurled
> In scattered fragments; but his head
> Down Hebrus' grieving stream was borne.[33]

Another victim was Hylas, whom Milton repeatedly evoked elsewhere as a mythic youth ravished to a watery grave, and who was worshipped as a dying god — one of the underlying archetypal aspects of Lycidas himself. "For what crime did Hylas die" the chorus in *Medea* asks.

> For he,
> Mid waters safe was done to death.
> Go then, and fearlessly the deep
> Plow with your daring ships; but fear
> The peaceful pools.   (647, 649–51)

Thus the Argo, as a cursed ship, earlier reminds the chorus of the former "guiltless golden age our fathers saw" (326), now gone. And, the chorus continues; "This impious bark its guilt in dread atoned" (340).

The fragmentary and deeply recessed nature of this context, as we come to it at first, seems to lack a coherent connection with the larger movement of *Lycidas*. Indeed, the allusion to the "fatal and perfidious bark" can stand by itself, without reference to the Argonauts, to suggest the curse of bodily death that hangs over humanity in its mortal, fallen condition.[34] At that level, its association with the earlier Orphic image of death is sufficiently sustained by the image-pattern that brings together water and the death of the body. Nonetheless, a further latent element in the covert connecting structure becomes evident when the poem moves from its third to its fourth stage and to the fourth degree of death. In the *Christian Doctrine* Milton described the fourth degree of death as the final death man experiences, namely, eternal death, the death from which the blessed are to be triumphantly spared by their resurrection. Here the meaning of the other most enigmatic passage in *Lycidas* is crucial, the evocation of Alpheus at the turning point of the fourth stage of the poem, the underlying context of which coherently relates to the contexts of Senecan primal sin and the voyage of the Argonauts.

Since the Christian understanding of death is at first impeded, then deeply enhanced, by the pastoral and mythological disguise, there must be some implicit equation working throughout. Death must be figured imaginatively in terms that can modulate freely back and forth from pagan allegory to Christian symbolism. The Argonautic myth, evoked allusively by the "perfidious Bark / . . . rigg'd with curses dark," allegorically suggests a latent moral pattern in the association of ships and watery death with primordial guilt and punishment.[35] But in turn these symbolize in Christian terms original sin, spiritual death, and finally the death of the body, which is the point reached by the end of the third, Apollonian stage of *Lycidas*. Now, as we noted, each of the poem's four movements begins with the evocation of an inspirational stream which somehow, in each movement, becomes involved with the actual development of the theme of death by water. Correspondingly, as the poem moves toward its climax, with the mind's turmoil turning into hope, and hope into triumphant faith, the underlying theological aspect of death's degrees turns inside out, from death to resurrection. And, within the thematic pattern of imagery of death and water flowing from movement to movement, there is a corresponding transposition of the symbols of death and water into symbols of life and regenerative streams. These transformations are exactly what the chorus in *Samson Agonistes* called them, "consolations from above / Secret refreshings, that repair . . . strength / And fainting spirits uphold" (664–66). They are musically the ground bass to the consort of explicit meanings, the song of the poem.

After the "fatal and perfidious Bark" allusively identifies a primal curse akin to that original sin by which, spiritually and bodily, all are afflicted, the ecclesiastical passage assimilates the thwarting of fulfillment for Lycidas, the dead priest, with the frustration of fulfillment for Christ's body on earth, the visible Church. The imagery here is pastoral but keyed to Peter's identification as both the shepherd of the Church and "The Pilot of the *Galilean* Lake." And implicitly the sustaining association is one common in patristic writings, that the ship of the individual soul and the ship of the Church's soul, in their earthly lives, undergo the same ordeal of peril, where the decision is made for life or death. In such journeys, writes Ambrose, "Victory is no more than the guerdon of return." But the note that sounds the outcome for the Church and the possible transformation of the individual's death into eternal life is apocalyptic — "that two-handed engine at the door" which "stands ready to smite once and smite no more." The least enigmatic feature of this image is that it is two-handed, separating by cleavage the damned from the saved. Just as St. Peter indignantly denounces the ongoing effects of the primal curse, which reaches into and perverts even the Church, the vehicle of grace itself, so too, as the fisher of souls, he anticipates the open triumph of the last movement, with its "dear might of him that walked the waves," who saved Peter himself from drowning when he stepped from the ship on the Sea of Galilee. Thus Peter's last prophetic words signify a twofold fulfillment in judgment and love. "In mystical divinity," wrote Edward Benlowes, Milton's contemporary, God's "two-handed sword is the Word and the Spirit, which wounds and heals; and what is shed in this holy war is not blood but love."[36]

What then is the meaning of the sudden transition from this note of wrathful and compassionate finality to the invocation of the fourth and last stage of the poem?

> Return *Alpheus*, the dread voice is past
> That shrunk thy streams; Return *Sicilian* Muse.

Surely this dread voice is not that of St. Peter, except insofar as his words are overlaid by another, a mythological voice of judgment. But whose? And in what context? The first most evident lead is the well-known mythological association of Alpheus with Arethusa, both figures who, in mortal danger, by metamorphosis became flowing streams and sources of poetic inspiration. Fountain Arethuse, invoked at the beginning of the preceding or third stage, was originally a nymph pursued by Alpheus, to escape whom she turned herself into an underground stream, but he followed, as a stream from the *Peloponnesus*, and caught up with her in Arcadian Sicily, where their waters mingled and were said to symbolize the tempering of imperfection by virtue. Another legend has Arethusa become a healing nymph whose waters cured deep distress. This gives an added dimension to Plutarch's story that Alpheus, a primal criminal descended from the Sun, killed his brother and now, being pursued by the Furies, threw himself into a river thenceforth called Alpheus. Plutarch goes on to say that along the banks of this river grows a plant that cures the madness and passion of grief and great distress. Alpheus then, whether impelled or pursued by love or furious judgment, is a god transformed into an underground-flowing, inspirational stream whose powers symbolically ease grief, especially in the form of flowers watered by his streams.[37]

But this cannot be all, since Alpheus is bid to return because some voice is past that *shrunk* his stream. The meaning of this most enigmatic line becomes fully clear only in the context of another passage from Seneca, this time his tragedy *Thyestes*, which like *Medea* takes tragic death to be the consequence of an inherited curse in a pattern that makes the primal fault a type of original sin. Now Seneca, well into the Renaissance, benefited from the supposition that he had been a friend and correspondent of St. Paul and one whose moral interpretations of pagan myth and tragic themes were suffused throughout with a kind of sympathetic crypto-Christianity. Indeed, conclusive proof that Seneca was not a Christian or a Christian sympathizer was published only as late as 1668. This explains the readiness with which his influence penetrated Renaissance drama and lent itself to Christian symbolization. And among Milton's many references to Seneca or his tragedies, significantly, his most striking is his metaphor for the consequences of original sin in *Paradise Lost*, when, as Adam and Eve complete the eating of the

apple, "At that tasted Fruit / The Sun, as from *Thyéstean* Banquet
turn'd / His course intended" (X, 688–89). The figure is from *Thyestes*,
where, at the banquet of the flesh of Atreus' children offered to him by
his brother Thyestes, the sun is wrenched from its course and all the
order of the universe plunged into chaos. A second and more recessed
use of the Senecan metaphor for original sin is in *Samson Agonistes*,
where Samson curiously condemns his own divulgence of the secret
source of his strength as a betrayal of God, hence a form of original sin.
Such a betrayal was the unnamed sin of Tantalus (himself unnamed), "a
sin / That Gentiles in thir Parables condemn / To thir abyss and horrid
pain confin'd" (*SA* 499–501).[38]

The betrayal by Tantalus, and its connection with a type of original sin, is explicit in Seneca's *Thyestes*, which opens with the confrontation in Hell between Tantalus and a heaven-sent Fury, for Tantalus had
once been admitted to the companionship of the gods, and lived among
them in paradisal bliss, until he betrayed Zeus by stealing divine food to
share with mortal companions. But a more grisly horror followed when
he butchered his son Pelops to serve as a dish to the gods. For this he was
damned to a hellish stream from which he could not drink to allay his
thirst nor reach up to eat fruits dangling above him. Elsewhere we learn
that Pelops was miraculously reconstituted, yet even he carried on the
inherited taint, compounding it by other crimes.[39] In Seneca's play, the
rivalry between Thyestes and Atreus is central. They are the descendants of Tantalus, and at the play's outset the Fury goads Tantalus
with a horrible curse that foretells the universal miseries his crime has
produced, relief from which becomes identified with the waters he
longs to drink but cannot. In one last burst of execration all restorative
streams are banished by the dread voice of the Fury, "Dost thou not see
how . . . / The waters flee their springs? How river banks / Are empty."
(108–10). And he goes on to gloat over the shriveled waters:

> Now Lerna backward shrinks,
> The streams of Inachus have hidden away,
> The sacred Alpheus sends his waters forth
> No longer. (115–18)

But, when the Fury passes, the chorus implores forgiveness and restoration from "any god" for all the waters, but singles out only one river by
name, the one even the Fury had distinguished above all other streams
as "sacred."

> if Alpheus bright
> With its cool, clear stream moves any god,
> Far favored for its Olympic course —

> Let him his peaceful godhead turn
> To our affairs; let him avert
> This dread inheritance of crime.   (129–34)

The essence of the whole choral passage is summed up in its one great yearning cry, a lament expressing the longing for a return at last to original innocence and perfection: "Enough of sin!" They ask chorally for the permanent passing of the voice of that Fury of vengeful justice that shrunk Alpheus' streams, almost as if Alpheus were one of the lost rivers that flowed originally, in the Christian scheme, from Eden.[40]

It must have been immaterial to Milton's purpose if the underlying context of this most obscure of all allusions went consciously unrecognized, to say nothing of the larger pattern by which Alpheus and Arethusa's restorative powers were linked to both Seneca's *Thyestes* and the primal curse of death by water in his *Medea*. What mattered is an effect which is imagistically rather like the abrupt montage of film technique, where one powerful and only symbolically reinforcing image, without apparent continuity, is spliced with another. Or, in the musical vein of the poem's technical development, what matters is the swelling of sound from the chords and instrumental accompaniment that sustains the vocal surface. The fact is that by virtue of its otherwise inexplicable resonance this transition masterfully controls the modulations of mood into the poem's next section, but not entirely without an even more subtle link to the final warning uttered by St. Peter a moment earlier. We cannot even possibly begin to suspect that this link is in Milton's mind until, halfway through the following passage, we encounter, as the next and last of the poem's enigma variations, the angel of the guarded Mount.

VI

After the cryptic invocation to Alpheus the poem enters on its fourth and last stage. There judgment is turned into love, and, in the last degree of death, the blessed, by the realization of eternal life, are separated from the damned in the eternity of their death in hell. The first intent is to invoke the restorative effect of Alpheus and its now well-watered flowers upon all of nature, conceived again in happier union with heaven and in sympathy with the human condition. Yet this sympathy, figured as the imagined tribute of Nature to the lost body of Lycidas, is a pathetic fallacy, and, dwelling still upon the body, is thus in several senses a "false surmise." Even Milton's apparent musical figuration carries a deeper latent sense, since the words suggesting an intermezzo, "For so to interpose a little ease" (152), ironically translate al-

most exactly a line in the *Enchiridion* of Augustine where he writes that
the dead in hell, "to interpose some little respite," imagine themselves
out of it.[41] (This phrase, assuming it stuck in Milton's mind from his
reading of Augustine, links this last section to its thematic equivalence
with the fourth degree of death.) The thematic movement thus modu-
lates from below the "whelming tide / . . . of the monstrous world"
(157–58) to a rising curve coming upward, at the horizon of sea and
land. There stands the angel,

> Where the great vision of the guarded Mount
> Looks towards *Namancos* and *Bayona*'s hold.

The angel now becomes the symbolic bearer of the inspirational power
which, with prophetic mercy, is the compassionate revelation of love
following wrath shown the grieving poet.

The militant angel, locally identified with St. Michael's Mount
and representing Protestant England facing Catholic Europe, resonates
with overtones still sounding from the implied Apocalyptic consummation promised by that two-handed engine image of judgment and love
climaxing the earlier movement. Now the emphasis is on love, as the
echo of judgment recedes. In its primary aspect, St. Michael's Mount,
like all the other indications of place, relates to the imaginative quest
for the mortal remains of Edward King, who — directly under the eye of
St. Michael, as it were — is now finally consigned to the compassionate
dolphins.

But, at less obvious levels, St. Michael's Mount, and the softening
of the archangel's militant aspect, evoke a cognate image in the Apocalypse of John of Patmos. There seven angels sound trumpets of doom,
the last of which must usher in that Day of Judgment intimated by
Peter's last words in Milton's poem. The six angels in turn sound their
blasts, which destroy forests and shrink seas; but, intervening before
the seventh and last blast, there is a mighty angel, the archangel
Michael himself, who descends from heaven to stand on the margin of
sea and shore, responding in his own voice to the thundering waters
that time should soon have an end. The rainbow of covenantal forgiveness and love is upon his head, the glory of the rising sun on his face, and
the fires of judgment at his feet. He communes with the visionary who
beholds him, prophesies the struggles of the saints and the resurrection
of the martyrs of God underneath God's altar, who, like Lycidas, are
unburied. His final words in part anticipate the cry sounded in *Lycidas*
for the return of Alpheus: "The second woe is past" (Rev. 11:14). The
third and last woe will come, perhaps shortly, with the end of the

world, an excitation of mood toward which Milton was clearly predisposed by 1637.[42]

The chord sounded here is the fully consonant harmonization of justice and love, and on the associative level the angel of the sea and land draws together all the linked undercurrents of shrinking and healing waters, original sin, primal curses, and heavenly forgiveness. And, as a soaring figure bringing all together — the elements, the heavens and earth, God's throne and the bowels of Hell — the angel is the symbolic center of all movements in the poem. At the evocation of his figure the fourth rapture of love itself is achieved, and the visionary intuition that follows in triumphant steadiness seems meant to heal the last trace of spiritual perturbation:

> Weep no more, woeful shepherds, weep no more,
> For *Lycidas* your sorrow is not dead,
> Sunk though he be beneath the wat'ry floor,
> So sinks the day-star in the Ocean bed,
> And yet anon repairs his drooping head,
> And tricks his beams, and with new-spangled Ore,
> Flames in the forehead of the morning sky.   (165–171)

Theme, chords, *basso continuo*, all harmonically resound now to "the unexpressive nuptial Song / In the blest Kingdoms meek of joy and love," where music, consolation, and love all meet. With this image there is the utter repose of the regenerate mind, and the mere recollection of the mortal part of dead Lycidas becomes for mortals a benign influence, a genius of the shore. The tetrachord, or fourfold chord of cosmic harmony signifying the divine justice and love governing the universe, is now completely sounded, its grandeur scaled to within the compass of the inner spirit through which it has been experienced.

In the movement back to the pastoral context the beginning is evoked again: the day-labour of the poem now is done, and the nature of the artistic enterprise, the monody wedding music and words, and the alacrity of mind thereby produced, is set before us formally, as, in the shift in pronoun from the first person singular to the third, we are firmly set outside the work, no longer participants but observers. For all along we had been identified with the internal workings of Milton's mind and art in his use of the first person. But now he too stands apart and sees himself as "the uncouth swain" who, in the last lines' composure, departs the scene.

Lycidas then is a theodicy that at the level of our conscious understanding can be expected to justify God's ways, for God's providential justice had been called into question by the death of Edward King. Yet, for Milton, God's providence signified his *"hidden ways,"* which "we adore and question not,"[43] so that even the insistent pastoral inquiry after the meaning of death in *Lycidas* cannot but obliquely face the questions raised by history and mortal peril. The poem itself translates that graphically horizontal experience of time and mortality into an ascent, as it were spatially, into immortality, an ascent that becomes an affirmation of faith in the Christian mystery of death. History and time itself, however, are the ground of that real world behind the Arcadian disguise, and with this real world the poem is evidently connected, despite the mystery of God's providence. Since Milton believed he was inspired when he wrote the poem, he could look back upon it when it was republished in 1645 and note how, presumably unbeknownst to himself in 1637, it *did* "by occasion" foretell "the ruin of our corrupted Clergy then in their height."

But the prophetic character of *Lycidas* is only the reflection of Milton's faith in the harmony of discordant experience under the aspect of Christian eternity. It is a poem which takes the commonplace yet bitter trauma of death when it is near to us and makes it unfamiliar in order to restore to it its primal mystery. When we have been brought in tune again with the woe and wonder of death as a tragedy, we may hear, sustaining that sense, the music of consolation that Milton apparently heard as he composed his monody.

Tufts University

NOTES

1. The last phrase is from *At a Solemn Music* (5). The text of this and other poems are from *John Milton, Complete Poetry and Major Prose*, ed. Merritt Y. Hughes (New York, 1957), but the translations from *Ad Patrem* and the *Ad Leonoram* poems are those of Douglas Bush, in his edition of *The Complete Poetical Works of John Milton* (Boston, 1965).

2. See my study of Milton's experiments with "The hidden soul of harmony" (*L'Allegro*, 144), in "The Orphic Technique of 'L'Allegro' and 'Il Penseroso,'" *English Literary Renaissance*, I (Spring, 1971), 165–77.

3. For the first quotation from Milton's *Commonplace Book*, a text translated and edited by Ruth Mohl, see *The Complete Prose Works of John Milton* (henceforth designated *YP*), ed. Don M. Wolfe et al. (New Haven, 1953–), I, 382. The Greek word translated as "unconsciously" is *lanthanontos*. The second quotation is from Milton's digression on poetry in *The Reason of Church Government*, *YP*, I, pp. 816–17.

4. Paula Johnson, *Form and Transformation in Renaissance Poetry and Music* (New Haven, 1972), p. 150, apropos "The gradually quickening tempo, increasing tension, and sudden release" in climactic progressions in music and poetry, analogous to "the most compelling" rhythms of human life. She takes up here and cites an idea discussed earlier by Suzanne Langer in *Feeling and Form* (New York, 1953), p. 312. On spirit see the Elder Brother's lines in *Comus*, 453–69. Equally relevant is the Angel Raphael's account of the circuit of spirit in the great chain of being, *PL*, V, 469–500, and the passage in *Animadversions* (see also end of n. 29 below), where Milton writes of the worthy minister, one who has a "cleare spirit nurst up from brighter influences with a soul inlarg'd to the dimensions of spacious art and high knowledge" (*YP*, I, p. 719). Such references (and there are others in Milton's writings) to the rising and clarification of spirit are more literal than metaphorical.

5. "Plato's Four Furors and the Real Structure of *Paradise Lost*," *PMLA*, XCII (1977), 952–62.

6. Samuel Johnson, certainly as wide ranging in his learning as any of Milton's readers, noted with displeasure the "remote allusions and obscure opinions" particularly evident in *Lycidas*. See the *Life of Milton*, relevant passages reprinted in Scott Elledge, *Milton's "Lycidas," Edited to Serve as an Introduction to Criticism* (New York, 1966), p. 229.

7. Just about all the apparently interminable list of answers to that question assume that Milton did not really mean to be obscure. One of the key premises of this study is that I assume he was being deliberately obscure while appearing not to be.

8. Hunt, *"Lycidas" and the Italian Critics* (New Haven and London, 1979), posthumously published; Wittreich, "From Pastoral to Prophecy: The Genres of *Lycidas*," in *Milton Studies*, XIII, ed. James D. Simmonds (Pittsburgh, Pa., 1979), pp. 59–80; and *Visionary Poetics: Milton's Tradition and His Legacy* (San Marino, Cal., 1979), ch. 2. Others have discussed meaningfully the musicality of the poem, notably Gretchen Finney, *Musical Backgrounds for English Literature* (New Brunswick, N.J., 1962), ch. 10, where she sets out the structural character of its musical nature and suggests a connection to Monteverdi's *Orfeo*. To the extent that the poem relates to a whole class of such contemporary monodic lamentations as occur also in the opera, I think Finney may be right. But in every respect her work remains the most valuable introduction to the musical background not only of *Lycidas* but of the rest of Milton's poetry as well. See also the seminal discussion of the *canzone*-like structural form of *Lycidas* in F. T. Prince's *The Italian Element in Milton's Verse* (Oxford, 1954), ch. 5. Wayne Shumaker's "Flowerets and Sounding Seas: A Study in the Affective Structure of *Lycidas*," *PMLA*, LXVI (1951), 485–94, relates the musical themes of *Lycidas* to aspects of its design. And while Sigmund Spaeth's *Milton's Knowledge of Music* (Princeton, 1913) is outdated, it is still useful, though not as much as the brief but illuminating essay by Mortimer H. Frank, "Milton's Knowledge of Music: Some Speculations," in *Milton and the Art of Sacred Song*, ed. J. Max Patrick and R. H. Sundell (Madison, Wis., 1979), pp. 83–98.

9. Seriatim: Scaliger, from *The Poetics*, and Puttenham, from *The Arte of English Poesie*, relevant passages both reprinted in Elledge, *Milton's "Lycidas,"* pp. 109, 114; on lyric effects' being a species of grace working as a transitive power, see my "Plato's Four Furors," p. 952 and n. 1, pp. 959–60; for Milton's characterization of inspired poetry as a power "besides the office of a pulpit," and his account in *Animadversions* of the transitive cycle of such spiritual work, see *YP*, I, pp. 816–21, 721.

10. *"Lycidas" and the Italian Critics*, p. 24.

11. Ibid., pp. 52–54, while the discussion of the evolution of the lyric in theory and

practice takes up all of ch. 4, or more than half of the book. It is regrettable that not all of Hunt's work on *Lycidas* was published, since his discussion of the poem itself is tantalizingly brief.

12. "The Orphic Technique of 'L'Allegro' and 'Il Penseroso,'" 165–77, and Milton's *Animadversions*, n. 9 above.

13. *"Lycidas" and the Italian Critics*, p. 151.

14. Seriatim: Marsilio Ficino's commentaries on Plato, *Commen. in Ion*, and *Commen. in Conviv.*, and *in Phaedrum*, *Opera Omnia* (Basel, 1576; facs. rpt. Torino, 1959, 1962), II, 1282, 1361, 1365. Frances Yates writes how Ficino used to "sing the Orphic songs, accompanying himself on a *lira da braccio*. They were set to some kind of simple monodic music which Ficino believed echoed the musical notes emitted by the planetary spheres, to form that music of the spheres of which Pythagoras spoke." The instrument he played was "decorated with the figure of Orpheus taming the animals." In her *Giordano Bruno and the Hermetic Tradition* (Chicago, 1964), pp. 78, 80. On Ficino see also D. P. Walker, *Spiritual and Demonic Magic from Ficino to Campanella* (London, 1958), pp. 10–24. And on Pontus de Tyard, see Walker, pp. 120–21; Frances Yates, *The French Academies of the Sixteenth Century* (London, 1947), pp. 58, 114. On musical humanism and monody more generally, see James E. Phillips' contribution to *Music and Literature in England in the Seventeenth and Eighteenth Centuries*, papers delivered by James E. Phillips and Bertrand H. Bronson at the Second Clark Library Seminar, 24 Oct. 1953 (Los Angeles, 1954); and especially the articles by D. P. Walker, both called "Musical Humanism in the Sixteenth and Early Seventeenth Centuries," *The Music Review*, II (1941), 1–3, and III (1942), 55–71. On the separate artistic spheres of influence of words and music, see John Hollander, *The Untuning of the Sky* (Princeton, 1961), p. 175. Finally, I should note that the specific aims of monody tend to weaken somewhat Wittreich's original suggestion in "Milton's Destin'd Urn: The Art of *Lycidas*," *PMLA*, LXXXIV (1969), 60–70, that the rhyme patterns and stanzaic organization of the poem derive from the madrigal, since monodic theory was specifically aimed at displacing the madrigal's contrary subordination of words to music, and succeeded so well that the madrigal was all but dead by 1630. When Milton visited London from Horton in the early 1630s, we know he was particularly interested in mathematics and "avant-garde" music which he could not acquire elsewhere. At this time the music would not likely have been the old madrigal writing, but rather the new avant-garde monodic theory and practice. In his own words, he "took the keenest pleasure" in the new music. See the personal account of his Horton years in *A Second Defence of the English People*, trans. Helen North, YP, IV, pt. 1, p. 614.

15. Donald F. Tovey, "The Monodic Revolution and Its Results," in his article "Music," *The Encyclopedia Britannica*, 11th ed. (1910).

16. For Hunt's musical analysis of *Lycidas*, see *"Lycidas" and the Italian Critics*, ch. 5.

17. Since the indications are implicit and intermittent I invert here Northrop Frye's term "continuous allegory," used where "a poet explicitly indicates the relationship of his images to examples and precepts," in *Anatomy of Criticism* (Princeton, 1957), p. 90.

18. *PL* V, 627. The phrase describes an effect of the "mystical dance" in heaven celebrating the Son's annunciation, where the "harmony divine" absorbs, as a *concordia discors*, the movement of the faithful and the already fallen angels ("All seem'd well pleas'd, but were not all"). Hence their dance resembled the irregular but harmonic Copernican movement of the heavenly bodies, "mazes intricate / Eccentric, intervolv'd, yet regular / Then most, when most irregular they seem" (622–24). Cf. the unheard music evoked in the Nativity Ode, 126–32.

19. On inaudible, and invisible, effects in music, as well as in the other arts of the Renaissance period and later, see Manfred E. Bukofzer, "Allegory in Baroque Music," *Journal of the Warburg Institute*, III (1939–40), 1–21; Edward Lowinsky, *Secret Chromatic Art in the Netherlands Motet*, trans. Carl Buchanan (New York, 1946), esp. ch. 9, "The Meaning of Double Meaning in the Sixteenth Century"; Irwin Panofsky, *Studies in Iconology* (New York, 1962), p. 89; Ernst Gombrich, *Symbolic Images* (London, 1972), passim; and Rudolf Wittkower, *Architectural Principles in the Age of Humanism* (London, 1967), pp. 8–21, 95–98, 108–11, 114 ff.

20. See Courtland Baker, "Certain Religious Elements in the Doctrine of the Inspired Poet During the Renaissance," *ELH*, VI (1939), 309–10.

21. "Plato's Four Furors and the Real Structure of *Paradise Lost*," pp. 952–56.

22. *Mythomystes*, rpt. in *Literary Criticism of Seventeenth-Century England*, ed. E. W. Tayler (New York, 1967), pp. 232–36, 247, 253–54; *Prolusion II, YP*, I, p. 236. On the interchangeability of all tetradic systems, see S. K. Heninger, Jr., *Touches of Sweet Harmony: Pythagorean Cosmology and Renaissance Poetics* (San Marino, Cal., 1974), passim.

23. *The Christian Doctrine*, ed. Maurice Kelley and trans. John Carey, Bk. I, chs. xii–xiii, *CPW*, VI, pp. 393–414.

24. It is appropriately Socrates, who, of the seven who speak of love in the *Symposium* (208–09), has Diotima distinguish between the parents' love of children for the sake of their own immortality through them, and the creative souls who aspire rather, through a different love, for an immortality of fame. But this in itself is but one higher (that is, a second stage) in the quest for the highest or heavenly love (210–12). Cf. *Laws* (721) on marrying for procreative immortality, the corollary of which is "the desire of every man that he may become famous and not lie in the grave without a name."

25. On the tensions involved in Milton's vocational crisis and their relevance to *Lycidas*, see my *Milton and the Kingdoms of God* (Evanston, Ill., and London, 1964), ch. 2.

26. On the symbolism of coronal leaves see J. B. Trapp, "The Owl's Ivy and the Poet's Bays: An Enquiry into Poetic Garlands," *Journal of the Warburg Institute*, XXI (1958), 227–55, specifically p. 255 where Trapp comments on the opening lines of *Lycidas*. See also the dialogue on coronal symbolism in Giordano Bruno's *Heroic Frenzies*, trans. and ed. Paul E. Memmo, Jr. (Chapel Hill, N.C., 1964), pp. 84–88.

27. In "The Pattern of Milton's Nativity Ode," *UTQ*, X (1941), 171–72. See also Kathleen Swaim, "Retributive Justice in *Lycidas*: The Two-Handed Engine," *Milton Studies*, II ed. James D. Simmonds (Pittsburgh, Pa., 1970), pp. 119–29, for another three-part analysis of the poem. See also Alastair Fowler's numerological discussion, "'To Shepherd's Ear': The Form of Milton's *Lycidas*," in *Silent Poetry*, ed. Fowler (London, 1970), pp. 170–84, where stanzaic, rhyming and other patterns that seem numerologically significant are, perhaps, meaningful in terms of the poem's relationship to the *canzone*, and the poem's architectonic intricacies are seen as expressing "the structural ambiguities of mannerist art" (p. 179). Of all "musical" effects in the poem these are possibly the most inaudible.

28. Referring to the ascent and descent through the hierarchy of the "Socratic frenzies," or four raptures, Pico della Mirandola is very eloquent on the effect of the Dionysian reversal. While the upward movement is integrative, toward contemplative unitive vision, to descend may involve a "titanic force rending the unity like Osiris into many parts." *Oration on the Dignity of Man*, ed. E. Cassirer et al. (Chicago, 1948), p. 230, para. 11. See also Edgar Wind, *Pagan Myths and Christian Mysteries* (New York, 1968), p. 115, on the archetype of Orphic and Dionysian dismemberment in Renaissance art, signifying the disintegration of the One, as Truth, the Church, or any whole, by the inversion of the power in-

volved in integration. The relevance of Pico's Osiris image and the passage in his Oration to the same image in *Areopagitica* is clear enough to have been often noted. Less obvious, but a subject that must await another discussion, is the relationship of the fourfold structure of Pico's Oration to the fourfold structure and thematic development of *Areopagitica*.

29. *Eumenides*, 189–90, trans. Philip Vellacott, in *The Oresteian Trilogy* (Baltimore, 1967). The linkage between the clear spirit and the sublimed desire for an immortality of fame (see n. 24 above) is plainer if we remember that in Renaissance physiology clear spirit was in part a distillation of the potency for life and the linkage between the bodily kind of spirit and the ethereal element of the soul. Clear spirit inhered in male sperm and seminal fluid, which is why Ficino, commenting on the desire for fame as a sublimation of the procreative drive for immortality, writes that those who aspire through the love of fame to a higher love should live chastely and not exhaust their clear spirit in coitus. *Commentary on Plato's Symposium*, trans. and ed. Sears Jayne, Univ. of Missouri Studies, XIX, No. 1 (Columbia, Mo., 1944), p. 227. Cf. Shakespeare's repudiation of lust in Sonnet 129, "The expense of spirit in a waste of shame / Is lust in action," where "expense" bears a partial sense of sexual depletion and "spirit" certainly refers in part to the vitality of the seminal fluid. One could make a small essay of Milton's references to spirit, with their varying degrees of sexualized significance. Here we need but note his imagistic contrast of the spiritually depraved clergy in *Of Reformation*, with their "sordid sperm," as against the procreative power of true preachers of the Gospel, who themselves had had "cleare spirit" infused in them by evangelical virility and who in turn procreate souls, making a "creation like to Gods, by infusing his spirit and likenesse into them, to their salvation." *Animadversions*, YP, I, pp. 719–22.

30. Apollonian illumination can be concurrently intellectual, spiritual, and prophetic. Thus it is worth remarking that in this section of the poem Milton's striking reference to the "blind mouths" of the corrupted clergy precisely inverts the implicit synesthetic character of his account elsewhere of the illumination of the will, which endows the regenerate man with clear vision, a transformation of his capabilities that, by responding "to the call [of God] . . . is sometimes called *hearing*, or listening . . . sometimes called a *taste*." Italics are Milton's, in *The Christian Doctrine* I, xvii, YP, VI, p. 457.

31. The phrase is G. W. O'Brien's, in *Renaissance Poetics and the Problem of Power* (Chicago, 1956), p. 82.

32. YP, VI, pp. 393–94.

33. Trans. and ed. F. J. Miller, *The Tragedies of Seneca* (Chicago, 1907), ll. 625–33. Throughout this edition, and hence in my citations, the line numbering of the Latin original is applied, without exact match, to the translations.

34. See *The Argonautica of Apollonius of Rhodes*, I, 1340–50, trans. E. V. Rieu (Baltimore, 1959), p. 72; Robert Graves, *The Greek Myths* (Baltimore, 1955), I, 150; and Northrop Frye, "Literature as Context: Milton's *Lycidas*," rpt. in *Milton's "Lycidas," The Tradition and the Poem*, ed. C. A. Patrides (New York, 1961), p. 201. Orpheus figures very prominently in *The Argonautica*, since prophecy had it that without his presence particular dangers at sea would destroy the Argo. Hence in Milton's earlier evocation of Orpheus' death, the futility of his song takes on an added, near ironic meaning, in the context of the journey in which Lycidas was drowned, an action related, as we shall see more clearly later, to a type of original sin.

35. See my earlier discussion of *Lycidas*, in *Milton and the Kingdoms of God*, pp. 58–60.

36. Ambrose, cited by Hugo Rahner, in *Greek Myths and Christian Mysteries*, trans. Brian Battershaw (London, 1963), p. 349; Benlowes, Introduction to his poem, *The-*

ophilia, rpt. in *Minor Poets of the Caroline Period*, ed. George B. Saintsbury (Oxford, 1905–21), I, p. 321.

37. Seriatim: On the mingled waters symbolizing imperfection, see Natalis Comes, *Mythologiae*, cited by Merritt Y. Hughes in his note on this passage in *John Milton, The Complete Poems and Major Prose*, p. 119. On the healing waters of Alpheus, see Graves, *The Greek Myths*, I, p 278. On Plutarch see "On the Names of Rivers and Mountains," in *Plutarch's Morals*, trans. R. White, and ed. W. W. Gooding (Boston, 1871), V, p. 501.

38. See D. C. Allen, *Mysteriously Meant* (Baltimore, 1970), pp. 47–51, on the Renaissance and seventeenth-century Christianizing of Seneca; and *Thyestes*, in *Tragedies of Seneca*, esp. ll. 784–85 and 789–884.

39. See Graves, *The Greek Myths*, II, 31–39. In winning his bride by a chariot race against Myrtilius, the course running over the sea, Pelops tricked his opponent who, cast into the waters, drowned, but not before he laid a curse on Pelops and all his line. One of Pelops' sons, a brother to Atreus and Thyestes, was Lysidice, whose name signifies the dispensing of justice (*The Greek Myths*, II, 40, 398).

40. *The Variorum Commentary on the Poems of John Milton*, II, Pt. 2, ed. A. S. P. Woodhouse and Douglas Bush (New York, 1972), pp. 707–08, surveys the problem and those who have written on it, hewing to the allegorical line that figures clearly in the Alpheus-Arethusa connection, as far as Alpheus is concerned, and identifying the "dread voice" with St. Peter in the immediately preceding action. On the other hand, Mother M. Christopher Pecheux, in the most direct and coherent approach to the problem I have come across, sees St. Peter's as only part of the "dread voice," which, with ingenious stitching of patristic and other passages together, she blends with allusions to the voices of Moses and Christ; see "The Dread Voice in *Lycidas*," *Milton Studies*, IX, ed. James D. Simmonds (Pittsburgh, Pa., 1976), pp. 221–42. Her point is well argued and since the Fury whose voice is past is indeed an allegorical stand-in for some embodiment of God's judgment on original sin, I would think Peter, Moses, and Jesus would do. But an interpretation which does not recognize the very particular provenance of *the* dread voice of the Fury who shrunk Alpheus' streams simply gropes in the dark in which Milton so long and so thoroughly left his readers. Of general relevance to the question of calculated obscurity in Milton's longer poems is his cryptic practice at this juncture in *Lycidas*, obscuring the nature of the connection which underlies the transition from Peter's warning to the "dread voice." The precise technique is justified by Milton in his *Art of Logic* as one of a number of techniques of "crypsis of concealment" appropriate to poetry and involving the suppression of clear indications of disposition or sequence by avoiding clarity in,"partitions and transitions." *The Works of John Milton*, ed. Frank A. Patterson (New York, 1931–1940), XI, p. 485. Milton did by artistic instinct what he could justify by theory.

41. *The Enchiridion*, in *Library of Christian Classics* (Philadelphia, 1955), VII, pp. 400–72. In Augustine's text the phrase refers to the gradation of torment in Hell, so that "some will have a more tolerable burden of misery than others."

42. Seriatim: On·Michael, the angel of Revelation X, 1, see my discussion in "The Apocalypse Within *Paradise Lost*," in *New Essays on "Paradise Lost*,"ed. Thomas Kranidas (Berkeley and Los Angeles, 1969), pp. 161–63. The same apocalyptic angel, straddling sea and land, appears in a passage of Renaissance French Protestant poetry. See Gilbert Gadoffre, "Structures des Mythes de Du Bellay," *Bibliothèque D'Humanisme et Renaissance*, XXXVI (Geneva, 1974), 285, where the apocalyptic angel's association with the shore is related to similar biblical images in Daniel and Ezekiel. On Milton's millennial mood in 1637, see my *Milton and the Kingdoms of God*, ch. 2.

43. *The Doctrine and Discipline of Divorce*, YP, II, p. 292, emphasis added. With reference to the musical use I attribute to the "enigma variations" as a *basso continuo*, accompanying by unscored chords the overt "song" of Milton's "Doric lay," I am content if others find them analogically but not actually musical. We cannot any longer question, however, the poem's intentionally monodic and therefore its formal musical character. With that in mind, how else can these linked but apparently discrete allusions be seen as organically coherent? What else can we call them?